Mapping Warsaw

Mapping Warsaw

The Spatial Poetics of a Postwar City

✦

Ewa Wampuszyc

NORTHWESTERN UNIVERSITY PRESS
EVANSTON, ILLINOIS

Northwestern University Press
www.nupress.northwestern.edu

"*Warsaw 1956*: Rewriting Ruins and the Palace of Culture," which now appears as part of chapter 4, appeared previously in Polish as part of the essay "Normalizacja a odbudowa Warszawy," 98–109. Copyright © 2014 for Authors and Dom Wydawniczy ELIPSA. Used with permission.

Another part of chapter 4, "Reappropriating Warsaw and the Palace of Culture," was originally published as Ewa Wampuszyc, "Socialism, Synecdoche, and Tadeusz Konwicki's Palace of Culture" in *East European Politics and Societies* 27, no. 2 (2013): 224–40. Copyright © 2013 by the American Council of Learned Societies. Reprinted by permission of SAGE Publications. DOI: 10.1177/0888325412469664. Some revisions have been introduced.

Publication of this book was made possible, in part, by a grant from the First Book Subvention Program of the Association for Slavic, East European, and Eurasian Studies.

Printed in the United States of America

10 9 8 7 6 5 4 3 2 1

ISBN 978-0-8101-3789-9 (paper)
ISBN 978-0-8101-3790-5 (cloth)
ISBN 978-0-8101-3791-2 (ebook)

Cataloging-in-Publication data are available from the Library of Congress.

For my father, Jan.

In memory of Teresa, my mother.

That which once was is never to be seen again, and that which is current occupies the present one hundred percent.

—Siegfried Kracauer

CONTENTS

ACKNOWLEDGMENTS

I have had a number of travel companions on this journey through Warsaw. Many thanks to my colleagues for conversations and comments. Alphabetically, they are: Karen Auerbach, Ruth von Bernuth, Eric Downing, Beth Holmgren, Bill Johnston, Ingrid Kleespies, Clayton Koelb, Elżbieta Konończuk, Priscilla Layne, Madeline Levine, Mike Levine, Ewa Pasek, Chris Putney, Bożena Shallcross, Mariusz Szajnert, Ewa Thompson, Kirill Tolpygo, Silvia Tomášková, and Piotr Zwierzchowski. Special thanks to Louise McReynolds and Hana Píchová. Gene Fishel, Bożena Karwowska, Irene Masing-Delic, and the anonymous reviewers engaged by Northwestern University Press provided invaluable comments. Lisl Hampton and Helen Halva conscientiously edited portions of the book. Many thanks to Anne Gendler of Northwestern University Press. Special thanks to Katarzyna Koła-Bielawska and Justyna Turczynowicz of the Repozytorium Cyfrowe Filmoteki Narodowej for their assistance with the Polska Kronika Filmowa (PKF) catalog and website.

No project of this sort comes to fruition without the support of family and friends. Many thanks to Bożena, Ewa, Gina, Hana, Holly, and Jen. My heartfelt gratitude to Eleanor and Michael Fishel for their encouragement, and to James Fishel, for his healthy perspective. I am grateful to my father, Jan Wampuszyc, for many things, including starting me on this road, and to my sister, Maja Wampuszyc, with whom I first explored Warsaw. I am indebted to Fiszek, who read it all and listened.

Research for this project was supported by grants from The Center for Slavic, Eurasian and East European Studies at the University of North Carolina-Chapel Hill, the UNC-CH Center for European Studies, and the UNC-CH Department of Germanic and Slavic Languages and Literatures, as well as a Junior Faculty Development Award from the UNC-CH College of Arts and Sciences. This book's maps and visualizations are by Lorin Bruckner (Data Visualization Services Librarian, Digital Research Services Department, University Library, UNC-CH). Assistance with maps and data was provided by Phil McDaniels (GIS Librarian, Digital Research Services Department, University Library, UNC-CH).

Mapping Warsaw

Figure 1. Old Town rooftops, Warsaw, May 2017. Photo by the author.

Figure 2. Zamkowy Square, Warsaw, May 2017. Photo by the author.

PROLOGUE

Take 1. *Half asleep, I heard "Warsaw" and looked through the window. I couldn't believe my eyes. I couldn't connect what I saw with what I remembered from the past. All around, there were only makeshift buildings and rubble . . . Overcome by the horror of what I saw, I wondered how I would find the place where I was supposed to deliver some "documents." Otherwise buried by ruins, a few streets were usable and had almost normal traffic. Those streets that were narrow to begin with had even more narrow paths running through the rubble. I still remember the tiny little lights that flickered among the ruins and in destroyed buildings, even in the upper stories. Surprised by this and curious, I asked some passersby what the lights meant. The people responded with no less surprise: "You don't know? People live there." I had been told—but until then couldn't imagine—that people actually lived in such ruins.*

> This is how my father remembers seeing Warsaw in 1945.
> He did not return to the Polish capital again until 1998.

Take 2. Imagine walking along cobblestone streets between colorful, historic buildings decorated with wrought-iron or baroque-like details and being transported to a Europe of the past by the atmosphere of the architecture. Now imagine—after being vested in the authenticity of this experience—finding out that what you have endowed with history is, in fact, only a reproduction. This was my experience of Warsaw.

Take 3. August 2013. I sit at my computer looking at a satellite image on Google Maps. It is the intersection of Marszałkowska Street and Jerozolimskie Avenue in downtown Warsaw. There is a river of cars, the Palace of Culture and Science, billboards advertising the movie *Transformers 3*, the hotels Novotel and Marriott, and numerous shops. This cityscape is a far cry from the streets I remember during trips to Poland in the 1970s when Warsaw was the capital of communist Poland. At the time there was no Marriott, let alone other signs of capitalism. From the perspective of a child, the magic of the colorful buildings, called *kamienice*, the cobblestone streets, and the aristocratic grandeur of Łazienki Park obscured the historical vicissitudes of the city.[1] I looked at the Old Town Market Square and did not see these "historical" buildings as the mid-twentieth-century life-sized replicas that they are. As for the contrast between the architecture of the Old Town and the Palace of Culture? That was a contrast I seamlessly embraced. The view of Warsaw provided by twenty-first-century technology is even further removed from the image of the same street corner filmed for a 1945 newsreel that shows this intersection populated by shacks serving as a provisional shopping area amid the rubble of Poland's capital. Despite the difficult living conditions in the city in 1945, the intersection is crowded. People walk along the street, shoulder to shoulder, living their lives among Warsaw's ruins.

INTRODUCTION

In many cities, you can simply sightsee. All you need to get to
know Paris, Rome, Moscow, or New York is a good guide, a
map of the city, a bit of knowledge, and a certain amount of
receptiveness. In the case of Warsaw, this is not enough. You
need more than explanatory comments to understand the city.
You need a key.

—*Warsaw 1945 and Today*

The story of postwar Warsaw is not only a story of reconstructing the city's
physical topography after being nearly destroyed during World War II, but
also its discursive topography.[1] It is a story as much about the physical space
of the Polish capital as it is about the meaning attached to Warsaw's reconstruction and the way this was collectively understood, embraced, rejected, or
contested. At its core it is a story about the expressive capabilities of verbal
and visual texts to render spatiality. Warsaw's discursive topography was in
a state of transition after the war, prime for its own "reconstruction" or re-
narration. The story of Warsaw's genius loci, or its pervading spirit, is thus
a story of "writing" and "rewriting." The desire to understand this process
of (re)writing the city in a postwar, reconstruction, and totalitarian context
rests at the core of this project. *Mapping Warsaw* posits that postwar Warsaw was (re)built not only as the physical space that we experience or that is
worthy of cartographic representation but also as the abstract space, which
we encounter textually in such sources as newspapers, literature, photography, film, or as metadata on Google Maps. It is this abstract, textual space of
the city that is the main topic of this book.[2] This book is an interdisciplinary
study that analyzes the Warsaw of photobooks, the newsreels of communist
Poland called the Polish Film Chronicle (Polska Kronika Filmowa, PKF), feature films, and select literary works, particularly those of the author-director
Tadeusz Konwicki. Above all, *Mapping Warsaw* seeks to elucidate the way in
which the Polish capital was rebuilt discursively and textualized in the aftermath of World War II. This is a spatial study that looks beyond the material
facade of Warsaw and grapples with how space was represented in written
and visual forms when the city was rising from the ashes of war and in the
following decade as the "socialist path" to "communism" was established in
the People's Republic of Poland (Polska Rzeczpospolita Ludowa, PRL).[3]

Mapping Warsaw posits the coexistence of multiple Varsovian discourses that intersected with one another across genres to create a rhetorical space that was appropriated and reappropriated *textually* by official and dissenting spheres responding to historical and political changes.[4] It elucidates how Warsaw was "reconstructed" by photographers, cinematographers, directors, and writers who formulated their own versions of the city in a totalitarian context. The main focus of this study, however, is the analysis of how these narratives were adopted by an official communist-era discourse to create a Varsovian spatiality that blended individual artistic choices, preexisting cultural paradigms, and postwar cultural policies of a People's Republic. Specifically, I look at the intersection between official narratives promoted by communist authorities and narrative counterpoints that developed in response to, or in lieu of, the geospatial narratives promoted by ideology and propaganda.[5] Such an approach not only reveals the evolution of Warsaw's postwar spatiality, but also shows how the discursive appropriation of the city was a dynamic process that crossed boundaries between genres during the communist period.

Throughout this study, I maintain both diachronic and synchronic approaches to the topic of Warsaw in the process of (re)construction. This results in a fluid time frame. From the synchronic perspective, the focus is from 1945 until the Thaw of 1956, a period during which various organs of the communist party intensely promoted a "socialist" narrative about Warsaw. However, from a diachronic point of view, I analyze materials from later decades of the communist period in order to demonstrate the impact and persistence of a Varsovian narrative that developed synchronically during the decade after the war. The core official narrative on the postwar capital reconstructed here is based primarily on texts that coincide with representations of a Warsaw contemporary to the years 1945 through 1956. This means that some texts traditionally considered pivotal to the Varsovian narrative and set in Warsaw do not appear as part of this study, because their narratives take place before or during the war.[6] Furthermore, the materials analyzed in this book continue to be relevant and in circulation up to today. Photobooks, newsreels, films, and fiction have remained popular or their popularity has been renewed through YouTube, e-books, online used booksellers, and digitized archives. With such accessibility, these sources continue to influence Warsaw's spatiality.

Theoretically, I locate this study in the context of the "spatial turn" in the humanities and social sciences, a line of academic inquiry that has gained resonance in literary and cultural studies since the mid-twentieth century following the devastation caused by the Second World War. Add to the war what Karl Schlögel identifies as a radical change in the relationship between time and space through globalization and new technologies, and the twentieth century was ripe for this "spatial turn."[7] With the wartime reconfiguration or loss of iconic and meaning-filled spaces, it is not surprising that academic inquiry has sought to interrogate how we represent the experience of space, both that which was destroyed and that which remained intact. In addition to the ideas suggested by the spatial turn, I have allowed my primary sources to refine my methodology, reading each text at its word.[8] This means that each chapter draws on theories relevant to the material at hand: film and media studies, theories of photography and photographic composition, narrative history, literary criticism, and cultural studies. Such a hybrid approach is necessary, because developing a dynamic postwar Varsovian narrative by rhetorically appropriating the capital across genres was central to the project of constructing socialism in Poland. Official texts often promoted a core Varsovian narrative, and thus the spatiality created in photobooks, newsreels, and certain feature films often intersected. At the same time, each source communicated its message according to its own stylistic code shaped by the possibilities and limits of its genre, and reached different audiences. This meant that Varsovian spatiality was "filled" from a variety of perspectives. One of the goals of this project is to better grasp how different textual forms or genres analyzed, adopted, interpreted, and then translated the ideological message according to their own rules. Another is to understand how the chaotic postwar Varsovian space (here I mean the abstract, conceptual one) became inscribed with meaning and textualized.

The juxtaposition of heterogeneous sources also allows me to identify the strongest and most persistent narrative threads of Warsaw's postwar story as it emerged in officially published or produced texts under communism, as well as to identify how this narrative interlocks with other postwar discourses about the city. What emerges is a discursive map that outlines the socialist meanings of "Warsaw" and "Varsovian," meanings that became integrated into Polish culture, but which also served to spur dissent and inspire counter-discourses. The implications of this study, however, are broader than understanding the narrative dynamics of Warsaw itself. The combination of sources from various genres points to the way that cultural texts, while functioning according to their own "rules of engagement," also absorb and react to (often conflicting) discourses. In reacting to one another, these narratives likewise shape one another and become part of a greater whole. While this may seem somewhat obvious, such interlocking and integrated cultural discourses can be complicated to map and their threads difficult to tease out. This project is an attempt to understand some of those threads as they relate to Warsaw, as well as to better understand how seemingly incompatible discourses not only coexist but feed off one another.

Textualizing Warsaw and the Spatial Turn

Regardless of the academic discipline, be it geography, cultural studies, or philosophy, scholars engaged in the study of space and how it is represented differentiate between spatial practice and theory, concrete space and abstract spatiality, the physical and the experiential. Maurice Merleau-Ponty considers, for example, the concept of space from a phenomenological-philosophical point of view. He distinguishes between "geometrical space" as homogenous and isotropic, and "spatiality" as the *experience* of the body in relative or subjective relation to the surrounding material world.[9] For Merleau-Ponty, spatiality is a practice that manifests itself as a description or explanation of how we perform within the world around us and how we relate to the physical world in which our bodies exist. In comparison, Michel de Certeau considers the way humans physically or narratively move through space while taking the concept of "space" itself for granted. De Certeau defines "place" as the equivalent of order, rule, location, and stability, while "space" refers to the practice of place and our interaction with it. His definition of space relies on changing variables such as time, direction, and relative orientations that are then narratively represented.[10] For him, "every story is a travel story—a spatial practice" that is expressed either as a tour or as a map.[11]

Analogous distinctions between space and spatiality are adopted in literary and cultural studies. For example, J. Hillis Miller's *Topographies* investigates the transposition of topographical descriptions and terminology onto literary and philosophical texts, suggesting that the act of mapping occurs on both cartographic and linguistic planes.[12] He argues that the topography of place "is made, performatively, by word or other signs."[13] And Svetlana Boym, the cultural theorist, makes a distinction between physical and narrative manifestations of space when she explores the "topography of the urban myth together with the physical spaces of the city." In particular, she considers the concept of topos as it "refers both to a place in discourse and a place in the world." She makes a point of distinguishing between "physical *topoi*" and "rhetorical *topoi*," pointing out the connection between them as "arbitrary, semiotic rather than symbolic," and traces this distinction as far back as Aristotle.[14] These models of space/spatiality have one thing in common: they distinguish between an identifiable, physical point on the globe marked by coordinates on which we can stand, walk, build, and live in contrast to spatiality, which refers to the way in which we experience and interpret this physical space and then "rebuild" it through textualization—that is, describing or naming it in speech acts and codifying it in cultural or anthropological artifacts (maps, books, photographs, films, etc.).

Space and spatiality can be considered two distinct spheres that exist independently of each another. For example, geographers criticize scholars from other disciplines who use geography terms such as "mapping" and "space" to describe culture. They see such an application of these terms to culture as amorphous, ill-defined, and overly metaphorical. In turn, they question whether the sociocultural and subjective meanings created by texts actually become "part of the material's content."[15] Correspondingly, the historian

Karl Schlögel contends that space is not a text to be read. His argument rests on the scientifically measurable dimensions of space and the necessity to visit a place, to walk around it, to experience its dimensions, proportions, and shapes. He correctly points out that buildings, squares, and interior spaces are distinct from their reproductions in novels or other cultural artifacts. He argues that spaces and places set conditions which can only be satisfied by seeing and feeling, conditions that cannot be satisfied by reading a book.[16] In each case, the perspective of the geographer or the historian stands apart from Jacques Derrida's famous theoretical deconstructionist and provocative proclamation that "everything is a text." And if everything is a text, then shouldn't the physical and rhetorical spaces be somehow dependent on one another?

So which is it? I am inclined to say "both." As we interact with a physical space, we inevitably attach meaning to it, whether that meaning is based on individual or communal experience. And this meaning is expressed in word and image. This does not mean that spatiality always physically becomes part of the material world we live in, but it certainly influences our evolving relationship to space and the way in which we determine how the space around us will evolve. This, in turn, has implications for both individual and communal identity. The redevelopment of the former site of the World Trade Center as a memorial to the victims of 9/11 is such an example. In this way, spatiality and space are inextricably linked. While we may be able to consider them separately, we cannot deny their tendency to intersect in meaningful and sometimes life-changing ways, nor can we deny the tendency for spatiality to "textualize" the world around us.

Warsaw is an excellent example of how a space can be textualized, yet difficult to read. To an unsuspecting tourist, the fact that Warsaw's Old Town (Stare Miasto) is actually "Old Town," and that the buildings on one of the main shopping streets, Nowy Świat (literally, "new world"), were built in the late 1940s rather than being centuries old might come as a surprise. The chasm between Warsaw's "old" architecture and the way in which the streets can be read outside the historical and cultural context is potentially vast, because walking the streets of Warsaw does not necessarily provide access to a specific Varsovian code that would make the city "legible" unless one is initiated into the cultural or textual narration of the space. Basically, without knowing Warsaw's history, one cannot read these buildings in their proper context. This might suggest that the sociocultural meanings of the city are not part of its material manifestation. Varsovian space, however, is highly textualized. On the most basic level, the Polish capital has hundreds of historical markers, cornerstones, or plaques installed on buildings throughout the city to commemorate or memorialize events or people, and provide mininarratives that "textualize" the space.

Another example: on a visit to Warsaw in 2013, I stood at the corner of Jerozolimskie Avenue (Aleje Jerozolimskie) and Nowy Świat Street (ulica

Figure 3. Former offices of the Civic Fund for the Reconstruction of the Capital, located on the northwest corner of Jerozolimskie Avenue and Nowy Świat Street, December 2013. Photo by the author.

Nowy Świat) where I recognized a building I had seen in a number of Warsaw-themed photobooks. It is a socialist realist building that in 1950 housed the Civic Fund for the Reconstruction of the Capital (Społeczny Fundusz Odbudowy Stolicy, SFOS), a government office that collected money for Warsaw's reconstruction through voluntary contributions and levies on income and vodka. Today, the building houses a cosmetics shop and a bookstore. In addition to the store signs that grace the roof and windows, the motto of SFOS is carved into the stone frieze of the building: "CAŁY NARÓD BUDUJE SWOJĄ STOLICĘ" ("The entire nation is building its capital"). (See figure 3.) It is a message from the past whose significance is being erased by time. Seeing this building after encountering it many times in photographs is thrilling. Maybe Schlögel is right? The real thing is almost always better. Yet without the textual, photobook experience of the city, I might not have noticed this building. I am even more excited when I notice reconstruction work being done on the former headquarters of the Central Committee of the Polish United Workers' Party, sometimes referred to as the "Party's House" or the "White House" (figure 4). It is located kitty-corner from what was once the SFOS office. After the fall of communism, this building became a financial and banking center,

Figure 4. The former headquarters of the Central Committee of the Polish United Workers' Party, located on the southeast corner of Jerozolimskie Avenue and Nowy Świat Street, June 2015. Photo by the author.

even housing the Warsaw Stock Exchange from 1991 to 2000. Under Prime Minister Tadeusz Mazowiecki's government in 1990, the proceeds from the rental of the former party headquarters were earmarked for a new library for the University of Warsaw.[17] In 2013 this building was cordoned off by a makeshift, temporary fence made of posters that read "we are building trust" ("budujemy zaufanie"). (See figure 5.) I wonder how many people read the signs on that fence and noted the irony of two such similar, yet different, claims intersecting at this corner of Warsaw. The old sign, carved into stone, seems permanent. But it is a message from Poland's communist past that has crumbled and given way to market capitalism and democracy. The other sign, made of paper and wood, sought to elicit trust in the economic constructs of twenty-first-century Poland. Both messages suggest that their respective buildings are vital physical manifestations of abstract ideas. But as the fate of communism shows, carving messages into stone, let alone on advertising placards, does not guarantee their permanence. Abstract ideas can evaporate; however, the use-value of physical edifices continues and textual traces sometimes remain firmly carved in stone, even if no one reads them.

Figure 5. Former headquarters of the Central Committee of the Polish United Workers'
Party under renovation in 2013. Photo by the author.

The City as Palimpsest

The former building of the Civic Fund for the Reconstruction of the Capital
and the former headquarters of the Polish United Workers' Party (Polska
Zjednoczona Partia Robotnicza, PZPR) described above exemplify the sometimes purposeful and, at other times, very unexpected textualization of a
space. They also point to the potential redefinition of the indexicality and
connotation of an object or image by its confrontation with text. Through
such juxtapositions, we can see how urban space and its spatiality combine to
form a palimpsest on which old "texts" are erased and replaced by new ones;
yet traces of these old texts remain present and can resurface or be actively
revived. In this way, a city is "palimpsestic," having layers of meaning. But a
city is also "palimpsestuous," continually reinventing itself through a complex relationality between the archeological layering of the built environment
(space) and archeological-like, intertextual connections (spatiality).[18]

Today the palimpsestuousness of space and spatiality is more heightened
than ever because of technology. Maps contain not only geographically
specific reference points, but also layer upon layer of metadata that create
simultaneity between the past and present through images or hypertext. But

twenty-first-century technology is not necessary for such an experience of space and spatiality. Palimpsestousness can be experienced within the physical space and transposed onto historic, cultural artifacts. A photograph taken by the photojournalist Chris Niedenthal on December 14, 1981, is a case in point.[19] It consists of three "texts." The first is a tank positioned in front of a movie theater deployed in the first days of Martial Law to keep order during the crackdown against the Solidarity movement. The second text is the name of the movie theater, "Kino Moskwa," which looms at the top of the photo over the tank and movie theater marquee.[20] The last is the marquee itself, which announces a screening of Francis Ford Coppola's 1979 film *Apocalypse Now*. Separately, each element possesses its own meaning and connotation. In combination with one another, however, they are pregnant with interpretative possibilities. When brought together into a single framed image, these three texts inscribe a synchronic moment of Warsaw's cityscape and spatiality with diachronic, historical implications that capture the clash between the oppressive political regime represented by the word "Moscow" and the tank, the connotations of the American film which achieved cult status in Poland, and the reinterpretation of the film's title as a speaker of truth about the heightened political oppression brought on by Martial Law.

Regarding the city as palimpsest also reveals an important aspect of the interaction between space and spatiality, namely, the potential for "newly inscribed" surface-level meanings to create narrative silences. Silence, however, does not mean absence, as the primary sources of this project demonstrate. This is the case, for example, with the neighborhood Muranów, which was inhabited primarily by the Jewish population of the city and became part of the Warsaw ghetto established by the Nazis during World War II and annihilated during the 1943 Warsaw Ghetto Uprising. In the 1950s, the ghetto rubble was used to build a socialist housing complex and the Jewish experience of this place was minimally commemorated. The Jewish presence (or absence?) in this neighborhood would be obliterated if not for a number of greater or smaller efforts tightly associated with the landscape. On a smaller scale, I am thinking of markers throughout the city that outline the borders of the wartime ghetto; on a larger scale we can look to the POLIN Museum of the History of Polish Jews located in Muranów. Such memorialization textualizes the city. At the same time, silences persist on a narrative level. For example, the narrative of prewar "Jewish" Warsaw in the postwar period was for the most part erased from the "Polish" memory of the city and was generally silenced both in socialist discourse and in narratives that resisted the communist regime. In areas of cultural discourse where the Jewish narrative remained on the surface of the official narrative (as in photobooks), it was often present to support the socialist message being constructed, not to reinscribe a Jewish presence onto the city. This was particularly evident in the commemorations of the 1943 Ghetto Uprising in the immediate postwar years, with monuments built in 1946 and 1948, over forty years before a monument to the 1944 Warsaw Uprising was erected.

In other areas of cultural discourse, the Jewish narrative was simply non-existent. For example, in Pola Gojawiczyńska's novel *Stolica* (1945; *The Capital*), the Jewish spatiality of Warsaw, including the ruins of the Nazi-established ghetto, is narratively absent despite its proximity to the action of the novel, its centrality to the city, and the extent of human and material devastation suffered there.[21] Gojawiczyńska's silence about Jewish Warsaw becomes all the more obvious when we read Adolf Rudnicki's story "Czysty nurt" ("Crystal Stream") about the destruction of prewar life and the impossibility of its postwar reconstruction. Rudnicki calls attention to the area of the Warsaw ghetto that was completely pulverized during the 1943 uprising and contrasts it with other parts of the postwar city. Set immediately after the war, the story begins with the main character, Abel, looking at the former ghetto where he

> expected to see destruction, but on the same scale as in the other districts . . . Here the city had been rubbed out, removed from the surface of the earth like a tent from a meadow. On other districts there were dead bodies; here there was not even a dead body. In this place the capital had been crushed to powder, not one stone was left on another. And though beneath these fields of rubble rested more dead than in a hundred cemeteries, there was nothing to suggest a cemetery.[22]

When Gojawiczyńska's Warsaw is contrasted with Rudnicki's city or, to broaden the perspective, Isaac Bashevis Singer's Warsaw from novels set in the prewar capital, we can only conclude that we are reading about three very different Warsaws.[23] At the same time, all three representations of Warsaw belong to a broadly defined Varsovian spatiality that includes spatial articulations, as well as silences.

Spatiality, Propaganda, and the Semiosphere

In considering the palimpsestic polyphony of space and spatiality, Yuri Lotman's later, post-structuralist concept of the semiosphere is particularly useful.[24] Defined as the space in which languages and discourses meet and function (here, "space" is a conceptual locus), Lotman's semiosphere accounts for contingent, diachronic, and nonlinguistic manifestations of culture.[25] Lotman describes the semiosphere as "a working mechanism whose separate elements are in complex dynamic relationships. This mechanism on a vast scale functions to circulate information, preserve it and to produce new messages."[26] Lotman's semiosphere "possesses memory" and "thus includes also the whole mass of texts ever created by mankind as well as programs for generating future texts."[27] Those languages or discourses which exist in the semiosphere of a cultural system thus constantly collide and conflict with one another regardless of their temporal location within history.[28] According to Lotman, such clashes are productive and create a sum greater than the whole. As Ernest Hess-Lüttich suggests, Lotman sees texts as generating spatiality. He points out that for Lotman, aesthetic objects (traditional texts, as well as pictures or buildings) that are parts of a semiotic system "design models of possible worlds" where "space works as a sign system through which social reality can be constructed."[29]

At the same time, however, if the semiosphere is the sum total of discourse that includes the past and the present, then it stands to reason that there is always a disjuncture between the actual physical space in the here and now and the language that describes it. Thus, space and spatiality overlap, but they are incongruous. If we are to consider "Warsaw" from this perspective, then Warsaw becomes the sum total of its physical and rhetorical manifestation over time. It is the continual rewriting of a Varsovian semiosphere that is dynamically driven by clashes between physical transformations of the space and the constantly generated rhetorical topoi of the city.[30] This also explains the disjuncture between the textual construction of Warsaw in propaganda under communism and the real experience of living in a city of ruins after the war. Hence the Varsovian semiosphere is, on the one hand, always greater than its physical boundaries, because from the perspective of time the resulting intersections of space and spatialities are potentially infinite. On the other hand, the Varsovian semiosphere is an abstraction limited by a geographic (albeit murky) border (i.e., the "boundaries" of the city).

For example, today's material and discursive manifestation of the place we call "Warsaw" is predated by a no longer existing material entity (prewar Warsaw) and a narrative spatiality that was shaped and determined by the prewar experience of the space. Literary examples illustrate this phenomenon well. Such novels as Bolesław Prus's *Lalka* (1890; *The Doll*), Zbigniew Uniłowski's *Wspólny pokój* (1932; *Shared Room*), or Isaac Bashevis Singer's *The Family Moskat* (1945), feature the Polish capital as a means of defining political and social constructs prior to World War II. These narratives textualize Warsaw and contribute to the meaning of the place while creating an alternative, narrative locus.[31] Warsaw narratives set after World War II, however, contend with a spatiality that refers to prewar Warsaw, a physical space that no longer exists, as well as with spatialities engendered by wartime destruction and the postwar reconstruction of the city. These narrative constructions refer to approximately the same geospatial coordinates; however, the narrative result is determined by the intersection between location, history, the experience of place, and the multitude of conceptions about Warsaw that develop as part of communal memory over time. Furthermore, the various textualizations of Warsaw result in polyphonic expressions of the capital that coexist, complement one another, or collide: Jewish Warsaw,[32] the Warsaw of the resistance movement or the Home Army, literary Warsaw of the interwar period, and the Warsaw of ruins and rubble, to name a few. Yet, despite this multitude of possibilities, we can talk about the specificity brought about by the experience of a space and how we express ourselves about it. "Warsaw" is thus a combination of its geospatial spot on the globe, its architecture, streets, people, and the discursive space of language, stories, and histories that are written about it. What is Paris, after all, without Proust or Balzac? Manchester or London without Dickens? Dublin without Joyce? New York without the sum of its geospatial points and the seemingly infinite iconic images of the American metropolis in films, and on postcards or T-shirts?

Lotman's concept of the semiosphere also refines our understanding of propaganda and how it functions. If we see propaganda as an attempt to control discourses or the clashes within the semiosphere, then we can begin to understand how seemingly incongruent ideas can discursively coexist even within a purportedly "unified" message. In an attempt to make an ideologically driven narrative of Warsaw a dominant discourse, propaganda sought to re-create Varsovian spatiality while physically reconstructing the capital. This circumstance changed the relationship between space and its textual representation. In most conceptions of the interaction between space and narrative, geospatial points as determined by their fixed position on the globe come first. In the case of Warsaw and other postwar socialist cities like Nowa Huta, the relative temporal distance between the (re-)creation of a physical space and its spatiality was compressed, if not reversed. In my view, Warsaw's "socialist" spatiality predated Warsaw as a "socialist" city, while the concept of a "socialist Warsaw" continued to be challenged by prewar or wartime conceptions of the capital. The ostensible necessity for socialist Warsaw to be read and experienced according to a socialist ideological framework forced propaganda to craft a spatiality that would shape the experience of the place before it was constructed, rather than allow the prewar sense of place to dominate the discursive semiosphere, or allow the postwar space to develop a spatiality independent of an official narrative.

The concepts of "semiosphere" and "palimpsest" help explain the interaction between the experience of physical space when we do not possess the code or "key" to understanding it, and spatiality, which provides us with the ability to decode messages of the past and present that linger in the urban landscape. *Mapping Warsaw* analyzes portions of the Varsovian semiosphere to provide a glimpse into the greater semiotic space that is "Warsaw," elucidating how clashes or conflicts within the semiosphere manifest themselves in cultural texts. At the same time, I tease out the many layers that have intertwined over time to create the Varsovian city-palimpsest. In this study, spatiality thus includes a wide range of narrative possibilities that can be considered representational (descriptions of space), discursive (how the space is "talked about" and what can or cannot be said about the space), and semiotic (the code or symbolic meanings attached to specific loci). Thus, rather than expressing a cartographic, bird's-eye view offered by modern atlases and road maps, spatiality refers to the way that written and visual narratives express our relationship to the physical world. In this way, I narrow my focus on the discursive mapping of space, or the representation of space in narration. As we shall see, such discursive, spatial mapping is a dynamic process that functions over time (diachronic perspective); simultaneously, it can be fragmentary and episodic, reflecting the nature of narration by calling attention to select geospatial points and often ignoring others (synchronic perspective).

Warsaw: A Capital City

Despite its near complete destruction by the end of World War II, Warsaw was rebuilt and remains Poland's capital to this day. But knowing that Warsaw was reconstructed at the geographic coordinates 52°13'47″ N and 21°00'42″ E after the war is not sufficient to understand the city. Geospatial markers do not help us decipher conflicting aesthetic registers of aristocratic palaces, secession-style *kamienice*, communist-era buildings, or new glass skyscrapers and malls. Nor do these coordinates help the average tourist understand the cultural significance attached to individual places in the city or the space of Warsaw itself. On a casual stroll through Warsaw, the uninitiated cannot know that after World War II parts of the city had been carefully rebuilt according to eighteenth-century paintings and interwar photographs, while other areas were built according to the socialist principles outlined by the Moscow-established postwar communist regime. Today, it is almost impossible to imagine that in 1945 the city lay in ruins, the victim of a systematic campaign by the Germans to wipe the Polish capital off the face of the Earth.

The decimation of Warsaw was a pivotal element of the Nazi *Generalplan Ost* which aimed to Germanize Central and Eastern Europe by expanding German territories to include occupied Poland, the Baltic states, Belarus, Russia, and Ukraine; annihilating the Jewish population of Europe; and enslaving, expelling, or resettling those considered "racially undesirable" (in this case, mostly Slavs). In one version of the plan to demolish the Polish capital, Warsaw was to be razed and rebuilt as a German enclave serviced by ethnic Poles housed in camps encircling the city. The bombing of Warsaw by the Germans in 1939 was the first effort in achieving this goal. As the war proceeded, the destruction of Warsaw occurred in two additional phases that had not been formally part of the plan:[33] the annihilation of the Nazi-imposed Warsaw ghetto after the 1943 uprising, which led to the death of over 350,000 Jews and left the area in rubble and ashes;[34] and the aftermath of the 1944 Warsaw Uprising, when German demolition squads set fire to the city, building by building, endeavoring to destroy anything left standing in the Polish capital. This effort was facilitated by the decision of the Soviet Army not to assist the insurgents of the 1944 uprising and instead to wait on the east bank of the Vistula River (Wisła) until the uprising was put down by the Germans; the Soviets nominally "liberated" Warsaw on January 17, 1945. While exact statistics on the extent of destruction vary depending on the sources, most agree that by the end of the war 80 to 85 percent of the city was damaged or destroyed. In 1945, Warsaw was a cemetery covered by 20 million meters³ of rubble, enough to fill 8,000 Olympic-sized swimming pools.[35]

Few would disagree that rebuilding Warsaw in the context of such vast devastation defied practical decisions based on economic or logistical factors; however, the cultural and symbolic value of the geographically specific point called "Warsaw" was much stronger than any challenge posed by the systematic destruction of the city. Hitler, who wanted to make Warsaw disappear, and Stalin, who encouraged and even supported Warsaw's postwar reconstruction, were both acutely aware of the capital's significance as a symbol of Polish national identity.[36] Established as the Polish capital under King Sigismund III Vasa in 1596, the city maintained its symbolic, if not actual, political role for over three centuries. During the period of the partitions when Poland disappeared as a state from the map of Europe,[37] Warsaw existed as the Duchy of Warsaw (1807–15) under Napoleon I; as the capital of the Congress Kingdom of Poland (1815–64), a quasi-sovereign state under the Russian tsar; and finally as the capital of the Privislansky Kraj (Vistulaland), subject to intense Russification. Despite its political marginalization at this time, Warsaw remained an important urban center, becoming the third largest city in the Russian Empire by the end of the nineteenth century.[38] Warsaw's location between East and West was considered its greatest attribute, making it an important stop along train routes between Europe and the Russian Empire.[39] Architects like Ferdinand de Lesseps, the builder of the Suez Canal, envisioned Warsaw as the largest European city of the twentieth century.[40] Between the world wars, it was also one of the most ethnically diverse cities of the region, consisting of about half Poles (mostly Catholic) and one-third to two-fifths Jews.[41] When Poland was reconstituted in 1918 as an independent state after the First World War according to Woodrow Wilson's Fourteen Points, the interwar government was faced with wartime destruction, a legacy of overcrowding and poor housing, and neglected infrastructure exacerbated by Warsaw's role as a fortress city with little autonomy under tsarist rule. Russified politically and architecturally, Warsaw's landscape was marked by such edifices of the ruling Russian Empire as the Citadel that housed tsarist troops stationed there in response to the 1830–31 November Uprising, whose insurgents sought Poland's independence.[42]

In 1918 Warsaw was established as the capital of the Second Polish Republic, which was tasked with unifying a politically, economically, and legally fragmented country. In addition to serving as the seat of government, interwar Warsaw was a place of great promise from an urban planning perspective. The 1934 concept of "Warszawa Funkcjonalna" (Functional Warsaw) proposed a modernized, holistic vision of Warsaw's development as a rationally organized European metropolis; it shaped urban planning in the capital until the start of World War II.[43] In addition to its political role and its prominence as an up-and-coming modern city, Warsaw possessed symbolic value. From the moment Poland lost its independence in the late eighteenth century, Warsaw was at the heart of resistance and patriotism. It was the place of successive uprisings in the nineteenth and twentieth centuries, including the already mentioned November Uprising and the later January Uprising in 1863, both against the Russian Empire. On the eve of World War II, Warsaw was thus the space where many of its most cherished national heroes had met defeat and death, marking "a central point of the national graveyard."[44] The fate of Warsaw and Poland during World War II would only intensify the symbolic value of the Polish capital, with the 1943 Warsaw ghetto and 1944 Warsaw uprisings against the German occupiers leading to the greatest human and material losses the capital had ever witnessed.

Warsaw, a Socialist Capital?

Formally governed during the war from London by the Polish government-in-exile and within the country through the activities of the Home Army (Armia Krajowa), Poland fought the war on two fronts: against Germany in the west and the Soviet Union in the east.[45] While the Nazi leadership sought to annihilate Poland, with Warsaw as one of its main military targets, the Soviets took measures to establish a communist regime by occupying the country and setting up a puppet government with the help of the communist Polish Workers' Party (Polska Partia Robotnicza, PPR). On January 1, 1944, the PPR established the National Home Council (Krajowa Rada Narodowa, KRN), a self-proclaimed "parliamentary" governing body subservient to Moscow that actively sought to displace the internationally recognized government-in-exile. From today's perspective, the KRN can be seen as the genesis of the future People's Republic.[46] With the formalization of Moscow's de facto control over Poland during the Yalta Conference in February 1945, the country became a Soviet satellite state and found itself behind the Iron Curtain under the Provisional Government of National Unity (Tymczasowy Rząd Jedności Narodowej, TRJN) formed by a decree of the KRN.

After the war, the communist leadership in Poland exerted control through rigged elections, persecution and repression of the opposition, and other totalitarian strategies like censorship and propaganda. The reconstruction of Warsaw played an important role in the legitimization of communist power. Rebuilding the Polish capital became a postwar focal point and an important goal of the new socialist government, which sought to conflate the reconstruction of the city with the process of "building a socialist state." Through Warsaw's reconstruction and the discursive recoding of the city as a "socialist" capital, the communist leadership wanted to legitimize their power and prove their efficacy, domestically and internationally.[47] In 1944, however, before the final decision to rebuild Warsaw was made, communist leaders debated where and how a new socialist capital for Poland should be built. With Warsaw in ruins, some wanted to return the Polish capital to Kraków, considered Poland's historical center of governance. Others proposed Lublin, where the communist KRN was located. Yet another proposal suggested moving the capital to Łódź, a city located about eighty-five miles southwest of Warsaw. Compared to Warsaw, Łódź was minimally destroyed during the war and provided a ready infrastructure. Furthermore, it was a centrally located industrial center with a large working class and, thus, an ideologically convenient contrast to Warsaw's deeply entrenched aristocratic, noble, and middle-class traditions. Supposedly, however, Stalin believed that the reconstruction of Warsaw was of utmost importance to the establishment of a communist regime after the war. According to some sources, even before the Yalta Conference, the Soviet leader met with Bolesław Bierut, then chairman of the KRN and later Poland's president and prime minister, in Moscow and explicitly told him that not only should Warsaw remain the capital of a communist Poland, but that the KRN should move to Warsaw as quickly as possible; he promised financial assistance from the Soviet Union for the reconstruction process.[48]

Although the Sejm, the Polish parliament, did not pass the official decree to rebuild the city until July 3, 1947,[49] plans for reconstruction and early efforts to clean up Warsaw began before the war ended and before the communist authorities could set up a government in Warsaw. Once German forces withdrew from Warsaw in January 1945, the city returned to life despite the devastation. Thousands came to the capital and settled in bombed-out buildings and dangerous, unsanitary ruins. Of those who came to the capital, many were Varsovians, who had survived the war and were returning home; but many were from other areas of Poland seeking new lives in the postwar era. Regardless of who returned for whatever reason, these (new) Varsovians were the first to tackle the chaos of a war-torn landscape and to reclaim the physical space for human habitation. They established provisionary shopping districts and cleared rubble by hand. With time, such grassroots efforts would become co-opted by the communist regime, which organized monthly, and later annual, volunteer "de-rubbling" events. But the early unorganized efforts were a crucial testimony to Warsaw's symbolic importance, and were as consequential as political decisions. A "resurrected Warsaw" was a manifestation of resolve and a reified victory over Nazi Germany.

Warsaw's reconstruction was an obvious means of unifying Polish society despite the political differences that abounded after the war. Rebuilding the city held a positive value for communists and noncommunists alike. As such, it was a convenient symbol to be exploited by the new regime, which sought to construct a new, common identity for Varsovians through a rhetoric that did not differentiate between those who returned to the city and new migrants coming from the countryside or elsewhere. In official discourse, these were all "Varsovians." More importantly, however, appropriating the "idea" of Warsaw was an easy way for the communist leadership to establish a rallying point, rather than a point of division, in a society that—to a great extent—rejected the communists' newly seized power. Spearheading the reconstruction process meant legitimizing a political regime that was largely seen as installed by Moscow. Immediately upon the January 1945 decision that Warsaw would remain Poland's capital, the city's postwar reconstruction became conflated with the notion of "building socialism." By February of that year, the Office for the Reconstruction of the Capital (Biuro Odbudowy Stolicy, BOS) was established and organized efforts to rebuild Warsaw were set in motion. With the assistance of architects, engineers, urban planners, and historic preservationists, the Office for the Reconstruction of the Capital started designing a postwar Warsaw. But there was much to take into account in the reconstruction process. What would the new Warsaw look like? How would it represent the new, socialist society planned for Poland? How would the new Warsaw preserve what remained of the old? Should the ruins of "old" Warsaw be preserved and a new city be built in the vicinity? Preservationists debated with those who wanted a distinctly "socialist city" on how best to fuse Warsaw's prewar "historical" image with the ideal of creating a model socialist capital. The city's urban plan, its aesthetics, how it would refer to the past, and how it would "reflect" the future were deliberated. Some saw the rubble and ruins as an opportunity to construct a new socialist city divorced from the past. Others, led by sentiment and patriotism, were determined that the Polish capital should rise from the ashes as a testimony to Polish resolve against Germany's wartime attempts toward its annihilation and as a monument to the nation's past. Still others saw the opportunity to create a new city inspired by Western architecture and modernist principles of urban planning, while some looked east to Moscow.[50] In this way, Warsaw's future mirrored the political debates around Poland's future during the war and in the early postwar years: would Poland—and Warsaw—move westward toward the London government-in-exile or eastward toward the Soviet Union?

Ultimately, a compromise would be struck between preservationists and socialist ideologues. Warsaw would become a model socialist city worthy of a socialist country. Housing was to move away from the tight overcrowding attributed to a bourgeois social structure of the interwar period toward spaces that would cater to the working classes. The old *oficyny*, living spaces added to the back of *kamienice* for poorer residents or as servants' quarters, were to be eliminated. The proletariat was to have bright, spacious, and hygienic housing that would "produce" a new type of man, the socialist Pole, who rejected the prewar world and embraced a new mentality shaped by communist ideology.[51] In Warsaw, this transformation of Polish society was to be encouraged with the help of a city plan that privileged parade grounds, enormous stadiums or halls designated for mass rallies and meetings of workers, and broad avenues in lieu of narrow streets and bourgeois markets and shopping areas.[52] Despite this focus on building a socialist city, however, the socialist urban project often only changed the language of city planning but not its substance. The basic building blocks of the socialist city remained similar or comparable to "traditional" cities with a central "sacred" location, like the unrealized plan for a Palace of Soviets in Moscow that was to replace the Cathedral of Christ the Savior.[53] There remained a need for efficient transportation (mass transit, as well as other infrastructure), accessible and convenient housing, a workforce and jobs, the establishment of a central locus for the governing authority (needed for a capital), and the organization of places to "acquire" food, clothing, and other goods.

At the same time, support for preserving Warsaw's historical legacy would not be abandoned, even at the risk of re-creating select prewar middle-class and aristocratic spaces that might cast a shadow over the socialist building project. To preserve a sense of the authentic, building facades of the Old Town, New Town (Nowe Miasto), and Krakowskie Przedmieście (literally, "Kraków suburb"), one of the main Varsovian historic streets that is part of what is called the Trakt Królewski or Royal Route,[54] were meticulously reconstructed to evoke the city as recorded on canvas by the Venetian painter Bernardo "Canaletto" Bellotto in the eighteenth century. Hailed for their veracity, attention to detail, and documentary value, the younger Canaletto's paintings were crucial to the process of re-creating the "authentic" image of historic Warsaw by "artists and engineers, craftsmen and laborers."[55] The return to an older version of Warsaw came at the expense of urban development from the interwar period. For example, prior to the war, Nowy Świat had been transformed from a nineteenth-century street that connected the aristocratic manors in southern Warsaw with Old Town in the north into a thoroughfare of modernist architecture, shops, and restaurants. This area had been destroyed during the war, but the interwar modernist version of Nowy Świat was considered too "bourgeois" to be reconstructed in a postwar socialist capital. Thus Nowy Świat was returned to an older, more ideologically convenient, iteration and today exemplifies a selective return to "authenticity" in Warsaw's reconstruction process. Going further back in time, postwar ruins exposed the historical, material, urban palimpsest and revealed remnants of medieval architecture and infrastructure that had been buried or hidden by newer construction.

After the war, the archeological nature of the city became palpable and provided a means of reaching into Warsaw's past in order to legitimize present reconstruction efforts that consisted of selecting which "old" facades would become Warsaw's new architectural image. As de-rubbling efforts around war-torn and crumbled nineteenth-century neo-gothic facades gave way to evidence of architectural remnants from the late medieval period, the historical accuracy and authenticity of the reconstruction process became a new and pressing question.[56] These newly revealed historical elements were occasionally incorporated into the reconstruction by preservationists. And they were also sometimes exploited by propaganda to reconstitute a sense of Warsaw's authenticity as it rose from the rubble of war, underscoring the postwar city's historical continuity while masking the political intentions at the foundation of official reconstruction plans. In the end, postwar Warsaw became a fusion of two contradictory ideas: (1) to rebuild select historical buildings and sites, and (2) to develop the urban space according to socialist principles. And this fusion was influenced by practical considerations that took precedence over all else. Limited by the terrain and pressed for time, parts of the postwar city were redesigned according to extant plans, old foundations, existing street patterns, and urban development plans designed during the interwar period. As David Crowley aptly writes, reconstruction "proved, in practice, to be a synthesis of both restoration projects designed to reproduce facsimiles of the prewar urban fabric as well as new schemes to revive the city."[57]

With the chance to replan and restructure the space, communist officials saw the potential for transforming Warsaw into the ultimate physical manifestation of socialist (i.e., communist) ideology. But the new authorities' plans to take control of the reconstruction process and appropriate the *physical* space proved to be insufficient to overcome the resistance of the "reconstructivists." This struggle between the two factions translated into symbolically and discursively appropriating Warsaw by both those who wished to make the Polish capital one of the linchpins of communist propaganda in early postwar Poland and those who saw cultural continuity as an ineluctable component of modern visual and written culture. Warsaw's official narrative eventually established a cultural and historical continuity with the past *and* envisioned a Polish society propelled into the future, mirroring the debates about Warsaw's physical reconstruction. Material reconstruction meant rooting Warsaw's past in the present and showing that not all that was of the past had been rejected; socialist urban development was to show positive progress toward the reshaping and refashioning of Polish society from one based on aristocratic and bourgeois principles to one that placed the proletariat at the center of its concerns. As such, Warsaw's physical and rhetorical (re)constructions, together, were meant to redefine Polish identity through propaganda aimed at influencing the cultural and collective imagination.[58] These tensions would constitute the basis of the official narrative on Warsaw from the end of the war to the political Thaw in 1956.

Authenticity and "Stołeczność"

Placing Warsaw at the center of propaganda was a conscious discursive act of spatial (re)construction by postwar authorities. Just as Warsaw was reconstructed to a large extent on the remnants of the old city plan, the extant ruins, and remaining foundations in combination with new, "ideologically" construed edifices, the official *idea* of the postwar Polish capital was constructed according to a narrative of historical continuity in combination with a socialist projection of the future. While each primary source analyzed in this study presents Warsaw according to the rules and poetics of its specific genre, Varsovian-themed propaganda promoted specific narrative building blocks which were adapted and incorporated across sources. Two of these elements, particularly prominent in the immediate postwar years, worked towards legitimizing communist authority in Poland. The first was a reaffirmation of Warsaw's *stołeczność* or capital status as a *socialist* city for the average worker. The second was the affirmation of new Warsaw's "authenticity," a backward-looking narrative that posed a significant rhetorical problem for an ideology that was focused on bettering the future of the proletariat. Propaganda bridged this gap through carefully controlled language. According to this narrative, Warsaw was to become (in the future) a "socialist capital for every citizen," taking the best of Warsaw's past "aura" and "authenticity" while eliminating the excesses of bourgeois capitalism.

Closely intertwined, *stołeczność* and authenticity discursively embraced past, present, and future. They referred to the historical rationale and legacy of a city that symbolically and historically unified the Polish nation. In a socialist context, they were recast as new and better versions of a past historical legacy. And they were presented as a gift to future generations. This relationship between Warsaw's socialist *stołeczność* and its historical continuity was expressed on the pages of *Stolica: Warszawski Tygodnik Ilustrowany* (*The Capital: A Varsovian Illustrated Weekly*) throughout the late 1940s. In a September 1949 article, Warsaw's reconstruction was described as a process of preparing the city for "its role as the capital" and was seen as "an expression of the most vital interests of the popular masses [*masy ludowe*] and their battle for social justice, for a better life, for socialism."[59] While underscoring Warsaw's role as a new, socialist administrative center, maintaining a balance between the concepts of "old" and "new" was an important part of Varsovian discourse in the earliest days following the war. In the first issue of *The Capital*, an article responded to widely circulating criticism that the faithful reconstruction of Warsaw's historical buildings could never reconstitute the original. Stating that "it won't ever be the same," the author compared the reconstruction of historic buildings to a portrait of a deceased person. According to him, the reconstructed edifices would be pleasing to Varsovians and Poles in the same way as the portrait of a deceased person, which—though dramatically different from the living specimen—provides a sense of pleasure nonetheless.[60] The article acknowledged that at first, Warsaw's reconstructed beauty might seem artificial (*sztuczne*), but that over time

> the fresh walls will once again absorb the atmosphere of Old Town, an atmosphere which continues there till this day; a patina will cover the fresh copper, and countless surviving fragments, portals, lattices, entablatures, door frames—woven into buildings reconstructed according to their previous forms—will permeate the entire resurrected Old Town, with its Cathedral and Royal Castle.[61]

According to this article, Warsaw's authenticity was to be provided by recycled and salvaged *material* remnants that were incorporated into new (re)constructions. The reconstruction was to re-create a "portrait" of the "original" city that would evoke pleasure and memory but substantially differ from the original by its socialist content. The full-scale reconstruction of architectural history differed from the portrait in many ways, particularly in that the new, old Warsaw would become a self-reflexive image, vessel, and space for the aura of authenticity, and over time would soak in the atmosphere or "rhetorical *topos*"[62] of the capital to reestablish its narrative (if not physical) genius loci. In this way, Warsaw was to become an image or reflection of its past self, but one that had been purged of its negative, class-based qualities. This problem of authenticity was negotiated particularly saliently in the photobooks and newsreels, which combined visual and verbal techniques to elide the contradictions inherent to a discourse that simultaneously rejected and embraced the past (see chapters 1 and 2). Debates in the Office for the Reconstruction of the Capital continued long into the 1970s on how and what historical buildings should be preserved; however, the *discourse* on new-old Warsaw was already codified during this postwar decade, and remnants of it remain up to today.

1949: Socialist Realism and the Six-Year Plan for Warsaw's Reconstruction

Until 1949, the "new old" oxymoron permeated Varsovian discourse, with Warsaw's official narrative focusing on a balance between the capital's new socialist image and the assurance of Warsaw as an authentic inheritor of the past. In 1949, however, the balance in propaganda between the "old, authentic Warsaw" and the "new socialist Warsaw" shifted toward the capital as a model *socialist* city. This shift was precipitated by Bolesław Bierut's July 3, 1949 announcement of the Six-Year Plan for Warsaw's Reconstruction (Sześcioletni plan odbudowy Warszawy), which marked the end of the first phase of reconstruction and the beginning of the next stage of (socialist) development, summarized the reconstruction progress made between 1945 and 1949, and outlined future development plans for the city.[63] According to Bierut, the first stage of reconstruction had been focused on clearing the city of rubble and salvaging construction materials. This phase was now complete, and so a new phase of construction was ensuing.[64] For Warsaw to be a well-ordered, rational "factory of culture,"[65] he explained, this next phase required "planned management from the Party and People's Republic more than ever before" and would constitute a "conscious and increasingly wide-ranging application of socialist economic management and socialist construction of not only the Capital but the entire country."[66] Bierut further underscored that as part of the general economic, cultural, and social development planned for Poland, Warsaw's six-year plan would result in "new, better, and more rational living conditions for the working man, addressing both individual and social needs."[67]

Bierut's Six-Year Plan for Warsaw's Reconstruction coincided with the adoption of socialist realism in the arts that same year.[68] Though officially lasting until 1956, a mere seven years,[69] socialist realism undoubtedly left its mark on Polish arts and letters. Though often assessed as a cataclysmic moment in Polish culture, the 1949 adoption of socialist realism inspired a flurry of ideologically correct works of prose, poetry, film, painting, sculpture, and architecture.[70] According to a March 1950 newsreel, the First All-Poland Exhibit of Fine Arts (I Ogólnopolska Wystawa Plastyki) at the National Museum featured over 600 paintings and sculptures that called attention to "concrete topics associated with the socialist reconstruction of the country" and presented "the work and life of the people [naród] in a simple way that is understandable to all." These artistic works depicted "charming and beautiful subjects" such as "work in the fields," "work in the mines," and the construction of major infrastructure projects (PKF 14/50:11).[71]

According to the 1950 nonfiction film Nowa sztuka (New Art), socialist realism dictated that art "must serve and educate. It must serve the great idea of Socialism. It must be a weapon in the fight for freedom, for the happiness of tomorrow's world."[72] As an aesthetic meant for the worker and peasant, the artistic form had to be easily accessible and understandable.[73] With these goals in mind, literature led the way. Adopting a tendentious formula prescribed in the 1930s in the Soviet Union, writers of prose works borrowed from nineteenth-century realism, rejected the experimentation of modernism, and adopted a politically correct stance through an ideologically motivated plot. "Positive heroes" possessed the ideal virtues of a typical socialist worker and exhibited faith in a future socialist society.[74] Formulaic and artistically inferior, such literature was eventually pejoratively labeled "literature of production."[75] Despite the shortcomings of socialist realism as demonstrated by prose, similar principles were adopted in other art forms. As in the Soviet Union, poetry rejected modernist and avant-garde forms and embraced didacticism. It glorified labor and featured steelworks, construction sites, and Warsaw reconstruction. Odes exalting Stalin and Bierut were common. Such verse was rhythmic and sing-songy, and—per the requirements of the aesthetic—"easily accessible."[76] This principle of simplicity also applied to music. Considered too abstract to carry a socialist message on its own, music was often deployed in connection with other art forms, finding its most common expression in the pieśń masowa (song for the masses)—catchy, folk-like melodies with easy-to-memorize lyrics that glorified socialism. In film, the production novel was adapted for the screen with plots about workers, the countryside, labor competitions, and the elimination of "reactionary bourgeois" ideology.[77] Because screenplays determined the ideological value of a proposed project, films often portrayed cinematic versions of positive heroes and rejected experimentation for the sake of "correct realism" or in order to portray Polish reality "as it should be," not as it was.

In painting and sculpture, a socialist realist iconography developed. It focused on socialist leaders, revolutionary activity, and labor. Workers were portrayed as strong, healthy, happy, optimistic, and young representatives of ideology, and their labor was contextualized within the Marxist class struggle and the fight for a better future. Images of The Worker abounded on propaganda posters designed by such artists as Waldemar Świerzy and Wiktor Górka that promoted Warsaw's reconstruction or in such paintings as Aleksander Kobzdej's *Podaj cegłę* (1950; *Pass the Brick*), which depicts three masons laying bricks. With the masons' facial features barely distinguishable from each other, this painting exemplifies a tendency toward de-individualization encoded in the visual iconography of socialist realism. This inclination was likewise visible in freestanding sculptures, as well as those installed on the facades of socialist realist buildings. But the application of this loosely defined aesthetic in architecture did not stop with decorative elements. New buildings were designed as monumental, adapting neoclassical styles meant to assist in engineering a new society and to affirm the power of the communist authorities by evoking a mythologized and venerable antiquity.[78]

Though 1949 was the official start of socialist realism in Poland, it did not appear out of nowhere. As the literary critic Hanna Gosk points out, the Polish "cultural worker" was assigned the role of "engineer of the human soul" as early as 1944 in Lublin, with authorities reiterating Stalin's notion that the writer and artist were as important to the construction of a socialist state as were the steelworker, mason, and engineer.[79] She explains that "culture was recognized as equally important to other areas of socio-civic [*społeczno-państwowe*] life, and the cultural worker . . . became conscious of his societal importance."[80] Of note is that the Main Office of the Control of Press, Publications, and Public Performances (Główny Urząd Kontroli Prasy, Publikacji i Widowisk, GUKP-PiW) was already established in 1946 after an earlier iteration created in 1945. GUKPPiW looked to Soviet models for how best to disseminate ideology, and it became key to the process of "socializing" Polish culture.[81] Such control over artistic production was bolstered by official statements on the importance of art in building a socialist state. For example, in a 1947 speech at the opening of a Wrocław radio station, Bierut stated that "the nation has a right to set expectations of artists" and that artistic works should "correspond to the needs of the community" rather than "awaken doubts when inspiration [*zapał*] and faith in victory are needed."[82] Soon after in 1948, Jakub Berman, who was second only to Bierut with close ties to Stalin and head of the Security Apparatus (Urząd Bezpieczeństwa), stated that the "class struggle" demanded battle-like "creative explorations in literature, art, and scholarly inquiry."[83]

As official representations of Warsaw demonstrate, socialist goals drove propaganda and censorship from the earliest postwar years, which meant a *progressive* (rather than sudden) adoption of socialist realist aesthetic

principles from 1945 to 1949. During this period, socialist realist-like propaganda about the capital's reconstruction predated the official adoption of the
aesthetic and utilized many of the later-defined precepts in the iconic images it
promoted. As a "socialist city," Warsaw was a place of industry, construction
workers, construction sites, and new housing projects that were supposed to
raise socialist children, provide improved living conditions and health care,
and offer a workers' haven, in comparison to capitalist societies that were
depicted as depraved, fascist, and raising "cannon fodder" by indulging in
bourgeois habits and modern art that deformed the human psyche.[84] Socialist
themes prepared the ground for a wholesale adoption of socialist realism by
the late 1940s. The Varsovian narrative highlighted generic construction topics as symbols of "building socialism." These shaped Warsaw's official image
even before the adoption of a socialist realist aesthetic and were meant to
allay the negative connotations caused by the challenges of reconstruction, as
well as to ameliorate the tensions between communists and anticommunists.
By focusing on the redevelopment of Warsaw, urban progress on a mass scale
was at the forefront of propaganda, while the trials of hard living and working conditions besetting the individual worker were effectively ignored. This
idealized propaganda image of reconstruction neglected to account for the
reality of poverty, crime, a persistent lack of housing, and other shortages
that contradicted the sanitized images of Warsaw and its reconstruction that
were presented officially.

This "lacquered" quality (to borrow a term popularized by the Soviet
Thaw) was tempered by promoting Warsaw's uniqueness as a capital of the
past, present, and future. Warsaw's symbolic value in cultural discourse was
addressed by a narrative that highlighted its distinctiveness as the *supreme*
example of a socialist (capital) city. This exceptionality came through in
the rhetorical, yet anachronistic, formulation of a "new" historical Warsaw
endowed with a socialist significance. To control this discourse of "new old,"
the dominant Varsovian narrative narrowed its focus on specific geospatial
reference points around which spatiality was aggressively constructed. On
the one hand, there was a focus on such "historic" areas as Mariensztat, a
former *jurydyka*[85] founded by the nobleman Eustachy Potocki, the Old Town
Market Square (Rynek Starego Miasta), Nowy Świat Street, and Łazienki
Park. However, these historical reconstructions were often juxtaposed with or
overshadowed by a discursive focus on major socialist urban planning projects like the Marszałkowska Residential District (Marszałkowska Dzielnica
Mieszkaniowa, MDM); the Trasa W-Z (literally, "east-west thoroughfare"),
the largest infrastructure project of the late 1940s that connects the banks
of the Vistula River via a tunnel that runs under the streets Krakowskie
Przedmieście and Miodowa near Zamkowy Square (plac Zamkowy); Stalin's
"gift" of the Palace of Culture and Science (Pałac Kultury i Nauki) and the
adjacent Defilad Square (plac Defilad), the largest parade square in Europe to
this day; and "rational" housing projects in the neighborhoods of Muranów,

Koło, and Wola. These specific historic and socialist geospatial reference points and "textualizations" of Warsaw in official publications throughout the first postwar decade were balanced with generic socialist aspects planned for the city and were continually contrasted with one another. Such juxtapositions created a Warsaw-specific definition of the space that embraced conflicting or incongruous architectural and narrative registers and outlined a uniquely Varsovian spatiality. But this also meant that areas physically located between these specific geospatial points were subject to narrative generalizations or silences, creating "peripheral" spatialities of places that were sometimes geographically within the very center of the city but absent from discourse.

War had not only disturbed Warsaw's physical manifestation, but it also dramatically transformed its spatiality by attaching new symbolic meanings to the city. Warsaw became an important presence in every sphere of postwar reconstruction: political, social, ideological, national, and cultural. In particular, there was a strong trend toward memorializing the Warsaw of the past through memoirs, historical films set in prewar or wartime Warsaw, and in photography. Representations of the contemporary city as it was being reconstructed, however, were the purview of propaganda and walked hand-in-hand with official reconstruction goals. The official narrative of Warsaw, while coming from the political center, intersected with other conceptions of Warsaw not only by the very nature of the dynamics of a cultural semiosphere, but by the nature of urban space as a material and symbolic construct; as a place with a use-value; as well as a symbolic space of power, authority, patriotism, and trauma. Postwar narratives attempted to create a new language of Warsaw within a preexisting semiotic sphere, where conceptions of the city were bound to clash.[86] These narrative representations of Warsaw in the immediate decade after the war were simultaneously articulating and creating versions of the physical space *as it was being built and created*; this entailed adopting and adapting old discourses, as well as developing new ones. In the following chapters, I demonstrate how this occurred across genres.

Note on Street Names

For those readers who are unfamiliar with Warsaw or the Polish language, street names appear in Polish (as they would on a map) in combination with their English designations ("avenue(s)," "square," or "street" for the Polish *aleja/aleje*, *plac*, and *ulica*). Thus, "ulica Marszałkowska" is rendered as "Marszałkowska Street," and "plac Konstytucji" (literally, "square of the constitution") is rendered as "Konstytucji Square." I hope this will assist readers in locating streets on a map, be it a paper or digital one.

Chapter 1

Re-creating Warsaw in Photobooks

In 1949, the Civic Fund for the Reconstruction of the Capital published *Warszawa, stolica Polski* (*Warsaw, the Capital of Poland*), which it claimed was the first photobook on the city of Warsaw in the postwar period.[1] Printed in three editions in just one year, the photobook presented a collection of approximately 400 sepia-toned photographs with one to six images per two-page spread, and was printed on heavy stock paper about 9.5 by 13.5 inches. The photobook covered the history of Warsaw in illustration from the fourteenth century to the period of reconstruction in the late 1940s and presented a future, socialist vision of the city using photographs, copies of renderings, and images of small-scale models of building projects. Following a full-page portrait of President Bolesław Bierut and a long quote from a speech he gave on January 17, 1946, in which he lauded the exceptional nature of the Polish capital and its destruction, the authors of the photobook described their rationale for publishing *Warsaw, the Capital of Poland* as fulfilling the need for "a publication that simply and through images reminds us of old Warsaw, her experiences of war," "present[s] information about the reconstruction that has been completed," and describes "plans for future development of the city in an accessible and illustrated way." In service of this task were "images rather than words," which were to "reproduce the form and life of the capital." The written text, according to the authors, was simply a "means of connecting and supplementing the illustrated content."[2]

In claiming the primacy of the image over the word, the authors of *Warsaw, the Capital of Poland* implied that the images could and should speak for themselves. This was certainly not a new concept, with early photobooks exploiting the seeming superiority of the image over language.[3] At the same time, the authors called attention to a central conundrum of photography. While the images in the text *could* tell a visual narrative of Warsaw's history from before, during, and after the war, by themselves they imparted little information that could be constructed into a cohesive historical narrative by readers perusing the photobook. The sepia tone of the photographs made their age and date unclear, occasionally rendering images of prewar buildings and their postwar reconstructions indistinguishable from one another and requiring captions to locate the photographs within time, if not place. Likewise, the photographs of postwar rubble relied on the symbiosis between text and image for historicizing and contextualizing. To piece together the visual history of Warsaw required the expression of this context through language. When analyzing the captions and essays of the photobook, it also becomes apparent that despite the purported secondary function of the written text, there were carefully constructed narratives and ideas being promoted or "taught" between the images published. Without the written text, some of the images were "unreadable"; however, the text, which provided a space-time context often integrated with a tendentious political message, had limited impact without the photographic illustrations. This fundamental symbiosis between text and image is one of the most important aspects of Warsaw's postwar reconstruction of spatiality, particularly in the late 1940s and early 1950s; however, as the postwar narrative became more and more entrenched in public consciousness and politics influenced the parameters of propaganda, the balance between text and image changed in favor of the photographs, with the captions primarily expressing geospatial markers.

In light of Warsaw's twenty-first-century economic, urban, and architectural prosperity, the Polish capital's wartime devastation is difficult to imagine without the assistance of photographs. In 1945, however, it was almost equally difficult to imagine that a European capital had once stood where now rubble and ash served as the burial ground for thousands of Varsovians, both Christian and Jewish.[4] Add to this the tendency toward a domestic and international discourse that claimed Warsaw had ceased to exist, and photographic images served as some of the only material evidence of a once-vibrant capital city located at these particular geographic coordinates. Of course, it was not the space itself that had disappeared. As Adolf Ciborowski, chief architect of Warsaw from 1956 to 1964,[5] wrote: "The buildings lay in ruins. But the humble marker engraved with [Warsaw's] geographic coordinates [located on Teatralny Square] survived. The city could be destroyed, but its geographic location could not be changed."[6] To rephrase Ciborowski's statement, Warsaw's spatiality, rather than the space or place, was the real victim of German destruction.

At a time when words failed to express the memory of prewar Warsaw, the degree of human and urban devastation of the war, and the colossal reconstruction project undertaken after the war, photographs of the city were some of the seemingly most objective means to describe the pre-1939 capital and the extensive destruction left by the Germans. These photographs created a "virtual" map of Poland's capital by combining photographic verisimilitude with cultural connotations in book form and using captions and sequencing to locate the images in time and space. Exploiting the documentary value of the medium, photographic representations of the city were an obvious means of establishing new city icons, as well as broadly disseminating material proof that Warsaw had indeed risen from the ashes. They were important, thus, for resuscitating Warsaw as an anthropological place and were used for (re)constructing Varsovian spatiality by communists and noncommunists alike. *Warsaw, the Capital of Poland* may have been communist Poland's first Varsovian photobook, but it certainly was not the last.

From the earliest days following the war, photography and, later, photobooks were integral to (re-)creating the meaning and symbolism of the city. They represent some of the first attempts at discursively and visually reconstructing the Polish capital from its wartime destruction and helped define what today are considered iconic Varsovian spaces. While other cities have their Eiffel Towers, Statues of Liberty, and Towers of London, postwar Warsaw was bereft of comparable significations and had the challenge and, some may say, the opportunity to redefine the capital's architectural icons and narrative discourses. In the postwar decade, such loci as the Łazienki Park, the reconstructed Old Town (Stare Miasto), Zamkowy Square (plac Zamkowy) with a 72-foot column topped by a statue of King Sigismund III Vasa, the communist-era infrastructure project called Trasa W-Z photographed from the left bank of the Vistula River (Wisła), and the socialist realist Palace of Culture and Science (Pałac Kultury i Nauki) became Warsaw's best-known visual icons. Overtime, Varsovian photobooks, which often distilled the messages of the communist regime into a succinct visual-verbal hybrid, were an important means of disseminating and constructing the meanings of these iconic spaces.

The photobook has been defined as a "book—with or without text—in which the work's primary message is carried by photographs" and "authored by a photographer or by someone editing and sequencing the work of a photographer, or even a number of photographers." Photobooks demonstrate a coherent design and a specific theme or subject that is followed through with "intention, logic, continuity, climax, sense, and perfection."[7] From the artist's photobook that presents a selection of one photographer's oeuvre to collaborative photographic reportage or picture-stories that purport to document objectively an event or place, the photobook is at first glance a visual medium that grants more importance to pictures than written text. Upon further consideration, however, the separation of image from word quickly reveals itself as a fallacy. Combining photographs, exposition or narrative, captioning, and sequencing, the photobook is at its very core a visual-verbal text.[8] As Patrizia Di Bello and Shamoon Zamir point out, although the photographs within a photobook have a greater role than simply illustrating text or transmitting evidence, "they do not transcend the texts that accompany them; rather, image and text work within a dialectical relationship."[9]

Because of this union between text and image, photobooks were a convenient means of reconstructing Varsovian spatiality in the aftermath of war, and *albumy fotograficzne* or, in other words, photobooks featuring Warsaw, were published in Poland by state-owned publishing houses, as well as abroad by Poles exiled after the war and often opposed to the communist government. Whether communist-sanctioned or diaspora-sponsored, these Varsovian-themed photobooks generated multiple "mini" Warsaws. They transcended time and space through narrative simultaneity that embraced past, present, and future. They created an "eternal now" that was only possible within the binding of a book. Mirroring the nature of urban space, the photobooks portrayed buildings and city streets in archeological layers.[10] Archival photographs from the prewar period brought the past into the present in a real and palpable way, provided a means of depicting Warsaw "as it was" before the war, and attempted to capture the city's prewar energy and atmosphere. Images of postwar rubble and ruins recorded the devastation that resulted from Nazi policies toward Warsaw, and served as a reminder of the starting point for postwar reconstruction efforts. In the People's Republic of Poland, photographs of newly (re)built buildings and populated urban squares and plazas became evidence of Polish determination to overcome the devastation of war and functioned as proof of postwar normalization, reconstruction, and social and urban revitalization, in turn validating the postwar socialist government's reconstruction efforts. The proposed narrative of the material past reflected the goals of the new regime, echoed and reiterated propaganda about postwar Warsaw and set the parameters of an easily disseminated and popular visual-textual narrative about the Polish capital.

This chapter draws on photobooks published in Poland from the 1940s to the 1970s, focusing primarily on *Warsaw, the Capital of Poland*. Published in 1949, the same year communist authorities imposed socialist realism not only on photography but on all arts and letters, this book exemplified the basic outline of a Varsovian photobook narrative that became almost obligatory in later photobooks. Unlike other genres that pushed the topic of Warsaw into the background after 1956, photobooks about the capital continued to be regularly published by state-owned publishing houses well past the Thaw. While seeking to differentiate themselves from the basic model set in 1949, these later photobooks contended with the parameters set by *Warsaw, the Capital of Poland*, and thus I treat them as an extension of the 1949 text in order to show the continuity of the narrative. *Warsaw, the Capital of Poland*, though less overtly ideological than the 1950 photobook version of Bierut's 1949 Six-Year Plan for Warsaw's Reconstruction, delineated parameters and elements that were repeated in, adopted by, or consciously rejected by photobooks from later decades. As the analysis shows, the message of the photobooks—streamlined to fit the condensed parameters of the genre—became repetitive even if the images themselves were "new." Because of this condensed narrative, a specific Varsovian story was told and retold, and the limits of the photobook genre—further limited by ideological considerations—made it difficult to break established conventions and patterns.

As a point of contrast to the books published in Poland under communism, I also analyze *Warszawa Varsovie Warsaw Warschau 1945*, a photobook published in Switzerland by Polish expatriates. This photobook demonstrates the contrast between narratives of Warsaw developed after the war in Poland and those adopted among the diaspora. While the focus of this photobook was primarily on interwar Poland and the material losses caused by the war, it also subtly demonstrates points of intersection between the narratives developed by the communist government and the diaspora: both groups used photographs and photobooks as documentary evidence of Warsaw's past, and both desired to preserve a Warsaw of the past for the sake of the future. The differences, however, lay in the narrative thrust of these texts based on politics and ideology as represented by different visual focal points and distinct historical interpretations—that is, Poland as an aristocratic and middle-class haven versus Poland as a land of peasants and workers.

How, then, did the photobooks simultaneously express the "reality" of the geographic place while also developing a narrative, cultural spatiality that wrote the communist regime into the picture? What was encoded between the covers of these visual-verbal texts? And how did the spatial discourse of Warsaw shape both the historical and contemporaneous narratives in this context? The answer to these questions can be found in two different lines of inquiry. The first is a theoretical one that relies on the formal structure of the photographic image and photobooks as visual-verbal hybrids that can possess an indexical value meant to denote reality, as well as create cultural meaning through developing connotations. As I argue, the Varsovian photobooks, as visual-verbal texts, exploited the denotative, documentary value of the images and the denotative power of the accompanying text to create a synergistic result. The other line of inquiry is historical and considers the value of Warsaw's image before and immediately after the war. Both photographic and painted images were critical to postwar memory and reconstruction work. They were often the only documentary- or archeological-like evidence of a building's facade or existence. But it is the intersection of theoretical considerations and historical mappings that gives a multidimensional perspective on Varsovian poetics in the photobooks and reveals more precisely how photographic images could be exploited for propaganda purposes. In the photobooks, we can see how the symbiosis between photographic image and text was used (1) to build a series of narrative connotations in order to shape a new reality according to socialist principles; (2) to legitimize the authority of the party; (3) to unify its "constituency"; and (4) to "teach" Poles how to read and view the "socialist message" that was to become a part of the reconstructed space and postwar Varsovian spatiality.

The Varsovian Photobook

Beginning in the late 1940s, photobooks like *Warsaw, the Capital of Poland* were a popular genre that incorporated an official postwar story crafted

from official media, proclamations, and propaganda. Covering the historical and spatial breadth of the Polish capital, these photobooks presented
a visual-verbal narrative, both geographically and temporally. Published by
state-owned publishing houses such as Arkady, Polonia, and Interpress, these
photobooks relied on the juxtaposition of images of prewar Warsaw with
wartime ruins and later postwar reconstruction. Often beginning with the
appellation "Warsaw," the photobooks signified that a viewer/reader was
embarking on an urban tour constructed between book covers. Especially
in the late 1940s and early 1950s, the photobooks represented a communal
vision of the Polish capital that was constructed of hundreds of images taken
by dozens of photographers, who worked individually or for official Polish press and photographic agencies, such as the Polish Telegraphic Agency
(Polska Agencja Telegraficzna, PAT), the Military Photographic Agency
(Wojskowa Agencja Fotograficzna), the Photography Studio of the Central
Committee of the Polish United Workers' Party (Studio Fotograficzne KC
PZPR), or the photography division of Film Polski. These were far from artists' photobooks, focused on the work of individual photographers. Rather,
these books were creations of editorial teams, who selected images according
to their documentary, archival, and/or propaganda value.[11] The books did
not call attention to the photographers but were "marketed" and designed
as books on Warsaw. While the artistic merit of the images was not ignored,
the photographers were considered secondary to the topic.[12] For example,
Warsaw, the Capital of Poland was compiled of images made by such well-
known photographers as Zofia Chomętowska, Edward Falkowski, Leonard
Sempoliński, and at least forty-three others. Among these were cinematographers, who worked for the Polish Film Chronicle (Polska Kronika Filmowa,
PKF) and Film Polski, including Władysław Forbert, Karol Szczeciński, and
Stanisław Urbanowicz. Furthermore, both PAT and the Photography Studio
of the Central Committee of the Polish United Workers' Party contributed
images to this collection. In later decades, books featuring Sempoliński's photographs, as well as images by Edmund Kupiecki and Zbyszko Siemaszko
and compilations edited by the Varsovianists Olgierd Budrewicz and Adolf
Ciborowski, dominated the Warsaw photobook market. These books, however, did not claim to represent an individual artist's conception or view of
the city.[13] Instead, they represented the distilled, politically correct Varsovian
narrative, while at the same time continuing a Polish photography tradition
that dated back to the nineteenth century.

In the postwar context, the photobook on Warsaw embodied two broader
tensions related to photography's role in Polish culture, broadly speaking, and
the role of photography within a newly established socialist state. Already
in the nineteenth century, photographers like Karol Beyer (1818–1877) had
used photography to support the national aspirations of a partitioned Poland
through portraiture, the chronicling of events before and after the 1863
uprising against tsarist Russia, and photographing landscapes, cityscapes,

and historical monuments as a visual archive of "Poland."[14] A similar tendency can be noted in the interwar and postwar period with the photography of Jan Bułhak (1876–1950), whose photographic work had both artistic and patriotic goals. Alongside the concept of *fotografika* (artistic photography), he developed the idea of *fotografia ojczysta*, or "fatherland photography," as a tool for creating and maintaining cultural and national identity by documenting, like Beyer before him, historical landmarks, architecture, and monuments.[15] The main goal of *fotografia ojczysta* was delineated by a nineteenth-century ethos that focused on preserving, respecting, and propagating Poland's heritage through artistic and national engagement. In both Beyer's and Bułhak's cases, the patriotic goals of photography led to the publication of photobooks on Kraków, the Łódź Fabryczna Railway, and Polish painting (in Beyer's case) and on "historical monuments, nature, or the Polish landscape, which consisted of more than ten thousand photographs collected in 158 photobooks" (in Bułhak's case).[16]

In the postwar period, as the communist regime was being established, photographers worked within the parameters of the new regime to carve out a place for photography and highlight its importance and value. With the politicization of all aspects of public life, the work of photographers was quickly incorporated into the government's propaganda program. Even Bułhak expressed the value of this medium to the new regime, stating, "Propaganda is supported by photography. Without [photography], successful propaganda would be unthinkable."[17] Nonetheless, socialist realism in Polish photography never reached the scale or impact anticipated by the government in the postwar period.[18] This was partially due to the theoretical debates regarding the value of photography at the time, debates that rejected realism and focused on neo-pictorialism versus contemporary photography and surrealistic trends.[19] More directly, however, the general lack of direct political engagement by photographers in the mid- to late 1940s contributed to the marginal success of socialist realism in Polish photography.[20] Unlike the filmmakers who will be discussed in the following chapters, the majority of Polish photographers were amateurs before the war, were never associated with avant-garde circles or art photography, and did not identify with the communist party. Nonetheless, the tendency to focus on pictorialism and the "preservation of the nation," as well as the relative conservatism of the Polish photography world that continued the trend of *fotografia ojczysta* in the postwar period, made the photobooks on Warsaw popular publications despite the influences of the state-owned publishing houses and the socialist Varsovian spatiality that the images-texts promoted.

Under communism, the physical format of the photobooks varied from publication to publication, influenced as much by the editors' conceptualization as by the availability of quality paper and ink. Photobooks were published in all shapes and sizes and were printed primarily in black and white, with color photographs appearing more and more often beginning in the 1960s. The very physical experience of holding Warsaw in book form was accompanied by such formal photobook elements as their visual-verbal narrative, the organization and sequencing of photographs, and the captioning strategies adopted by the editors. Taken together, each book took a reader on a trip through Warsaw's space and history that was mapped not according to geographic coordinates, but through narrative elements and themes required by propaganda. Regardless of a photobook's size, shape, and quality, it was sequencing, organization, captioning, and succinctly written introductions and commentaries that time and again re-created Warsaw's space and history through text and image. From decade to decade, however, these building blocks were shuffled to create ever new manifestations of Warsaw that not only reflected progress in the building of the capital, but also mirrored shifts in the political situation and party politics. Each photobook constructed its own narrative shape by connecting the blocks in different and creative ways. But before we turn to the specific elements of the Varsovian photobook, let's take a look at some theoretical considerations.

"No Streets, Only Names Remain . . .": Symbiosis between Text and Image

In his 1961 essay "The Photographic Message," Roland Barthes called attention to the synergy between image and text when he posited that for every image that represents a real-world object or possesses a denotative meaning, there is a textual, connotative message or meaning that can be expressed only linguistically.[21] In this way, Barthes differentiated between the image as "an object endowed with structural autonomy" and the meaning or connotations constructed around the image by "the 'writing,' or the rhetoric, of the photograph."[22] In the first case, Barthes suggested that the photograph has the potential to be read as an "objective" reflection of reality and possesses a documentary power due to its analogous nature. Writing about press photography, in particular, Barthes argued that the photograph attempts to reduce the object it portrays to an image without stylistic "commentary" or code that exists beyond the image, and it assists or even teaches the viewer how to read it. In the second case, the photograph loses its structural autonomy by being placed into a cultural context. For Barthes, this duality of the photographic image represented both a structural and an ethical paradox that rests at the core of the purported verisimilitude of realism. It led him to ask how a photograph could simultaneously possess a sense of objectivity and be heavily "invested" with cultural or historical meaning or code.[23]

While it is not my task to resolve Barthes's ethical dilemma, his structural analysis of the image provides a starting point for understanding the complexity of Warsaw's photographic image after World War II and how it could be both documentary evidence and a tool of propaganda. A similar duality

Figure 6. Hoża Street, Warsaw, 1945. Photo by Edward Falkowski. Reproduced by permission from Centrum Fotografii Krajoznawczej PTTK.

exists in photobooks where the synergy between text and image creates multiple layers of meaning by simultaneously communicating documentary and discursive (cultural) information. To illustrate how this works, let's begin with a single image: a photograph of rubble taken after the war in 1945 by the photographer Edward Falkowski (1913–1998) and published in a 1970 photobook (figure 6). The photograph is composed of three basic visual elements. Along the bottom half of the photograph is a pile of rubble, remnants of a brick wall, and other pulverized building debris. This bottom half is contrasted and outlined by the border of an empty gray sky that fills the upper areas of the photograph. But it is the third element that draws the viewer's attention. Framed by the empty sky and hanging above the devastation below is a sign with the words "ulica Hoża" ("Hoża Street") on a rectangular plate tied by three wires to a distorted metal pole. The curved pole sweeps from left to right across the photograph with the name of the street centered in the vacant sky. The sign has been clearly ravaged by war, and some of the letters are no longer legible.

This photograph possesses many formal, aesthetic qualities that add to its indexicality or documentary value. Its triangular composition prevents it from being too symmetrical; the contrast between the ruins and sky highlights the devastation; and the curve of the metal pole acts as a unifying, visual force. Such a formal description, however, fails to account for another layer of meaning in the photograph, a meaning intensified by the street sign in the image, as well as by the connotation suggested by the caption: "No streets, only names remain: Hoża Street" ("Ulic nie ma, nazwy zostały: Ulica Hoża").[24] Without the street sign or the caption in the photobook, this photograph is a photograph of rubble like any other. After all, one pile of rubble is indistinguishable from the next unless it is placed within a context of space and time through framing, labeling, or explanation. Without the street sign, the rubble represents the devastation of war but is otherwise spatially non-referential. With the street sign as the focal point of the photograph, however, the rubble is named and an approximate geographical point is identified. We are able to "place" the photograph on a map, specifically in Warsaw's central district, Śródmieście. The street sign orients the viewer and changes the photograph from one of many images of wartime rubble into a geospatial marker that makes this photograph cartographically productive. The sign "Hoża Street" provides a geographic reference point, a means of locating the debris shown in the bottom portion of the image. For those who knew Warsaw before the war, the sign triggers not only the memory of physical space but also the area's spatiality. It conjures up an internal map of the mind's eye and may elicit an image of Hoża Street as an elegant residential area. The street represents previous "normalcy" and acts as a synecdoche for Warsaw's downtown. For those who know reconstructed Warsaw, the photograph is a reminder of the contrast between wartime devastation and the reconstructed spaces of today. The image can serve as a trigger of memory and a reminder of the lived experience of urban space. And even if a reader has never been to Warsaw, the street sign gives life to the photograph. By attaching a name to the rubble, the image suggests a broader spatial and temporal reality of place than that represented by a pile of bricks. The street sign communicates that once there was a street called "Hoża" whose skyline was filled with buildings, and at the instant when the image was taken, nothing but a sign and rubble remained. The caption takes the cartographic work a step further by stating outright that despite the destruction of place, there is a reality that continues to supersede the physical disarray of Warsaw, and it can be found in the memory of street names, in language and culture.

These meanings of the photograph are further augmented in the context of the photobook. The picture of Hoża Street is the *third* photograph in a series of six images printed on a two-page spread. The first photograph on the left page, taken by Falkowski in 1947, is a wide-angle shot of a barren cityscape in which the left background portion of the skyline is dominated by the skeleton of a skyscraper (figure 7). This skeleton-skyscraper is counterbalanced by a dead tree in the foreground on the right side of the photograph. In the photograph, the tree and the building are almost the same size, an indication of the distance from which Falkowski took the picture. Connecting these two focal points are other bombed-out buildings, debris, and barely visible Varsovians walking around the square. For those who know Warsaw,

Figure 7. Napoleon Plaza and Prudential Building in Warsaw, 1947. Photograph by Edward Falkowski. Reproduced by permission from Centrum Fotografii Krajoznawczej PTTK.

the skyscraper is easily recognizable as the sixteen-story art deco Pruden-tial building, the tallest edifice in Warsaw before the war. Here, the editors of the photobook deem it unnecessary to name the building. Built in the early 1930s, the Prudential symbolized interwar Poland's modernization, achieving legendary status when Polish partisans occupied it throughout the duration of the Warsaw Uprising in 1944.[25] Its postwar skeleton, the result of repeated bombings by the Germans during the uprising, remained none-theless easily identifiable. The caption, however, does not note the building's importance during the interwar period or its role in 1944. Rather, it simply states, "Warecki[ego] Square: houses and people."[26]

Between the images of the Prudential and Hoża Street is a photograph of Varsovians being transported in a horse and buggy through the rubble of Warsaw's streets. This caption reads: "Somehow the life of the city revives: transport . . ." Image four shows a close-up of Władysław Gomułka, then first secretary of the Polish Workers' Party (Polska Partia Robotnicza, PPR), captioned with the phrases "Władysław Gomułka in Marszałkowska Street. Yes, the capital will be here." This picture is followed by a wide-angle shot of a military parade in downtown Warsaw celebrating the "liberation" of the capital on January 17, 1945. This last caption reads: "Vast crowds at the parade of January 19th, 1945. Where do they all live?" Through the juxta-position with these other photographs, the picture of rubble on Hoża Street,

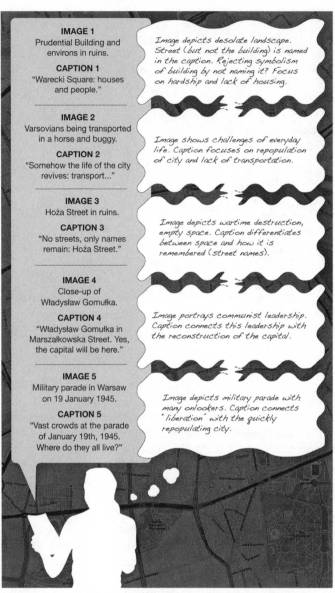

Figure 8. Mind map based on two-page layout from *Warsaw 1945–1970* (pages 32–33). The left column lists the captions and describes the denotative value of the images. The right column represents the connotative value of the two-page layout created by the interaction between text and image. Visualization by Lorin Bruckner.

which represents Warsaw's Śródmieście, becomes part of a larger, multilay-ered visual-verbal message. The denotative and connotative meanings of the photographs dynamically collide, merge, and mix to create a mini-Warsaw narrative that includes such typical elements as wartime destruction, Varso-vian spirit and resilience, communist control over the reconstruction of the capital, and the valorization of Soviet brotherhood in the form of Warsaw's liberation and the military parade. With the help of a mind-map, we can see how the visual-verbal form of the photobook inundates a reader with mul-tiple layers of meaning that exploit the duality of the photograph as both a document and a culturally imbued text (figure 8). Individually, each image possesses its own meaning. Together, the photographs and captions have the power to (re-)create Warsaw's spatiality through a series of connotations that might eventually merge into one narrative.

The Documentary Value of Images

Though cultural connotations are inevitably part of a photograph, as Barthes and others have rightfully demonstrated, there persists a common percep-tion that photos possess objective, evidentiary value. This was even more so the case in the early twentieth century when photography was consid-ered primarily to be a documentary medium that was "perceived as more immediate, powerful and universally accessible than other media" and a more direct form of communication than text and language.[27] This denota-tive, "objective" value of images was underscored by the events of the war with photographs serving as "witnesses" to Nazi cruelty, human trauma, and material and human losses. This is particularly true of Holocaust images. Barthes himself described the primary, denotative role of such traumatic pho-tographs as "the photograph about which there is nothing to say."[28] Across Europe, such photographs were collected in photobooks that "bore powerful and irrefutable witness to what had happened in German-occupied countries, informing a shocked, almost disbelieving world."[29] While the text, captions, sequencing, and introductory material of these photobooks provided a his-torical context for the traumatic images of the Holocaust, the denotative meaning or documentary value of these images tended to take precedence over their potential connotative value and function.[30] Furthermore, photog-raphers as the creators of these images were often secondary to, or even absent from, the reading of these images, limiting their aesthetic implications. In short, these images functioned, first and foremost, as evidence of Nazi crimes. Over time, however, Holocaust and camp images have gained iconic and, therefore, connotative status. In addition to their documentary value, pictures of human suffering in ghettos, gas chambers, barbed wire, and the gate of Auschwitz with its ironic motto "Arbeit macht frei" ("Work sets you free") trigger connotations that work synecdochically—individual images stand in for the entirety of the Holocaust. While the Holocaust photograph is one of the most extreme examples of traumatic photography, it provides us with a relatively clear example of how photographs work as document and discourse, as evidence and culturally imbued icon.

On occasion, photobooks on Warsaw included photos that could be categorized as "traumatic." When they did, however, little commentary was included. In *Warszawa: Portret miasta* (1979; *Warsaw: A Portrait of a City*), the editor maintained that traumatic wartime images were eloquent in and of themselves, and did not require written commentary or explanation.[31] For the most part, however, the number of traumatic photographs was limited in most of the Varsovian photobooks. The authors of *Warsaw, the Capital of Poland* explained in their introduction that they had consciously chosen not to include images depicting German Nazis' "bestiality" and cruelty.[32] Perhaps because Varsovians had seen enough death and Warsaw was virtually a cemetery after the war, or maybe because of the capital's cultural and symbolic value, or maybe because of the aesthetics promoted under socialism, traumatic photographs of human losses were set aside in favor of images of material destruction. Rubble photographs are, of course, incomparable to the traumatic images of emaciated bodies in ghettoes and concentration camps. However, the postwar images of Warsaw and its ruins possessed their own traumatic and symbolic value, drawing attention to the devastation of the Polish capital and acting as a form of psychological displacement.

During the war, numerous professional and amateur Warsaw photographers risked their lives to document the experience of the German occupation. After the war, many of these same photographers recorded Warsaw's devastation by creating images of ruins and rubble.[33] Often focusing on the iconic, most symbolic and easily identifiable ruins, these photographs circulated broadly in the immediate postwar years. One might say there was even a fascination with the ruin in a nostalgic sense, as demonstrated by a tendency to photograph destroyed buildings rather than those which remained intact and standing. In fact, a majority of photographers concentrated their efforts on the city center, which—other than the former ghetto—was the most heavily destroyed part of the city. Furthermore, these photographers often framed their subjects in similar and, at times, even identical ways.[34]

In addition to documenting Warsaw during and after the war, the Varsovian photograph gained in value by its seeming scarcity and the difficult conditions of postwar photography. With the destruction of the city came the destruction of countless archival materials. For the most part, wartime photographic material was destroyed, and prewar private and archival collections were either destroyed or scattered across Poland and Europe.[35] Efforts to collect extant photographs of Warsaw from before the war abounded. Two important sources of Warsaw's prewar image were the photographs of Zofia Chomętowska, who was already a well-known Varsovian photographer before the war, and the archival collections of the Polish Museum in

Rapperswil, Switzerland.[36] In addition, *The Capital: A Varsovian Illustrated Weekly* organized a project called "Otwarte szkatuły" ("Open Coffers"), which requested that its readers submit photos of Warsaw from their personal collections to be published in the newspaper.[37] Creating new images of the postwar city was also a challenge. As with many aspects of postwar life when scarcity was the name of the game, there was a marked lack of photography equipment available in Warsaw until the late 1940s and early 1950s. Photojournalists lacked the necessary professional equipment to create quality images. They used old, prewar cameras like the German Leica III or Contax, set up darkrooms in bathrooms, printed photos in kitchens, and created negatives on discarded film stock rather than photographic film. Though the quality of photographs from this time was seen as lacking, it did not detract from the documentary value placed on these images even today.[38]

The documentary value of Varsovian images was underscored by the first exhibit organized immediately after the war. Despite numerous challenges, the badly destroyed National Museum in Warsaw did not waste time mounting the exhibit *Warszawa oskarża* (*Warsaw Accuses*), which opened on May 3, 1945, in a handful of least-damaged and hastily renovated exhibition halls under the direction of Stanisław Lorentz.[39] Rather than displaying art to be admired from an aesthetic perspective, the exhibit focused on summarizing Warsaw's cultural, artistic, and scholarly legacy that had been willfully destroyed by the Germans. The exhibit included burned books, paintings slashed by knives, fragmented marble statues, and numerous boxes of artwork prepared for shipment to the Third Reich.[40] A large part of the exhibit consisted of photographic documentation that juxtaposed images of Warsaw's architecture from the late 1930s with wartime and postwar devastation.[41] One hall was dedicated to the work of the Office for the Reconstruction of the Capital (Biuro Odbudowy Stolicy, BOS) and presented 179 photographs documenting the destruction of Warsaw's churches, palaces, streets, and monuments, as well as posters enumerating the percentages of destroyed buildings and outlining early reconstruction plans.

Warsaw Accuses presented the destruction of the Polish capital within an already familiar rhetorical framework. In the very first sentence of the museum guide prepared for the exhibit, Warsaw was called a "martyr city,"[42] with variations on the word "martyr" ("męczeński," "męczeństwo," and "martyrologia") appearing another five times in the guide and evoking the nineteenth-century notion of Poland as the "Christ of Nations."[43] The war had reinvigorated this martyrological narrative, and even the communist provisional government exploited it for propaganda purposes, calling Warsaw a martyr city.[44] In the exhibit guide, however, the martyrological discourse was displaced from its traditional locus—the Polish nation—onto the loss of a material, cultural legacy. The National Museum was described as witnessing during the war the "near-complete martyrology of the old culture of the Capital" ("całą niemal martyrologię dawnej kultury Stolicy"), while the suffering of "lifeless objects, the material indicators of Polish culture," was correlated with the "communal suffering of living Poles."[45] The documentary evidence presented in the exhibit easily pointed in this direction and formalized the shared expression of postwar indignation and outrage toward the Germans. *Warsaw Accuses* was an intervention in public life that channeled communal, emotional attention toward the devastation of war caused by Nazi Germany and away from the practical and political challenges of the moment. The emotional and documentary power of the exhibit drew an estimated 435,000 visitors. Though originally scheduled for two months, it was extended to nine.[46] The artist Ignacy Witz described the exhibit as simply shocking. He stated: "There is much that can be written about the destruction and damage done to Polish culture, but no words can express it so clearly, leave such an impression, as seeing it with one's own eyes."[47] When Witz said "seeing it," however, he was not referring to the rubble-filled streets just outside the museum doors; rather, he was referring to the exhibit itself. For Witz, condensing the wartime experience of Poland and her capital in a narrativized exhibit provided a means of expressing the trauma of the period in a way words could not.

In *Warsaw Accuses*, the traumatized urban space was represented by before-and-after diptychs, primarily shot by Chomętowska and her cousin-photographer, Edward Falkowski.[48] Chomętowska had been commissioned by the mayor of Warsaw, Stefan Starzyński, to author an exhibit in 1938 entitled *Warszawa wczoraj, dziś, jutro* (*Warsaw Yesterday, Today, Tomorrow*), which had also been mounted in the National Museum under Lorentz's direction. Attended by over 500,000 visitors, this prewar exhibit focused on the accomplishments of Poland's interwar government with regard to Warsaw's urban development, and presented dynamic plans for the Polish capital's future evolution.[49] Starzyński had tasked Chomętowska and another Warsaw photographer, Tadeusz Przypkowski, with photographing historical architecture and monuments, as well as capturing on film various aspects of everyday Varsovian life.[50] These prewar photographs possessed a rich medley of denotative documentary value and connotative messages. On the one hand, the images recorded an "objective" reality; on the other hand, they were consciously assigned a meaning beyond the "objective" by virtue of the museum context. They highlighted the interwar government's successes and exposed prewar urban problems that the city's mayor wanted to correct. Little did Starzyński, Lorentz, or Chomętowska realize that in just under seven years these same photographs would be significant in a wholly new and unexpected way, for they anchored the photography portion of *Warsaw Accuses*. In the postwar context, Chomętowska's prewar photographs were used in before-after sequencing to underscore the devastation of Warsaw by juxtaposing images of fully intact buildings with images of their ruins photographed primarily by Falkowski in the spring of 1945.[51] The impact of these before-after images set the tone for many future representations of Warsaw in pictorial form at home and abroad. The photography portion of *Warsaw Accuses* traveled not only to Katowice and Kalisz in Poland but also to Paris, London, New York, and Tokyo. It proved to be a source of financing reconstruction efforts, even inspiring the Polish diaspora to make financial contributions to the Office for the Reconstruction of the Capital despite their general opposition to the communist regime.[52]

Mapping Memory

As the case of the exhibit *Warsaw Accuses* shows, prewar photographic images of Warsaw acquired increased documentary value in the context of postwar devastation. Their prewar connotative function became defunct. The original messages and meanings attached to Chomętowska's and her colleagues' images, namely, to show interwar Poland's successes and document areas of Varsovian life in need of transformation, were no longer relevant. In the immediate postwar years, these photographs possessed an archeological dimension and acquired a memory value that was markedly different from their 1938 meanings. They preserved the image of Warsaw and served as evidence of the rich Polish culture that the Nazis had set out to destroy. Juxtaposed with early plans for Warsaw's reconstruction, they also represented an unflappable determination to return the city to its former status as a capital. While the images themselves did not change, their connotative value and meaning changed because of history. The before-and-after diptychs denoted a city left in ruins by war, but they also connoted a vast array of mostly justified ideas about Nazi German aggression and barbarism that became a constituent part of Warsaw's postwar narrative. In the first instance, images of Warsaw, in their denotative documentary function, articulated the experience of war which had touched the majority of the Polish population. In the second instance, a connotative value grew around the photography of Warsaw. This connotation was one of architectural, historical, and cultural victimization that functioned as a synecdoche for the overall trauma suffered by Poles and Poland during World War II. As such, however, the connotative value was not stable and could be subtly developed and charged with ideology at little risk of alienating the consumer of the image. Warsaw's image was susceptible to being appropriated and adopted for propaganda and other purposes, and the photobook was one of the most concrete manifestations of this adaptability.

Most immediately, however, images of Warsaw were a means of resuscitating and remembering space. A photograph "sees" or "registers" far more detail than the human eye and thus by its very nature skews the memory of place. In other words, memory work through photographs is a distortion of the memory of place. Perhaps this is what the cultural critic Siegfried Kracauer had in mind when before World War II he noted that photography and film replaced the type of memory work most common to human history. In the case of Warsaw, the vicissitudes of history would make photographs and photography an essential part of reconstructing the physical, cultural, and spiritual memory of the capital despite these distortions inherent to the medium. Prior to photography, the possibility of reconstituting memory through photographic verisimilitude was nearly impossible; with photography it became not only possible but de rigueur.

In the aftermath of the deadliest war known to mankind, photography was a vital part of both memory work and historical documentation. It helped grasp a degree of devastation that was beyond the human capacity to remember, synthesize, and imagine; it confirmed stories that words tried to tell but failed to fully express. Unsurprisingly, memory work in photobooks was not uncommon at this time. The postwar era introduced across Europe a wave of reconstruction, reconciliation, memory, and reflection in photography, as well as in other art forms.[53] Many of the best examples of postwar photobooks were conceptually driven and represented the artistic vision of the photographers or authors of the books. They tended to document wartime experiences and contextualize the photographs in very specific cultural or historical moments. Among these were Jean Cocteau and Pierre Jahan's *Death and the Statues* (1946) depicting the 1941 destruction of Parisian statuary in the service of German munitions;[54] Martien Coppens's *Impressions of Holland during 1945* (1947); Jindřich Heisler and Jindřich Štyrský's *On the Needles of These Days* (1945); and Zdenek Tmej's *Alphabet of Spiritual Emptiness* (1946), portraying Tmej's time as a forced laborer in what was then Breslau (now Wrocław, Poland).[55]

While less conceptually driven than the above enumerated texts, Warsaw photography and photobooks had an important role in postwar memory work. Photobooks published both in and outside of Poland treated prewar images as an integral means of preserving individual recollections of the past and allaying fears associated with the fragility of spatial memory. War had obliterated the physical space, and without photographic proof, memory was likewise eroding. Before the life-sized reconstruction of the Old Town and other prewar structures could function as memory aids, photographs were used as artifacts that could trigger recollections of "what used to be."[56] For example, the 1947 photobook *Warsaw: Album on the Polish Capital's Ancient Architecture* published in Stuttgart, Germany, began with the words "Warsaw. We remember her." Referring to the capital as "the city of rubble and smoldering ruins, nameless graves and crosses," the author of the text also wrote of a different, old Warsaw that was "shrouded in the fog of memory."[57] This photobook, whose structure was organized around the losses caused by war and the political agenda of an anticommunist Polish diaspora, differed from books published in Poland. It presented a narrow scope of black-and-white photographs of Warsaw architecture, focusing on the Old Town; ten churches in nineteen photographs showing interior and exterior shots; the interior of the Royal Castle (Zamek Królewski), and the exteriors of other symbols of aristocracy, such as the Brühl, Krasiński, and Saski palaces, Łazienki Park, and the district of Wilanów; as well as a handful of other culturally important locations, such as the old university library and the National Theater (Teatr Narodowy).

Such memory work also appeared in photobooks published in Poland; however, the geospatial reference points in the Stuttgart photobook differed from those of in-country publications, which avoided a focus on religious or aristocratic spaces. Nonetheless, the authors of *Warsaw, the Capital of Poland*, the first photobook on Warsaw in communist Poland, were keenly aware of the fragile nature of memory and saw photographs as one solution to preserving the past. In the opening pages of the volume, the authors explicitly expressed the angst caused by the devastation of war on the triad of space-identity-memory. They wrote of the erosion of the "image of old Warsaw" from collective memory. Here, "old Warsaw" was defined by historical moments selected to fit the process of making Polish society "socialist," and included uprisings and battles against oppressors, beginning with the "April days of 1794" (or in other words, the Kościuszko Uprising), the uprisings of 1830 and 1863, the labor protests in 1905, and the "heroic battles" of World War II.[58] The authors also underscored the difficulty of remembering streets, squares, and buildings as they were before they had been destroyed, the loss of familiar facades and vistas, and the process of forgetting what the space used to look like. The authors lamented that "as the years go by, when the rubble disappears and a new capital begins to develop in its place, the look of old Warsaw—the way it was yesterday, during our lifetime, during the lives of contemporary people—will fade from our memories."[59] Likewise, they expressed regret at not being able to represent all "fragments of Warsaw in their proper light" due to a lack of photographs that portray "the poverty of Warsaw's working-class neighborhoods," "the heroic battle and work of Warsaw's revolutionary people, images from the 1905 revolution, interwar protests and strikes," or "the liberation [of Warsaw] by the Soviet Army and the reborn Polish Army fighting at its side."[60] The historical moments listed were rhetorically associated with communist activists and soldiers, and the images in the photobook indeed followed this communist narrative history. The message, however, was notably skewed. For example, one caption gave credit for the defense of the Czerniaków bridgehead to Berling's Soviet-commanded First Polish Army during the 1944 Warsaw Uprising.[61] Completely eliminated from this version of the narrative was the fact that the Home Army, which answered to the Polish government-in-exile in London, led the insurgent force fighting alongside Berling's men.[62]

It was through such selective framing of Warsaw's history that photobooks published in communist Poland adapted the documentary and memory value of images, using them as the basis for constructing Warsaw's spatiality according to ideological parameters. This framing rewrote history to give primacy to communist party activists during the war. It was also used as a segue to remind readers that a *new* Warsaw was rising before their eyes thanks to the actions taken by communist partisans and soldiers. This new city, according to *Warsaw, the Capital of Poland*, would be filled with "big-city arteries planned on a contemporary scale" and "multilane roads and multistory buildings that impress with their breadth and height." Under the "rational planning" of socialism, the city would be filled with air, light, and greenery.[63] According to the authors, while the rebuilding of Warsaw was bound to erode memory of the old city, the photobook could be used as a documentary, archeological tool of preservation and elicit a past spatial reality, both physical and cultural. The introduction to the volume connected the fragility of spatial memory in the face of total destruction with the power of photography, presenting prewar images as indispensable to safeguarding what had come before. The authors wrote of protecting and cherishing the memory of an irretrievable past through the books' illustrations, which were "carefully chosen from among the most valuable photographs of the Warsaw of yesteryear—photographs that portray an image of the city, particularly those fragments which were completely destroyed."[64]

Capturing the Genius Loci

In addition to using photographs as memory triggers, the authors of photobooks relied on a verbal narrative to describe the seemingly indescribable: namely, the genius loci of Warsaw. Such was the case in *Warszawa Varsovie Warsaw Warschau 1945* (1945; henceforth referred to as *Warsaw 1945*), published immediately after the war by Polish infantrymen interned in Switzerland. This book walked readers through the interwar capital, giving a "glimpse" of the city through the eyes of a foreigner, and attempting to capture on paper the elusive qualities that made Warsaw "Warsaw." According to its author, a visitor to interwar Warsaw would have observed a socially and religiously diverse city, "united in its spirit, in its soul."[65] According to his description, prewar Warsaw was filled with contrasts of nineteenth-century partition-era provincialism and early twentieth-century progress, modern architecture, bustling crowds, lively cafes, flourishing businesses and restaurants, first-class theaters and concerts, well-stocked libraries and reading rooms, elegant, fashionable, and neatly dressed Varsovians, colorful flowers spilling over balcony railings, and parks filled with greenery. Beginning and ending the introduction with the phrase "Warsaw exists no more,"[66] the author made a point of contrasting the material losses of the war with the unquenchable spirit of Warsaw's spatiality, stating that "the soul of Warsaw is not dead. It has become multiple and unseizable; hundreds of thousands of exiled and dispersed people of Warsaw, have, each one, taken a particle away with them; wherever they are, this soul subsists, continues burning inextinguishably."[67]

In *Warsaw 1945*, the idea that the Polish capital continued to exist as an abstraction, scattered across the globe, was a poignant call for rhetorical unification of the diaspora across time and space, and for identification with the losses suffered by Poland during the war. The book presented photographs as a nostalgic, material record of Varsovian life. It rhetorically proclaimed the eventual emergence of a new city, stating that the "inhabitants will reference the old legacy" and attempt to carry on old Polish traditions. Here, "traditions" referred to patriotism, resistance to foreign oppression (in this case by the Soviets), and the fight for Poland's independence. Such a sentiment poetically summarized the Varsovian and Polish reality of the moment. In 1945, Poles were exiled to not only such places as London, Paris, Switzerland, displaced persons camps in U.S. sectors in Germany, and the United States, but also to the eastern edges of Siberia, China, North Africa, and the Middle East. At the time of publication, the future of Poland was still in flux as the London-based Polish government-in-exile and the Soviet-backed Polish Committee of National Liberation (Polski Komitet Wyzwolenia Narodowego, PKWN) struggled to establish authoritative control over Poland. As regards Warsaw, the communist authorities had decided by this time to designate Warsaw as the capital of the new People's Republic, yet whether or not the capital could even be rebuilt, and if so how, was still being debated.[68] This was the context in which a series of eclectic photographs and reproductions of prints and paintings portraying Warsaw were perused and nostalgically regarded.

Focusing on the memory of Warsaw and her spirit, however, was not only the domain of exiled patriots nostalgically remembering home. Such sentiment over the genius loci was also present in the 1949 *Warsaw, the Capital of Poland*. Its authors suggested that Warsaw "possessed a strange appeal, a charm that lured the hearts of its own people, as well as strangers."[69] Attempts to capture Warsaw's spirit of place continued well into the 1960s. For example, an introduction to the photobook *Warszawa: Krajobraz i architektura* (1963; *Warsaw: Landscape and Architecture*) spoke of an intangible atmosphere that, along with historical fate and material architecture, constitutes a part of a city's essence.[70] Similarly, in *Warszawa: O zniszczeniu i odbudowie miasta* (1964; *Warsaw: On the Destruction and Reconstruction of the City*), Warsaw's genius loci was presented as the very thing that drew Varsovians back to the city despite its devastation, and which could be "deciphered in the changed but nonetheless Varsovian image of our new capital."[71] Some photobooks claimed that this spirit was constituted by the people and their character; others, by historical vicissitudes. In addition to Warsaw's bewitching, siren-like laughter, Warsaw's genius loci—according to some—came from the "rhythm of a great city, the tempo of traffic and life, creative momentum, the pulse of a large, modern, true capital."[72] But rarely, if at all, in the communist-era publications was interwar Warsaw the bustling capital described in the expatriate *Warsaw 1945*. While the photobook of the soldiers interned in Switzerland painted a middle-class portrait of Warsaw's interwar spirit, *Warsaw, the Capital of Poland* and later photobooks published in the People's Republic of Poland rejected the interwar atmosphere, preferring to call attention to the dilapidated and unsanitary housing conditions for the working class during that time, while locating the spirit of the capital in a string of historical, revolutionary activity.[73]

Narrating, Sequencing, Captioning

In 1970, the writer and devoted communist party member Stanisław Ryszard Dobrowolski (1907–1985)[74] wrote that "it is more and more difficult to write about Warsaw, especially if you don't want to wallow in a pool of beautiful phrases or stick with stereotypical assertions that over time have taken on a banal character." Nonetheless, however, he stated that

> despite oneself, a tenacious, traditional paradigm forces itself upon the writer. Warsaw. A seven-hundred-year-old city; the burg of the mermaid; the heroic capital of a freedom-loving nation; an unvanquished city erased from the face of the earth, tormented by barbaric, fascist invaders, and—with heroic effort—returned to life through sacrificial labor. Oh! And let's not forget the inspiration of the world, the city of labor and peace.[75]

Written for the introduction to *Warszawa 1945–1970* (1970; *Warsaw 1945–1970*), a photobook published in honor of the socialist city's twenty-fifth anniversary, Dobrowolski's words seemingly rejected two and a half decades of other photobook introductions that had dutifully presented a Warsaw narrative sanctioned by the communist authorities. Dobrowolski called readers' attention to the platitudinal narrative that, according to him, had been fossilized in the immediate postwar years and frustrated creative attempts to write about the city. At the same time, however, his words also reinforced this typical storyline. Taking an ironic tone, he reinserted meaning into this "traditional" narrative by calling attention to the well-trodden discourse and pointing out that its basic building blocks continued to be valuable and inevitable in light of such obvious historical ruptures as World War II, the 1943 and 1944 uprisings, and the establishment of a communist regime. Finally, Dobrowolski deemed the narrative necessary to the education of a new generation of Varsovians who criticized Warsaw, compared it to other European or world capitals, or focused on issues of housing and work while ignoring the city's "heroism, martyrology, and triumph."[76]

Through ironizing the official Warsaw narrative that had been developing since 1945, Dobrowolski stripped it down to its bare essentials and described the basic building blocks of Varsovian-themed photobooks. The story presented in many introductions had predictably borrowed the most common formulations about the city from both propaganda and popular sentiment. Utilizing hyperbolic and mythmaking language, the photobook narrative often described Warsaw in legendary terms and condensed its history into single paragraphs or even sentences, or mediated between the contemporary moment and the archeological remnants found during the reconstruction process. Common narrative strategies included listing dates when Warsaw had been destroyed, and broad, sweeping statements about how the phoenix city had managed to grow into a thriving metropolis time and again. For example, one photobook described Warsaw's uniqueness as having "went twice through the course of growth and formation. For the first time, during the long seven centuries of its history; for the second time, under our eyes, in the very short period of rebuilding and reconstruction."[77] Such narrative time compression heightened a sense of spatiality. It called attention to the historical layering of the urban space that could not be seen in photographs or on a stroll through Warsaw's streets.

Another common theme in the photobook was the notion of Warsaw as a historically revolutionary city. The introduction to the photobook: *Warsaw: Landscape and Architecture*, for example, began by asserting that at the end of the war Warsaw was best described as "an embattled city"; this introduction further asserted that this was the case not only during World War II but "from the very beginning of the city's existence."[78] In yet another photobook, Varsovians who returned to live among the ruins were compared to "pioneers of Alaska" and a special species called *homo varsoviensis*.[79] The descriptive hyperbolic language allowed for a quick narrative turn to the experience of war, and wrote into the Varsovian legend the heroic actions of average people defending their capital during the war and the teeming repopulation of a city that was destroyed and nearly dead. In the photobook version of this narrative, members of the communist People's Army (Armia Ludowa) and People's Guard (Gwardia Ludowa) were granted heroic status as defenders of Warsaw alongside the average Varsovian, a perspective supported by the sequencing and juxtaposition of photographs and captions that eliminated the activities of the Home Army from the story. As could be predicted, the role of the Home Army was either omitted from the narrative or subtly criticized. The language of legend and the glorification of old Warsaw was a rhetorical setup for focusing on Germany's systematic plan to destroy Warsaw, a plan thwarted by the postwar "effort of reconstruction, which was of an equally unparalleled scope."[80] The narrative would generally turn toward indignation and fury at the violence meted out on the Polish capital under German occupation and the plan to turn it into a German provincial town. Rage was expressed at the human casualties of this plan, often pointing out that Warsaw was a vast cemetery where thousands had died in its defense.

By focusing on those aspects of history that were fundamental to a communist-friendly historical narrative, the photobooks were complicit in echoing the silences promoted by propaganda elsewhere. For example, the

1944 Warsaw Uprising was practically invisible in their narratives. Also, the photobooks rarely distinguished between the Polish and Jewish experiences of the war, adopting a rhetorical stance common in communist Poland that absorbed the Jewish experience of the war into a "specific national framework of the Polish collective memory" without distinguishing between Christians and Jews.[81] Nonetheless, the Warsaw Ghetto Uprising was more often present in the photobook narrative than the Warsaw Uprising of 1944, albeit in very specific and narrow ways. In *Warsaw, the Capital of Poland*, the Warsaw ghetto was presented on a two-page spread. The photos depicted Jews being captured on the streets of Warsaw by the Nazi occupation authorities; Jews being forced into the ghetto, which had been established by German authorities in 1942; and the pedestrian bridge over Chłodna Street (ulica Chłodna), which was described in the captions as being built by the German authorities in order to prevent "Jews from having contact with the rest of Warsaw's population."[82] On the following page were three photographs, one of Jews being rounded up for execution by Germans and two referring to the Ghetto Uprising, which in this caption was referred to as an "armed battle."[83]

One of the best examples, however, of how the Ghetto Uprising was incorporated into a photobook can be found on the pages of the *Sześcioletni plan odbudowy Warszawy* (*Six-Year Plan for Warsaw's Reconstruction*). In the context of presenting the latest plan for Warsaw's urban future, the photobook version of Bolesław Bierut's speech included short "chapters" on city districts under development. This included the transformation of the rubble in the area of the former Nazi-established Warsaw ghetto into the Muranów housing project, a central point in the socialist redevelopment of Warsaw's Śródmieście. In its photobook version, the transformation of the Warsaw ghetto rubble into socialist Muranów was represented on twelve pages, beginning with a two-page spread featuring Natan Rapoport's 1948 Monument to the Ghetto Heroes superimposed over an image of pulverized rubble. This image was followed by a full-page detail of the monument, followed by a visualization of how much rubble needed to be removed from the neighborhood—that is, sixty times the volume of the Prudential skyscraper. Another seven pages plus a folded insert represented the socialist planning and construction of Muranów.[84] In this sequence, the monument acted as a temporal bridge between "what was" (the ghetto and rubble) and "what will be" (a socialist housing complex), subtly leaving behind the traumatic past. In later photobooks, the Warsaw Ghetto Uprising was variously represented, sometimes calling attention to the uprising as a heroic act of a radical, leftist Jewish movement against the Nazis,[85] though most often it was either omitted or presented in a less ideological tone. The introduction to *Warszawa 1960* (1960; *Warsaw 1960*), for example, did not mention either the 1943 ghetto or the 1944 citywide uprising in its condensed history of wartime Warsaw.[86] And in the 1963 photobook *Warsaw: Landscape and Architecture*, the Monument to the Ghetto Heroes was depicted on the right half of a two-page spread and the caption simply referred to it by name. While the word "ghetto" evoked the association with Jews and the Holocaust, the caption itself did not go out of its way to call attention to this aspect of the memorial.[87] Instead, the image of the memorial was placed with an image of Pawiak that was described as the "prison of the Hitlerites."[88] Such a juxtaposition of images presented the ghetto memorial as part of a shared experience or story of the war.[89] It was only in the late 1970s that the uniqueness of the Jewish war experience started to be acknowledged. For example, in *Warsaw: A Portrait of a City* (1979), the monument was shown as part of the timeline of Warsaw's reconstruction and the caption called attention to sacrifice rather than politics, describing the monument as memorializing the "martyrology and battle of Varsovian Jews."[90] Other than through the one- or two-page references to the Warsaw ghetto and uprising, however, the photobooks did not contend with the former Jewish spaces of the city. In this way, they fed a silence about Warsaw's Jewish communities that had disappeared during the war and reinforced the absence of the Jewish community by omitting this history from their postwar visual-verbal narrative.

While silencing some aspects of Warsaw's past, the photobooks honed and outlined other basic historical building blocks and used them over the years to develop continuity between the past and the present. Once the historical foundation of the narrative was laid, it was often followed by a narrative turn toward renewal and rebuilding. First came the Soviet Army, without which— the narrative claimed—no return to life in postwar Warsaw would have been possible. Next came the process of de-mining the city of German explosives. This was followed by descriptions of the colossal effort of Varsovians spontaneously returning to Warsaw after the war to clear the streets of rubble and rebuild their capital. The fact that many of those returning were not originally from Warsaw was rarely, if ever, mentioned. And finally in the narrative came the "landmark" decision of the communist authorities to rebuild Warsaw as the Polish capital on its original site, as well as descriptions of the authorities' commitment to reconstructing important historical buildings and monuments while creating a new, socialist urban space that would satisfy the fundamental needs of the working class. This entailed a narrative rejection of Poland's interwar years, stating that the capitalist endeavors of that period had been reflected in Warsaw's cramped, dark, and dank working-class housing. These capitalist tendencies, according to the photobook narrative, would be countered by the new Warsaw that would provide healthy, bright, and spacious housing for all. This version of the Varsovian narrative often ended with a summary of the progress made in the reconstruction efforts up to the moment of publication, with a look at future housing and infrastructure plans for the continued expansion and development of the capital. The formulaic nature of the written narrative was counterbalanced by the photographs and other images published alongside the written texts. Without the photos, the written text belonged to the realm of propaganda with its use of hyperbolic and emotional language. The photographs, however, gave weight to these words, saving them from their repetitive vacuousness and rooting them in photographic verisimilitude.

Organization and Sequencing, Themes and Chronologies

While the Varsovian narrative remained relatively consistent in photobooks throughout the communist era, other elements, such as the organization and sequencing of photographs and captioning techniques, were more malleable and functioned as barometers of political and sociocultural change. They reflected the progress achieved in postwar reconstruction, eventually reflecting the nature of a renewed contemporary urban landscape. Images of the ruins juxtaposed against their prewar structures gave credence to the historical thread of the narrative; photographs of in-process or completed construction projects, scale models of future development plans, and candid shots of nondescript workers laboring for the reconstruction of the capital gave the future-oriented narrative a material presence in the here and now. At the same time, each book possessed a unique value through the organization and sequencing of its selected images.

Warsaw, the Capital of Poland (1949) was organized more or less chronologically, starting with an urban history of Warsaw from its earliest representation in sixteenth-century woodcuts and the eighteenth-century paintings of Bernardo "Canaletto" Bellotto, continuing with photographs of interwar Warsaw under the rubric "Warsaw of a Bygone Era," and culminating with sections entitled "Embattled Warsaw," "Warsaw in Ruins," "Liberated Warsaw," "Warsaw Under Reconstruction," "Warsaw of the Future," "The Revolutionary People of Warsaw," and "People of the Reconstruction." Such an ideologically flavored chronological approach to organizing images in the late 1940s helped to place the reconstruction efforts of the postwar government on a continuous timeline of Warsaw history, connecting the younger Canaletto's eighteenth-century images with the more contemporary ones presented in the book. Within each section, the photographs were also organized in a way that promoted a subtle, propaganda message.

In 1950 an illustrated version of President Bolesław Bierut's 1949 *Six-Year Plan for Warsaw's Reconstruction* was published. This photobook was organized according to the themes of Bierut's 1949 speech that expressed the precepts of "rational," "socialist" urban development in the context of other common messages promoted by the communist regime. The photobook was organized according to such categories as: "Soviet Assistance," "The Legacy of Capitalism," "The Ideological Face of the City," "Industry," "Housing Construction," "Executors of the Plan," "Socialist Competition," and "The Fight to Strengthen Peace." Published as socialist realism was being formally integrated into Polish arts and letters, *Warsaw, the Capital of Poland* and the *Six-Year Plan for Warsaw's Reconstruction* followed chronological temporal

and rationalized thematic structures; they resisted the fractured or ellipti-
cal visual narratives that had been part of the photobook genre since the
1920s in Europe[91] and presented a verbal narrative that was supported by
photographic illustrations. Other organizational categories in these and later
photobooks were dictated by concepts closely associated with urban planning, such as "people," "architecture," "daily life," and "education," which
often acted as secondary organizational principles and were meant to highlight the nature and flavor of contemporary Varsovian life. With socialist
realism already waning in 1955, however, Varsovian photobooks began
to replace this linear, "rational" configuration with chaotic organizational
and sequencing principles that evoked the nature of urban life itself. Editors
sought to adopt structures and sequencing that better represented the modern, urban metropolis that was the new socialist Warsaw.

One such technique was a renewed use of before-and-after sequencing.
Similar to the diptychs used in the exhibit *Warsaw Accuses*, many later photobooks relied extensively on sequencing that transgressed chronological order,
introduced temporal anachronies,[92] created a simulated Warsaw space, and
transgressed the boundaries of time. Both *Warsaw, the Capital of Poland* and
Bierut's *Six-Year Plan for Warsaw's Reconstruction* minimally used before-
and-after sequencing, juxtaposing images of 1930s Warsaw with those of
1945.[93] By 1954, however, before-and-after sequencing was used to juxta-
pose images from 1945 with those of 1954, underscoring the *reconstruction*
rather than the *destruction* of the city.[94] Such juxtapositions not only reflected
progress and success in rebuilding, but also underscored a temporal distanc-
ing from the past. Later photobooks exploited the before-and-after technique
even more extensively by juxtaposing in various constellations images of
prewar Warsaw, postwar rubble and ruins, rebuilt edifices, and construction
sites. Particularly effective were triptychs that juxtaposed prewar images
with wartime rubble and postwar reconstructions. While two-dimensional
on the page, the temporal, visual comparisons gave depth to Warsaw's story
that a written text alone could not offer. Such sequencing contributed greatly
to establishing an aura of authenticity that could only be elicited through the
merging of "objective" documentary and archival images of the past with
those of a new era.

Other creative sequencing techniques began to appear in the 1960s. The
photobook *Warsaw 1960*, for example, was sequenced neither historically
nor thematically. Rather, it utilized a geospatial approach that presented
images of the Old and New Towns followed by a "tour" of the approximately eight-mile Royal Route (Trakt Królewski) from Zamkowy Square to
Wilanowski Palace. The sequencing of the images then "looped" back north
along Niepodległości Avenue (aleja Niepodległości) to Dzierżyńskiego Square
(today Bankowy Square) and Teatralny Square (plac Teatralny) to showcase
the National Theater and the Tomb of the Unknown Soldier. To some, the
first part of the image sequence might sound like a very traditional tour of

Warsaw; however, the text itself did not verbally draw attention to the geo-spatial organization of the Royal Route that was present in the photobook. Furthermore, the traditional, historical sites "visited" in the photobook were seamlessly, and without commentary, juxtaposed with photographs of communist-era edifices. Such a composition presented a multilayered Warsaw that simultaneously embraced the past and present. This was also a "walking tour" through Warsaw, which included forays along roads less traveled—that is, it visually ventured into newly developed neighborhoods and districts on the outskirts of the city.

The sequencing and organization of photobooks from the 1970s reflected the next stage in Warsaw's photobook poetics. While they included a verbal narrative anchored by the obligatory elements outlined above, their introductions became succinct and laconic, sometimes summarizing the experience of the war in only a few sentences. The verbal text often acted only as a trigger to what was assumed was a well-known broader narrative that was strongly rooted in the discourse on Warsaw. This also meant that the organization of the texts took on a new dimension. The sequencing and organization of *Warsaw 1945–1970*, for example, defied the inclusion of a table of contents. With pre- and postwar photographs mixed together seemingly ad hoc and with almost every two pages presenting a new chapter of postwar Varso-vian life, the album created a dizzying spatial and temporal effect. A far cry from "rational," cartographic, chronological, historically determined, and socialist realist-influenced aesthetics of an earlier period, the book not only included wartime images that had not been previously presented in similar photobooks, such as the image of the first German bomber over Warsaw, but also inserted contemporary color images of a new and lively city from 1970 between the grim, black-and-white photos of rubble, deprivations, and wartime hangings of Poles by the Germans. If you peruse the photobook from beginning to end, the color photos "appear" quite sagaciously, just in time to give the viewer a mental and emotional break from the gravity of the other images. With no maps and the historical context and captions offered simultaneously in Polish, English, French, German, and Russian, reading and viewing the photobook elicits a simulated chaotic experience of wartime, the postwar period, and contemporary cosmopolitan urban space. Unlike the photobooks that came before it, *Warsaw 1945–1970* drew viewers' attention away from the accompanying text to the photographs portray-ing candid, informal images of postwar Varsovian life. The book included more images of people than other books and avoided the tendency to sepa-rate images of architecture from those of Varsovians and their daily lives. Thus, this 1970 photobook created a more intimate, visceral, human experi-ence of Poland's capital than had been constructed in earlier photobooks, like *Warsaw, the Capital of Poland* or Bierut's *Six-Year Plan for Warsaw's Reconstruction*.

The organization and sequencing of *Warsaw: A Portrait of a City* provides yet another example of a changing photobook landscape. This book exemplified the dynamism associated with the 1970s, or what was called the "Gierek Decade." Named after Edward Gierek, the first secretary of the Polish United Workers' Party from 1970 to 1980, the early 1970s were marked by an economic boom in Poland that included heavy investment in the housing sector and the growth and expansion of Warsaw's districts. *Warsaw: A Portrait of a City* consisted of 112 color images taken by Krzysztof Jabłoński. If the images are mapped according to their sequence in the photobook, they create a circle or spiral that increases in size. With each new page of the photobook, the visual focus moves further and further away from the city center toward the periphery of the city. Such an organization and sequencing shifted viewers' and readers' attention toward Warsaw's urban development on the city's periphery, rather than on the project of (re)building central Warsaw and the ruination and destruction that occurred during the war. This photobook and its structure exemplified urban and economic development in more "normal" circumstances, illustrating that the city was no longer focused on rebuilding but rather on developing and expanding its infrastructure. This visual narrative mirrored the ideological thrust of Gierek's policies, integrating into the portrayal of the city important milestones of industrial development. The album also portrayed the need to adjust the narrative of the capital so as to integrate the successes of the early 1970s into a Varsovian narrative that balanced all aspects of daily Varsovian life: spiritual, marked by the inclusion of images of renovated and new churches; physical, indicated by photos of an ice rink and a surprising number of swimming complexes; material, represented by new shopping areas and thus suggesting increased access to goods and merchandise; industrial; educational; and medical, exemplified by new oncology clinics and health care centers for children. This, however, was not the entire photobook. In contrast to the geospatial organization in the first third of the book represented by color photographs, *Warsaw: A Portrait of a City* included a black-and-white illustrated timeline of Warsaw from 1945 to 1977. Though consisting of photographs that had not been published previously, the timeline was organized according to the principles of chronology and themes established decades earlier. Despite many changes, the visual-verbal narratives established in the late 1940s and early 1950s continued to persist and remained the default for even the most unique Varsovian photobooks of the late communist period.

Captioning the Images

Like organization and sequencing, the captioning of Varsovian images evolved over the decades of communism. In the early photobooks, images and their captions often worked in direct correlation. On a formal level, this meant that the captions were printed directly next to or under images. They not only identified the geographic or architectural sites pictured, but included the rationale, concept, and raison d'être of the volumes. In the first decade after the war, the editors of the volumes deemed it insufficient to simply identify the geographic coordinates shown on the photographic image. Rather, the captions worked in conjunction with introductory essays to give each photo a rich meaning in historical, ideological, and spatial terms. For example, in addition to the geographic location, the captions in *Warsaw, the Capital of Poland* commented on the historical relevance of the place portrayed; expressed indignation toward, and denunciation of, German policies towards Poles and Jews alike; rejected the capitalist, bourgeois urban development plans of prewar Warsaw; and parroted propaganda statements that valorized the newly established socialist state. Thus the written texts that accompanied images rarely possessed a simple, straightforward message that described the photo. Rather, they combined a number of narrative threads that represented a distillation of official Varsovian poetics in the aftermath of war and in the infancy of the postwar regime. Attached to each image, the captions actively built new connotations and merged with or obliterated old ones.

Such was the case in the section "Warsaw of a Bygone Era" in *Warsaw, the Capital of Poland*. It consisted of undated photographs of buildings and streets. The seemingly objective captions set out to historicize the images by explaining when buildings were erected, describing the architectural styles and details of the edifices portrayed, highlighting dates of fires and destruction by accidents or foreign invasions, and indicating the location of the photograph, such as "Boduena Street, which joins Jasna Street with Szpitalna Street."[95] Captions underscored notable historical events that took place at the location pictured and offered succinct overviews of Polish history. These captions constituted an example of the archeological relationship between image and text. Many of the one- or two-sentence captions identifying buildings or streets traced historical iterations of the architectural subject, unmasking or peeling away layers hidden by time under the facades. Through the relationship of caption and photograph, this book reconstructed an architectural history of Warsaw that was invisible to the naked eye before the war and was either lost amid the postwar rubble or exposed by devastation.[96] A typical caption might give a century of architectural history in just one sentence. For example, the caption describing Warsaw's prewar Town Hall (Ratusz Warszawski) was constructed as follows: "Warsaw's Town Hall on Teatralny Square, once the Jabłonowski Palace, reconstructed in the neoclassical style by Merlini at the end of the eighteenth century, later restored after the fire of 1870 by the architect Orłowski."[97] On the one hand, this one sentence described the history of the building. On the other, its grammatical structure did not provide a temporal marker in relation to the present tense, making it feel as if the building still existed even though it had been destroyed during the war. In sum, the captions of the historical section remained temporally undefined, eternally present, unrelated to any particular moment, and ripe for rhetorical and spatial appropriation.

The images presented in this section of *Warsaw, the Capital of Poland* were not juxtaposed with correlated images of postwar ruins; there were no attempts to make a direct connection between a building that stood during the interwar period and what it looked like as a pile of rubble. Such juxtapositions were reserved for later photobooks published in the 1950s, 1960s, and 1970s that showed images of ruins next to brand-new buildings or freshly reconstructed edifices. Rather, the buildings and street scenes portrayed here represented a modest inventory of the past, with the text subtly redefining their meaning for a socialist present and a communist future. The image of the bell tower of the Church of the Visitation of the Blessed Virgin Mary, for example, offered the chance to highlight one of the best examples of gothic architecture in prewar Warsaw, as well as incorporate into the narrative of the photobook information about the destruction caused during the seventeenth-century Swedish invasion of Poland, called the Deluge. The caption underscored that the church had been completely destroyed and burned during the invasion and was "reconstructed under King Jan Sobieski through the efforts, and at the expense, of Varsovian townsfolk."[98] Cunningly, this caption historicized the contemporary moment, making a parallel with the fund-raising campaign organized by the Civic Fund for the Reconstruction of the Capital. While providing a broad array of historical reference points, the caption did not engage in rhetoric on the role of Christianity in Polish history and culture. Furthermore, despite the purportedly neutral tone of the captions and the inclusion of images that called attention to an aristocratic and Catholic nation, calling the section "a bygone age" underscored a break with the past, providing the volume with the correct ideological tone and suggesting that the aristocratic values of Old Warsaw were passé. Notably, this narrative ignored other important aspects of the city's history, namely the Jewish population of Warsaw, as well as the move of peasants from country to city in order to repopulate the capital after the war.

Other narrative threads introduced in the captions and longer expositions included references to symbols of communism, such as "Mały Franek" Zubrzycki, who was the commander of the first partisan division of the People's Guard, and Marian Buczek, who was incarcerated during the interwar period for communist activity and died in September 1939 in a battle with German forces.[99] Neither man was of particular importance to the war effort; however, they were used in the photobook to give a sympathetic face to communists, and they symbolized a patriotic commitment of communist activists and their actions. At the same time, however, the effect of these names in the photobook was, to some degree, incommensurable with the tone of the text and seemed more forced than "natural" in the context of the volume. In particular, the image of Buczek's grave that was included on the second page of the section entitled "Warsaw Embattled" was strategically laid out alongside photographs of volunteers organized by the Polish Socialist Party (Polska Partia Socjalistyczna, PPS); a homeless family living in the midst of a dusty, littered field; and a shot of Zamkowy Square framed on all sides by charred support beams and other rubble, with the Sigismund III Vasa Column as the focal point of the image.[100] The caption for the image of Buczek's grave, which was placed above the image of the digging volunteers, read as follows:

> The grave of Marian Buczek, an extraordinary communist, patriot, and unyielding freedom fighter, who immediately after leaving the Sanacja prison, fought as a volunteer against the Hitlerite invaders and died on September 10, 1939 in Ołtarzew on the outskirts of Warsaw. Below: the Volunteer Brigade of the Defense of Warsaw digs an anti-tank trench.[101]

The caption directly called attention to the visual juxtaposition on the page, lest a reader needed a more thorough explanation of what he or she was looking at. This two-page spread presented a mini-narrative of the embattled city by casting Buczek and a volunteer unit of communists as average people and juxtaposing their efforts and fate with stranded refugees and the city in ruins, all under the historical patronage of the Sigismund III Vasa Column that stood as a symbol of Warsaw. More importantly, the narrative presence of communists on the war-torn streets of the city from the early days of the war tried to reiterate and legitimize the presence of Polish socialists and communists in the fabric of society and called attention to the organizational benefits offered by members of the PPS or other left-minded groups, thus removing the role of the Home Army and the London-based government-in-exile from the broader narrative. Though the Home Army was not directly mentioned in the text, the explanatory prose of the caption indirectly blamed it for the tragedy of the Warsaw Uprising in 1944 by depicting everyday people as passive victims and active heroes of the conflict. The caption read:

> The simple man of the Warsaw street, who heard the thunder of the divisions across the Vistula River and took up his place at the barricades, did not know the real state of affairs, did not know for what goals he was pushed into battle; he heroically fought against the Hitlerites, not sensing the tragedy of which he became a casualty and a participant. Every Warsaw side street, almost every meter of road has its own history of battles that was written down by hundreds of thousands of Varsovians, who fought without water, without provisions, often with bare hands against tanks and regular divisions.[102]

Typical captioning techniques, however, found an exception in one photobook from this period, namely the *Six-Year Plan for Warsaw's Reconstruction*. On some levels, the illustrated version of Bierut's 1949 speech intersected and overlapped with *Warsaw, the Capital of Poland*. In particular, the *Six-Year Plan for Warsaw's Reconstruction* followed a set narrative pattern and outlined how socialist Warsaw would abandon the crowded conditions of a prewar capital. However, there were also departures from the general structure outlined in *Warsaw, the Capital of Poland* and adopted by later photobooks. As the formal articulation of what a socialist Warsaw was supposed to become—namely, a city with open spaces, broad avenues, and accessible housing that was designed for workers—this book was the apex of ideological expression in photobook form. It contained images of the past and photos of present reconstruction achievements, but it also illustrated the future Warsaw through maps, renderings, and pictures of scale models. Abstract topics, such as improved health care, were illustrated using symbolic photographs that stood in for future achievements. Despite (or maybe because of) its importance, the illustrated version of the *Six-Year Plan for Warsaw's Reconstruction* was not used as a model for future photobooks. Presenting over 500 images in a large, B4 format with a dark blue or maroon cover embossed with gold lettering, it utilized more refined sequencing and captioning techniques, taking liberties not found in other books.

Bierut's 1949 speech was a turning point, formally moving the capital's postwar development from reconstruction toward construction and expansion. In its photobook form, the speech was broken down into thirty-seven sections calling direct attention to the themes being promoted: Soviet assistance in the liberation and reconstruction of Warsaw, the ideological shape of the city, transportation developments, housing, education, parks, and more. Each section of the speech was followed by a rich selection of photographs symmetrically laid out with two to eight photographs on every two pages. Some photographs were captioned with direct quotes from the speech, in the same way an illustration in a novel might be captioned using a direct quote from the text. The captions condensed the speech and highlighted its most granular points. They took an already condensed developmental narrative about Warsaw found within Bierut's plan and distilled it to its most basic message, associating specific sentences with familiar scenes or attractive images of the future. These captions, however, almost all began and ended with ellipses, rather than standing alone as full sentences. Such punctuation called attention to these caption-quotes as part of a greater whole. Instead of providing geospatial coordinates, or the type of mini-histories found in the captions of *Warsaw, the Capital of Poland*, the *Six-Year Plan for Warsaw's Reconstruction* forged a symbiosis between written and visual text, building a series of visual associations with particular propaganda messages. Despite the importance of Bierut's speech to this photobook, photographs dominated the publication and were the primary means of communicating ideology. Of the book's 367 pages, only 45 contained written text; and of those pages, some contained as few as three or four sentences, often without an accompanying photograph, suggesting that the visual image possessed a greater power of persuasion than even the words of President Bierut. Such a truncated captioning technique ensured that even the person least likely to read the written text in its entirety might quickly skim a sentence or two of Bierut's speech and connect it with a photograph that captured his or her attention.

As Warsaw grew and developed, the need for an inextricable union between image and word subsided. By the late 1960s Warsaw was a functioning urban center, and the official obsession with controlling the language and discourse of the capital had eroded. Captions withered to direct geospatial identification, and were sometimes even printed on different pages than the image to which they referred. As Warsaw was rebuilt and urban icons carried value as both geospatial markers and discursive symbols, the need for written or linguistic explanation likewise subsided. Yet the basic shape of the official Varsovian narrative remained a part of the photobooks, albeit in condensed form, well past the Stalinist period. The memory value and genius loci of postwar Warsaw was a tangled thread. Based on the ideology of the communist regime, post-1945 photobooks rhetorically ignored or rejected Warsaw's "bourgeois" legacy, yet they could not ignore the deeply rooted memory of the city and its atmosphere within Polish collective memory and culture. As an article on the topic in *The Capital: A Varsovian Illustrated Weekly* stated: "Today, we are moved, without exaggeration, by photographs of those buildings which lie in ruins. They awaken in us memories; they pleasantly remind us of life in prewar Warsaw, all the more so because, with time, the negative aspects of the city will disappear."[103] A social intervention of sorts, the photobooks contributed to a distillation of the Varsovian narrative through their formal elements, manipulating the sequencing, organization, and verbal-visual connotations. They were one means of controlling what entered into the narrative memory of Warsaw. By hijacking the potential of memory work in photobooks and utilizing them in the narration of building a socialist Warsaw, the photobooks became complicit in constructing a new, postwar genius loci that merged recent historical events with such notions as legendary Varsovian commitment, sacrifice, humor, and heroism. Yet the communist-era books were far from nostalgic. As the war years were left behind, the future-oriented socialist narrative abandoned the notion of photography as a means of reconstituting national memory. Though the idea of the genius loci remained a part of Warsaw's photobook narrative, it was not the driving force or rationale behind the publications. As the temporal distance between World War II and the contemporary moment grew, so too did the photobook become less and less a memory book, and more and more a means of redefining Warsaw spatiality according to ideological parameters. Dominated by geospatial descriptors and sparse captioning, the later photobooks no longer negotiated the presentation of an aristocratic, "old" Warsaw, the events of the war, or the progress achieved in (re)construction since 1945. Instead, the photobooks focused on repeating a narrative that had been constructed over the years by propaganda on and about the Polish capital, while creatively sequencing images to offer a revitalized textual experience of place.

Chapter 2

Reconstructing Warsaw in Newsreels

The newsreel, a "potpourri of motion picture news footage," is an audiovisual artifact of the past.[1] The mere idea of the newsreel takes us back to an earlier era when the connection between the moving image, news, and its consumption by viewers was mediated by time and distance from the events it reported. A popular form of disseminating news in the United States and across Europe beginning in the first decades of the twentieth century, newsreels were limited to movie theaters, were screened prior to scheduled feature films, and were often secondary to the main attraction and audience interest. In most countries, the dawn of television brought the national traditions of newsreels to a close. Today, with news outlets broadcasting twenty-four hours a day on television, and updating information online from moment to moment, it is easy to forget that once access to filmed news and information required leaving home and entering into the magical space of the movie theater. While the spatiality of the movie theater is itself an intriguing topic, the goal of this chapter is to focus on how the spatiality of postwar Warsaw was created on screen by the Polish Film Chronicle (Polska Kronika Filmowa, PKF). Focusing on newsreels from the first postwar decade, I consider how Varsovian spaces were represented in news reports and special bulletins that underscored Warsaw as a functioning capital city and narrativized the process of Warsaw's physical transformation from rubble to reconstruction.

The Polish newsreels produced after World War II were similar to their Western counterparts: ten-minute reels consisting of shorter segments that juxtaposed serious news items with (sometimes) lighthearted stories.[2] Differences, however, between the newsreels of the West and those of Poland and other Eastern bloc countries such as Czechoslovakia, the Soviet Union, or Yugoslavia can be located in the sociopolitical context of communism and totalitarian states. Behind the Iron Curtain, newsreels were subject to the rules of state propaganda and ideological control. At the same time, as Joshua Malitsky demonstrates in his study of Soviet and Cuban postrevolutionary newsreels and documentaries, nonfiction film was subject to a "dynamic between the insistent and constant mandate from above and the (relative) open-endedness of the cinematic form," a dynamic that generated some degree of creative autonomy in the newsreels.[3] It is on this level of creative autonomy and cinematic malleability that the Polish Film Chronicle (PKF) intersects with newsreels from not only the Eastern bloc but also from the West. As scholars of the genre have demonstrated, regardless of time or place, the cinematic medium with all its components (sound, image, framing, etc.) makes nonfiction film, and especially newsreels, prone to manipulation and propaganda use.[4]

In the following pages, I show how the postwar regime in Poland utilized the newsreels to disseminate a Varsovian spatiality that attempted to counter the past and shape the socialist future by activating a national process of imagining a new Warsaw.[5] My analysis locates Warsaw's portrayal on the newsreel screen in its sociopolitical context, while elucidating how the formal elements of film were exploited to co-create a lasting image of the Polish capital that was written into the broader social consciousness, often along the lines determined by propaganda and, at other times, in surprisingly autonomous ways. This chapter demonstrates the complexity of nonfiction film as both a document and archival source by (1) looking at the particularities of newsreels and their production; (2) studying the way Warsaw's reconstruction was narrated, filmed, and promoted in the PKF; and (3) analyzing visual "counterpoints" that refute the official narrative on Warsaw in the newsreels. To this end, I pose some deceptively simple questions: How did the newsreels navigate their simultaneous roles as documentary, archive, and propaganda? What was the underlying narrative of Warsaw's reconstruction in the PKF? And how did this narrative intersect with other representations of the city? By answering these questions and tracing the Varsovian story in the PKF, the analysis sheds light on how this purportedly "nonfiction" genre is, at its core, subject to discursive narrativization.

Warsaw and the Polish Film Chronicle: Between Documentary and Propaganda

As a result of the decision that Warsaw should remain Poland's capital after the war, the city became an important topic and setting for many of the news segments covered by the Polish Film Chronicle (PKF). By focusing on Varsovian events related to the new authorities, the newsreels assured Poles of Warsaw's *stołeczność* or capital status. Furthermore, news segments about Warsaw's de-rubbling, renovation, and construction fulfilled a broader social need to reassure an information-starved public that the capital, and thus Poland, "had not yet perished." The newsreels served to document and archive wartime destruction, Polish fortitude in the immediate postwar period, and the communist government's plans for Warsaw's reconstruction. And finally, both the newsreels and the story of Warsaw were central to the propaganda goals of a newly established socialist state. The combination of these factors placed the capital at the center of the newsreels in the decade after the war and, as such, contributed to the (re)writing of Warsaw in parallel with its physical reconstruction. In this way, the PKF actively engaged in creating Warsaw's spatiality, a narrative act that relied on the purported documentary value of nonfiction film, as well as the propaganda value attached to it by the authorities.

The Varsovian segments of the PKF reflected a tendency toward nonfiction film that dominated the early cinema of communist Poland,[6] in part "to mobilize the nation to start reconstruction."[7] But this was not unusual for the time, place, or circumstances, since making documentaries and newsreels was cheaper than making feature films. After the war, film studios, distribution sources, and movie theaters across Poland were decimated, not to mention the human losses. And other than what was brought back to Poland in 1944 by the military film unit of the Polish Army in the Soviet Union, which was called Czołówka Filmowa Wojska Polskiego or simply "Czołówka," there was little or no remaining equipment.[8] According to one source, of the approximately 800 cinemas that existed before the war, only 200 were intact in June 1945.[9] The prewar and wartime experiences of filmmakers who remained in Poland after the war also contributed to the propensity for making documentary films and newsreels. Some of the leading postwar filmmakers, including those involved in producing the newsreels, started their careers in 1943 with "Czołówka" ("front rank"), which made documentaries while traveling "from Lenino to Berlin" with the First Polish Army under Soviet command.[10] Others were members of the interwar leftist-leaning Society for the Promotion of Art Film, or "START,"[11] which advocated for documentary film as an art form and as a means of exerting social influence.[12] Key players in this respect were Aleksander Ford, the first director of the state-owned Film Polski from 1945 to 1947; Jerzy Bossak, the editor-in-chief of the PKF until 1949;[13] the PKF cinematographers Stanisław Wohl and Adolf Forbert; and the directors Wanda Jakubowska and Ludwik Perski.[14]

The documentary tendency of the PKF was also encoded in the very name of the newsreels: Polska Kronika Filmowa. "Kronika" is defined as "a chronological record listing the more important events in the life of a state, institution, organization, and so on, without explaining their causal effect."[15] The importance of the genre in Polish culture dates to the twelfth-century Kronika polska, one of the earliest known records of Polish history, and attributed to Gallus Anonymous.[16] The word "kronika" was also used to describe a form of feuilleton perfected in the late nineteenth century by the author and journalist Bolesław Prus (1847–1912), whose weekly publications were famous for recording current political, social, and cultural events, as well as for their detailed observations of everyday life in Warsaw.[17] In this respect, the newsreels fit a pattern of recording Polish history and life, with the word "kronika" connoting a documentary and archival purpose.[18] The PKF filmmakers and crews embraced this archivist role. In addition to providing footage for news reports, they saw their work as document-ing the present and as archivization. As regards Warsaw, filming the capital city's reconstruction from the ground up was motivated by a desire to docu-ment changes that, over time, would be almost impossible to understand or remember unless recorded on film.

As I have already mentioned, the cinematic form allowed PKF filmmakers to maintain a certain amount of autonomy in producing newsreels. But as the film historian Marek Cieśliński demonstrates, this freedom was grossly curtailed with the PKF subject to censorship during the entire communist period.[19] Considered by Lenin and other Soviet ideologues as a core medium of education and communist propaganda, nonfiction film was seen as foun-dational to the mission of the new regime in Poland.[20] The communist-era film critic and historian Jerzy Toeplitz explained that after the war the gov-ernment "considered the film situation very important. Lenin's formula that film is the most important of all the arts probably had a very beneficial effect. He was especially interested in the educational aspects and the newsreel."[21] Based on this, resuscitating the film industry in postwar Poland and adapt-ing it to the pedagogical needs of propaganda became important aspects of the communist plan to indoctrinate Polish society. Despite the economic challenges, the authorities invested heavily in the film industry, supposedly sending the director and cinematographer Stanisław Wohl to Berlin to collect as much film equipment (cameras, lenses, cassette recorders, etc.) as pos-sible.[22] Investment in film continued throughout the first postwar decade, including in the newsreels, and the process of *kinofikacja* (cinefication) of the countryside resulted in a countrywide distribution network. By 1956, over 4,000 movie theaters across Poland were screening the newsreels, and the PKF was reaching an estimated four to five million viewers—a significantly higher number than newspaper circulation and later television viewership.[23]

Furthermore, even those PKF filmmakers who had aesthetic aspirations as part of START before the war were willing to forgo their artistic ideals and place their documentary experience in the service of ideology.[24] During the war, many of these filmmakers, including Ford, Bossak, Wohl, and Forbert, cooperated with Sojuzkino in the Soviet Union and were influenced by the Soviet documentarian Dziga Vertov's work from the 1920s. Vertov's docu-mentary style, called *kino-pravda* (film-truth), fostered "an attitude of active engagement from the viewer."[25] Though Vertov's style had fallen out of favor in the Soviet Union by the 1930s, his ideas about the transformative power of the cinematic image remained central to the ideals of PKF filmmakers. Other Soviet influences could be traced to former Sojuzkino cinematogra-phers, such as Eugeniusz Jefimow and Olgierd Samucewicz, who worked for the PKF in its early years.[26]

As documentary, the PKF nominally embraced the notion that raw footage represented "reality" and "truth." As propaganda, however, it exemplified communist Poland's most thorough and complete reflection of the reality that *was supposed* to exist under communism, and it corresponded directly to messages propagated in the state-owned and controlled press, radio, and later television.[27] Subject to censorship, the newsreels were used to build a socialist society through the messages they propagated.[28] They exploited their seemingly neutral role as recorders of history and presenters of fact, while deploying techniques of persuasion by adapting film language, dramaturgical principles, and other aspects of narrative cinema for the purpose of propaganda.[29] This was the case even before the official adoption of socialist realism at the 1949 conference of filmmakers. With the adoption of socialist realism, these techniques were honed even further. As Cieśliński points out, the PKF "filtered reality" by manipulating cinema and facts in such a way "that the reality portrayed on screen became more beautiful than the authentic one."[30]

The process of filtering information, making life under communism look better on screen than in reality, and adapting news items to propaganda goals were tactics of the PKF from the very start. Under Jerzy Bossak, the first editor-in-chief of the PKF, presenting an optimistic and positive interpretation of reality was the foundation of the PKF aesthetic, while selecting topics, themes, and footage that coincided with the needs of the state was compulsory. Perhaps Bossak's approach to choosing footage for the PKF is best typified by his response to camera operators, who in 1945 returned from an assignment in the newly annexed western territories (called the "Recovered Territories" in Polish) with no raw footage. When they claimed that they "did not want to contribute to creating a false image of territories dominated by chaos and disorder," Bossak explained the importance of their work and assured them of the "veracity" of the PKF's approach by underscoring and rationalizing the instrumental nature of propaganda as it related to documentary film. Alluding to Scottish documentarian John Grierson's theory of documentary as a "creative treatment of actuality,"[31] Bossak explained that the selective portrayal of reality "is not a lie but rather creative propaganda." He explained that "a camera operator's work does not varnish reality, even if the image does not coincide with the average situation dominating the country . . . The camera operator is more than a mechanical chronicler. He is a co-creator of this new and better reality." Bossak understood propaganda, and therefore the newsreels, as a pedagogical tool that "transforms itself into social behavior," "disseminates optimism," and "transforms bad things into good ones."[32] With the political Thaw in 1956 and during times of open protest and dissent, however, this "educational" potential often worked against the authorities, as the creators of the PKF used the malleability of nonfiction film to expose the shortcomings of the communist regime by incorporating into the newsreels ironic juxtapositions of voice-over, music, editing, and image.

Despite their commitment to propaganda, the PKF producers were intently aware of the pitfalls of heavy-handed ideological messages and Polish society's resistance to them. Thus, in order to keep the newsreels popular, they sought to impart their message while satisfying viewers' expectations for entertainment, variation, and news. As one document of the communist party from the mid-1950s explained:

> The PKF, as every direct tool of fleeting propaganda, is not a work of art; but by operating according to the means of film expression, it is subject to its basic aesthetic principles. . . . This does not mean that the newsreels can omit facts of political and state importance, but it must, after all, choose, shape, and arrange them in appropriate combinations. Particularly in film propaganda, a specific dramaturgy is required, as well as employing the right proportion of serious and lighter matters that do not require intellectual effort, attacking [the viewer's] attention at the moment it is distracted by surprise.[33]

This approach to producing the newsreels clearly worked to some extent. Despite their "pedagogical" function, their ephemerality and fleeting nature, and the rise of television culture, the newsreels remained popular in Poland under communism and even afterward, being produced until 1994.[34] The segments were short and quick-paced, lasting as little as 45 seconds and usually no longer than 90 seconds.[35] To maintain audience interest, the PKF fulfilled expectations by adopting visual and verbal structures, rhythm, and sound-signals that repeated themselves from edition to edition, segment to segment; however, the repetition was balanced by a diversity of topics generated by the journalistic function of the newsreel. The voices of narrators likewise played a role in audience expectations. In the early years after the war, the voice-over narration tended toward a graver, more propagandistic tone that underscored the drama and tragedy of the war era; with time and distance from the war, a lighthearted tone was introduced. When the news item permitted, the language and intonation entertained audiences. Most importantly, however, the voice of Andrzej Łapicki, who narrated the newsreels until 1956, became a recognizable cultural institution in the same way that Walter Cronkite's or Charles Kuralt's voices were across the Atlantic Ocean. The PKF musical signal, composed by Władysław Szpilman (author of the memoir *The Pianist* and the subject of Roman Polański's film by the same title), provided a node of aural familiarity. For special editions, like the *Biuletyn odbudowy stolicy* (*Bulletin of the Capital's Reconstruction*), theme music was selected as a means of unifying segments over a one- to two-year period. The speakers' voices, in combination with the music, gave life and rhythm to images that were otherwise silent.[36] Rarely did the newsreels include diegetic sound within a news story.

Between the "archivist" stance of film crews and the propaganda goals set by Bossak, the newsreels were an ideal mode to present to Polish audiences the new urban order planned for Warsaw and to capture the process of

material change as the reconstruction process evolved. One statistic suggests
that in 1946 almost half of the PKF segments produced were set in Warsaw or its environs.[37] Indeed, the PKF successfully chronicled a number of
building initiatives and created a film archive of what was deemed important
and newsworthy at the time. Like the photobooks discussed in the previous
chapter, newsreels contributed to the construction of a socialist Poland by
exploiting the tension between their documentary value, their potential as a
tool of propaganda, and their subjectivity as constructed forms of communication. The aesthetic and propaganda functions benefited from this flexibility
of the film form. The success of the "objective," albeit propagandized, news
image on screen relied heavily on subjective matters such as the relationship between text and image; musical selections that built aural connotations
and speakers' voices and intonations that became familiar (and expected)
over time; the organization and sequencing of news segments; and the editing
and sequencing of camera-takes that were first chosen by camera operators
and then sifted through by PKF managers, directors, editors, and censors. By
manipulating these elements, the PKF reinforced many of the same ideological principles being promoted in state-sponsored newspapers, photobooks,
and other official documents on Warsaw's reconstruction.

Throughout the postwar decade, the newsreel images of official events and
ceremonies occurring in the capital were foundational to documenting the
sense of Warsaw as a center of authority. They showed the city as the administrative center even at a time when many government institutions remained
in Lublin for practical reasons. News segments about pseudo-political life
built Warsaw's signification as a "socialist" city with numerous images of
communist party officials cutting ribbons at ceremonies to mark the opening
of tram lines, the groundbreaking on construction projects, or the completion
of new edifices. Reports on communist party conventions and congresses, and
military parades, as well as numerous segments featuring foreign dignitaries visiting Warsaw in the immediate postwar years all reinforced Warsaw's
capital status. At a time when photobooks, museum exhibits, and popular
sentiment envisioned Warsaw as "murdered," "no longer existing," or "resur-
recting" from the ashes, the PKF embraced Warsaw's capital status as a fait
accompli.[38]

In these news reports, Warsaw's urban space visually and thematically lin-
gered in the background. This space was treated passively by the camera
and endowed Warsaw with the gravitas of a capital despite its rubble state.
Spatial reference points that minimized attention to ruins such as the Vistula
River (Wisła), the nineteenth-century Belweder Palace where President Bierut
resided, or other still-recognizable areas of the city contextualized the activity of the new authorities. Though rejecting interwar Poland and what it
stood for, the communist authorities sought to locate themselves within the
context of Polish history and Warsaw by showing their physical presence in
the capital. The PKF reported on the activities of the communist government

in the context of symbolic Varsovian spatial reference points to create a sense of historical and cultural continuity, while redefining and developing new connotations between the city and the state. Underscoring historical continuity not only addressed the population's desire to refute Nazi Germany's plans to raze Warsaw to the ground, but also suggested that the communist party literally and figuratively was reconstructing and preserving—rather than rejecting—some of the basic material manifestations of Polish identity.

Thus the Varsovian segments of the PKF reinforced Warsaw as a setting that legitimized the new authorities, while the official activity of the communist government in Warsaw reinforced Warsaw's capital status. The newsreels countered static images of Warsaw's ruins and destruction, as well as the rhetoric of martyrdom, through their multidimensional chronicling of the slow but certain normalization of political and everyday life in the capital.[39] Varsovian news segments reported on concrete changes in the city landscape and provided a dynamic representation of reconstruction progress. In addition to showing changes in the urban landscape and disseminating these images quickly, film possessed the power to bring to life the propaganda phrase "The Entire Nation Is Building Its Capital," encouraging a sense of audience interaction with and participation in the building process.

From Legitimization to Normalization

In early 1945, the first newsreel of the PKF presented an item entitled "Dziennikarze zagraniczni na Pradze" ("Foreign Journalists in Praga") (PKF 1/45:4). The minute-and-a-half segment portrayed American, British, and French correspondents on a tour of the east bank of the Vistula River in the neighborhood of Saska Kępa in the Warsaw district of Praga, the same district where the Soviet Army positioned itself in early September 1944 during the Warsaw Uprising. The film showed the correspondents walking along Kawęczyńska Street (ulica Kawęczyńska) with the Basilica of the Sacred Heart of Jesus in the background, stopping at the graves of Polish and Soviet soldiers who were buried along the streets of Praga, walking along trenches, and conversing with soldiers who still remained stationed in the district. It was the dead of winter. The neighborhood was snow-covered. The streets were portrayed as empty, save for the journalists, Warsaw's mayor Colonel Marian Spychalski, General Stanisław Popławski of the Soviet-controlled First Polish Army, rank and file soldiers, and a couple of children. This newsreel was filmed before the so-called liberation of Warsaw on January 17, 1945, by the Soviets, and certainly before the reconstruction of the capital had begun. Yet, as the voice-over proudly related, plans for rebuilding the Polish state were already in the works and were cause for international admiration. According to the voice-over, "The process of rebuilding the Polish state which began in July '44 with the historical manifesto of the National Home Council [KRN] arouses great interest internationally." By citing the KRN's manifesto and showing the interaction of Spychalski and Popławski with foreign journalists, this image underscored the KRN's claim to legitimacy as the new authority in Poland. While it would seem at first glance that Warsaw as a space was of little importance in this segment, the fact that this was the first official image of the capital presented in the newsreels was significant. Praga's Saska Kępa had been minimally damaged during the war, and the obvious lack of ruins in this first news segment set in Warsaw is glaring. At the same time, however, setting a news segment in the capital—even if the setting was on the right bank of the Vistula River rather than in a central neighborhood on the left bank—was of vital importance. "Foreign Journalists in Praga" acted as a spatial counterpoint to the first segment of the edition, which reported on a French delegate visiting then Vice-Minister Jakub Berman of the communist provisional government in Lublin, the temporary location of the Polish capital. With the Warsaw segment as the fourth of five news items, the newsreel left viewers with a lingering image of Warsaw as a locus of authority despite its physical destruction.

The following month, the PKF presented Warsaw's liberation on the newsreel screen with a masterfully crafted seven-and-a-half-minute news report entitled "Warszawa wolna" ("Warsaw Is Free") (PKF 4/45:1). Directed by Jerzy Bossak and edited by Wacław Kaźmierczak, the segment exhibited a flawless montage of image, narration, and music that reached a dizzying speed of one- to three-second cuts. This news segment, however, was as much about the "liberation" of Warsaw as it was about (re)claiming the space from the Nazis for a new regime. In the course of seven minutes, the news segment rapidly summarized the war experience, beginning with the dynamic of victim vs. perpetrator, and ending with a visual statement of rightful and legitimate leadership. The segment played on viewers' emotions by stating "Warsaw is no more. Warsaw has been murdered" and referring to Germans as the "murderers," who were responsible for providing the physical labor to rebuild Warsaw.[40] Next, the news segment established an architectural pantheon of bombed and destroyed buildings, referring to prewar icons of the cityscape: churches, the Old Town (Stare Miasto), and the Warsaw Main Railway Station; the interwar Prudential skyscraper that symbolized the modern Warsaw of the Second Republic; the demolished Poniatowski Bridge (most Poniatowskiego); Teatralny Square (plac Teatralny); and the Sigismund III Vasa Column which was damaged by German bombs during the 1944 Warsaw Uprising. By the end of the segment, the ruins of Warsaw disappeared into the background, subsumed by the idea of a new leadership, embodied by President Bierut. The voice-over commentary was carefully matched with the images on screen. The commentary established the authority of the postwar communist leadership, calling them "legitimate administrators" ("prawi gospodarze") with Bierut at the helm.[41] The soundtrack filled the segment by matching or modulating the emotions elicited by the images. The victorious

music at the start of the segment offset the ruins shown on screen, majesti-
cally "filling" the empty spaces once occupied by buildings and monuments,
disallowing a single moment of silence during the entire seven-and-a-half
minutes. Even when the voice-over paused for dramatic effect (there are three
such pauses lasting from thirty to sixty seconds), the music dictated to the
viewer what he or she should be feeling: indignation, pride, elation. While
claiming to present news and information, this segment was outright propaganda, filled with persuasive, manipulative, and emotional language and
imagery. It carefully selected what was portrayed and just as carefully ignored
an important, potentially compromising fact: Soviet troops, who would soon
take over the city, are nowhere to be seen in the film.[42]

The following month a very different segment on Warsaw was presented
in the newsreels. Entitled "Pierwsze dni po wyzwoleniu Warszawy" ("The
First Days after Warsaw's Liberation"), the news segment showed throngs of
Varsovians returning to the city in overcrowded trains or walking shoulder-
to-shoulder across a makeshift wooden bridge from Praga, the district on the
right bank of the Vistula River, to the central district Śródmieście and other
left-bank districts of the capital (PKF 7/45:1). This segment included a view
of Zamkowy Square (plac Zamkowy) filmed from a similar perspective as
that portrayed in Bernardo "Canaletto" Bellotto's eighteenth-century paintings. The silhouettes of buildings were identifiable, and the poor quality of
the opening shots obscured the scars of war. Only the postwar context and
viewers' knowledge could fill in the reality, which remained unnamed and
unstated in the segment. Behind those walls, which from a distance seemed
to stand tall and intact, rested the remains of thousands who had died during
the war.

In this news segment, the victims of war were never mentioned. And only
halfway into the segment were the ruins of the city obviously visible on
screen. Even then, they were not the most important visual element within
the camera's frame. Rather, the people walking toward Warsaw, soldiers
marching on the streets, and the attempt to rebuild life in the capital were
highlighted as the most important elements of the return to Warsaw. The
voice-over stated that despite the bombed-out and burnt buildings, ruins, and
a lack of housing and public facilities, schools, stores, and artisan workshops
were appearing throughout the city. Only near the end of the segment, as the
camera panned along the crowded street, were the ruins of Warsaw visible in
the background. The narrator closed the segment with a statement in support
of the newly established communist regime: "All the preparations for the vast
and wide-ranging campaign to rebuild Warsaw are nearing completion. At
the service of this campaign are the Polish worker, the engineer, the heartfelt
offer of assistance from the allied nations of the Soviet Union, and the mighty
industry of the liberated territories of the Republic" (PKF 7/45:1).

Though the PKF segments described above differed from one another in
their goals and content, together they marked the start of a decade of Warsaw's

cinematization in the newsreels, casting in the main roles domestic dignitaries who participated in the reconstruction efforts; foreign visitors who were presented to Poles as a means of legitimizing the new government's reconstruction plans; and workers, soldiers, and children. The process of returning to normalcy would likewise remain an important narrative element in the PKF's representation of Warsaw from 1944 to 1956 (particularly in the early 1950s), and the obligatory message of Soviet brotherhood would accompany not only the news segments about Warsaw but many of the newsreels filmed until the fall of communism in 1989. Of importance to the PKF narrative of Warsaw was the idea of "process," or in other words, the active role played by the Soviet-backed KRN and the responsibility that the postwar authorities took upon themselves to rebuild the Polish capital as a socialist seat of power. By highlighting the role of communist officials and their activities, and tying these activities to the decisions made by the communist authorities, the PKF reiterated the message that the new regime was responsible for the reconstruction of the nation's capital and that the reconstruction of Warsaw could only be accomplished thanks to their plans. This rhetorical tautology of legitimization and normalization would become the basis for Warsaw's narrative reconstruction in the newsreels.

The PKF's reportage on the progress achieved in reconstruction, from the removal of rubble to fully navigable streets and erected buildings, was an active cartographic process that remapped Warsaw for audiences across Poland. It cinematically narrativized the reconstruction and expansion of the city by reporting on major and minor infrastructure projects, from new roads and bridges to the socialist Palace of Culture and Science (Pałac Kultury i Nauki) built in the early 1950s.[43] This remapping created a new, cinematic spatiality born of communist ideology that sought to establish historical continuity with pre-World War I Warsaw by circumventing references to Warsaw of the interwar period. It sought to demonstrate a correlation between attaining spatial order and establishing a communist regime; create new urban symbols by sidelining old iconic elements of the city; and reify ideology through new urban plans and construction projects.

In order to accomplish these goals, the notion of normalization underpinned many of the PKF news segments about Warsaw. In the early postwar years, portraying political stabilization was a primary goal of the newsreels.[44] In the Varsovian segments, this stabilization walked hand-in-hand with demonstrating a gradual normalization of life, understood as enabling Varsovians to take care of everyday needs. For example, in a city of rubble, the renovation of the second floor of a building was an occasion for both real-world and cinematic celebration, and the early newsreels reported on such seemingly small reconstruction accomplishments by the average Varsovian (PKF 17/46:6). Over time, the PKF moved from highlighting small changes in the city to showcasing major projects of Bierut's 1949 Six-Year Plan for Warsaw's Reconstruction. But as much as these projects were glorified and made exceptional, they were also narratively "normalized" and coded as spaces meant to ease the challenges of daily life for the worker and his family. Most importantly, the PKF fulfilled the goals of propaganda by attributing this normalization to the success of a rational, socialist plan, and—at least until 1956—by mostly ignoring the shortcomings of the reconstruction process. In aggregate, the newsreels demonstrated that Warsaw and everyday life in the capital were normalizing through the establishment of social(ist) order in the postwar period and space.

Where Has All the Rubble Gone?

In the years following the war, it was almost impossible to film the streets of Warsaw without capturing ruins hovering in the background. Despite this, and despite the purported realism of the newsreel, rubble quickly disappeared from the image of the capital promoted in the PKF even though it remained a part of the cityscape as late as the 1970s. Especially as the temporal distance from the war grew, ruins were an aspect of Varsovian everyday life that did not earn much screen time. Although their physical presence was mappable, the chaotic ruins had no place on Warsaw's ideological map, which demanded that an increasingly socialist space be portrayed as functional, organized, and "more beautiful than reality."[45] As a result, the PKF created a portrait of the capital based on renovated areas of the city, excising rubble from the newsreel screen and discursively marginalizing, and eventually historicizing, the ruins. The official Warsaw narrative moved forward on a linear path into the future, mirroring a Marxist view of history. This meant that the PKF "story" of Warsaw followed a path that began with the acknowledgment of ruins in the immediate postwar years and continued in subsequent stages: (1) the task of clearing rubble; (2) the reconstruction and achievement of normalization in daily life; and (3) the eventual fulfillment of socialist values and principles in the future. As many people who lived in Warsaw observed, however, reality was far from a straight path from rubble to renovation. Ruins coexisted alongside major renovation and reconstruction projects, making the official Varsovian narrative collide with reality. While on the ground the reconstruction process consisted of both forward movement and torpidity with the simultaneous presence of new construction and wartime ruins, the language of Warsaw's redevelopment in the PKF "moved forward" by focusing more and more on renovated parts of the city and ignoring those areas that remained in a rubble-state. Such a disjuncture rapidly increased the gap between the reality on the ground and the language and images shown on the PKF screen.

This contradiction could be seen already in 1945 when the ruins were featured as the backdrop for resurging life in the capital. The habitation of ruins and their creative adaptation for daily use served in the PKF as a sign of resilience and the desire to rebuild the capital. The mass return of Poles to a devastated city was presented as the result of the provisional government's decision to rebuild (PKF 7/45:1). Life in the city was described as "surging upon the demolished streets of the capital," and the newsreel cameras embraced the texture of a rubble city. The voice-over narration called attention to the creation of "a makeshift shopping district at the corner of Marszałkowska Street and Jerozolimskie Avenue," as well as the opening of schools and workshops "on the site of conflagration and ruins." But most importantly, the ruins were presented as an obstacle that was being overcome by Polish ingenuity and "the heartfelt offer of assistance from the allied peoples of the Soviet Union" (PKF 7/45:1). This same ingenuity, however, could also be problematic. With building after building barely standing, the dangers of living in the rubble were true enough, and stories of serious accidents and deaths circulated broadly. This led to public service announcements that warned of the dangers inherent in claiming unrenovated spaces for living quarters or private enterprises outside the scope of official reconstruction plans. One news segment, for example, warned of collapsing walls that killed a shop-owner and her daughter (PKF 17/46:6). "Private initiative" among the ruins—meaning anything that implied capitalist-like endeavors or "bourgeois" tendencies—was coded in the PKF as dangerous and risky, while demonstrating that life in the capital was (despite the dangers) moving forward. As the construction and renovation of buildings grew vertically, the image of a "ground floor Warsaw" ("parterowa Warszawa") transforming into a two- or three-story city became the measure of reconstruction success and of leaving the ruins behind (PKF 30/46:5 and 29/50:4). Private businesses established in the ruins of buildings were typically associated with prewar capitalism and described as "dwarf-like shacks" that "must disappear as quickly as possible" (PKF 37/51:4). In this way, the PKF reinforced the association between private enterprise, ruins, and dangerous or retrograde living conditions (PKF 39/50:3–7), while indirectly taking credit for earlier provisional shopping areas established on Marszałkowska Street (ulica Marszałkowska) right after the war.[46]

Reporting on new transportation and bridge construction was an important part of the PKF agenda for demonstrating construction progress, boosting morale, and appropriating the city space. Such news reports constructed a dynamic cartography of the city by highlighting bridges that connected Warsaw across the Vistula River or celebrating buses, trams, and trolleys traveling along streets cleared of rubble and thus demonstrating the existence of a navigable urban space. These news segments showed the connection between various points of the city and began to fill in otherwise "blank" spaces on the city map. By its very nature, however, transportation was a topic that required careful cinematographic framing. Reporting on new mass communication lines and bridge construction demanded wide-angle shots. But filming, for example, the opening of a tram line in the context of Warsaw's streets meant inevitably capturing images of rubble that had not yet been cleared, ruins that had not yet been demolished, or buildings that were far from renovated. To mitigate this problem, new transportation lines were often filmed in the least destroyed areas of the city or in places where some reconstruction had already taken place. More often, segments featuring transportation topics were filmed with tight shots that focused on the vehicles, passengers either getting into the vehicle or sitting inside, or—in the case of bridges—tight shots of support beams and building equipment.

In the transportation segments, such tight shots were combined with long shots where the primary visual subject, a bus or streetcar, was located in the foreground of a tracking shot that followed the vehicle's path through the city. Even though these long shots included ruins in the background, the movement of the camera in combination with rapid editing sequences prevented the camera from focusing on the ruins and rubble for very long. The camera takes remained concentrated on the basic topics of the news segments while avoiding filming ruins that might distract from the intended message. The lack of visual depth in such sequences contrasted greatly with the filming of construction sites which exploited the depth of field through deep-focus shots, long shots, and extreme long shots. And when cinematic techniques could not control the presence of ruins on screen, the voice-over was always ready to carry the correct message. For example, a segment on the completion of the Poniatowski Bridge showed ruins, but these images were countered by the voice-over that described the official opening of the bridge as "the first great holiday in the history of Warsaw's reconstruction, as well as a symbol of the achievements of Polish democracy" (PKF 24/46:1).

While rubble was avoided in certain news contexts, it was exploited in others. Domestic and foreign politicians, journalists, writers, international labor activists, and artists were portrayed touring the ruins, assessing the destruction of the Polish capital, and giving witness to the way the Polish capital was "lifting itself up from the rubble" (PKF 1/45:4, 19/45:4, 27/46:1, 27/46:2, and 11/47:1–2). Visitors included the former U.S. president Herbert Hoover (PKF 11/46:1); Marie Skłodowska-Curie's daughter (PKF 4/47:1); a youth delegation from China (PKF 46/49:7); and delegates from the Society of Franco-Polish Friendship (PKF 41/50:6–7). Screened in a domestic context, these segments reinforced the authority of the communist party by demonstrating far-reaching international cooperation with and support for the postwar Polish government. Unlike news segments that showed formal meetings between President Bierut and newly appointed ambassadors presenting their credentials at Belweder Palace,[47] the tours of ruins by officials or representatives of foreign governments and organizations moved the image of international cooperation onto the streets and appropriated Warsaw space more broadly. The walks of foreigners through the ruins legitimized Polish war trauma, as well as objectified the space by presenting it as a place to be toured. The focus of these segments was the visitors gazing upon the ruins as they walked between mounds of rubble, not the rubble itself. In these segments, the ruins were presented as an "objective reality," a perception that was reinforced by the "objective" gaze of the outsider confirming the tragedy and extent of destruction.

In yet another context, the PKF portrayed direct interaction with the ruins. Between 1946 and early 1949, entire news segments reported on clearing the streets of rubble and showed delegations or volunteers from across Poland and the Eastern bloc moving bricks, digging through wreckage, and clearing debris (PKF 38/49:2). Portraying the contribution of Polish students, socialist youth organizations, workers, intellectuals, and even Tito's former partisans was obligatory (PKF 16/46:7, 25/46:6, and 30/47:3). Other, similar segments showed prominent government and communist party officials like President Bolesław Bierut, Prime Minister Edward Osóbka-Morawski, and Józef Cyrankiewicz (then secretary of the Central Executive Committee of the PPS) (PKF 18/46:4, 30/46:5, and 19/46:3) or foreign dignitaries rolling up their sleeves to remove a brick or two. Moving between medium and close-up shots, such segments were meant to capture the cooperative effort required to rebuild the Polish capital. However, each segment also underscored the Sisyphean task of building a city from and upon its own carnage. Rarely did the portrayal of bare hands tossing bricks or shoveling rubble demonstrate a real dent in the cleanup process. Furthermore, this "heartfelt" communal effort was often staged and the participation of officials often seemed forced. The central figures, whether government officials or students, were clean, well-dressed, and rarely tired or sweaty. Men were often dressed in suits and ties, while women wore dresses and heels. But the basic message of these segments was clear. With groups of people moving one broken and burned brick after the next, the removal of rubble was an opportunity to forge socialist principles of work and cooperation. This was, according to the PKF, Soviet brotherhood in action.

While prior to 1949 the clearing of rubble was portrayed as the effort of the postwar authorities and volunteers, the announcement of Bolesław Bierut's Six-Year Plan for Warsaw's Reconstruction and the adoption of socialist realism in 1949 shifted the focus of the PKF away from the clearing of rubble and ruins toward their historicization. This is apparent, for example, in news segments that served as progress reports in which the rubble was no longer treated as a current problem but rather as something of the past. In a 1952 two-and-a-half minute news segment, rubble is mentioned twice in the voice-over narration, but only in conjunction with the value of salvaged bricks for current renovation projects (PKF 40/52:6–7). Entitled "Warszawskie wrześnie" ("Varsovian Septembers"), this segment presented a summary of reconstruction progress beginning with 1947 and commemorated the annual month of Warsaw during which volunteers from across Poland assisted in the reconstruction effort. Another news segment commemorating the anniversary of Warsaw's "liberation" treated the ruins as an element of the past, historicizing them in the context of Polish and Soviet soldiers who entered a city of ruins (PKF 4/51:1–2). And in reports on the construction of the Palace of Culture, the disappearance of the "final traces of war and ruins" was synonymous with the disappearance of the "old, destroyed Śródmieście [center] of capitalist Warsaw" (PKF 47/52:2–9).

Simply put, 1949 meant that the PKF segments on Warsaw shifted their focus from *odgruzowanie* (removal of rubble) toward *budowanie* (construction). Major construction projects such as the Trasa W-Z (literally, "east-west thoroughfare"), the Marszałkowska Residential District (MDM), and the Palace of Culture were not only hailed as symbols of a "new" Warsaw, but they also marked a turn away from rubble and communal clearing efforts toward the more officially organized and mechanized clearing of rubble and construction sites. Such a shift likewise presented the opportunity for using a language that historicized the rubble despite its persistence throughout the city. While this did not mean that ruins were completely cut out of the visual image of Warsaw, they appeared less and less often. Such historicization may seem like an obvious trajectory based on the real changes that had occurred in Warsaw since 1945. However, this discursive play with the prominence, presence, or absence of ruins in the newsreels of the late 1940s and early 1950s became the basis for a critical assessment of the official Varsovian narrative in the aftermath of the 1956 Thaw.

Counterpoint 1: Venerating the Ruin in *Suita Warszawska*

The Polish Film Chronicle's primary mode of representing rubble was in a documentary realist style, which dictated that ruins and rubble must make way for new construction. This followed the stance of Jan Zachwatowicz, Poland's general conservator of historic monuments beginning in 1945, who was determined to preserve Polish national and historical identity by *reconstructing* historic buildings and sites rather than venerating their ruins. His preservationist stance left little room for Warsaw to become a melancholic site of reflection on the trauma of war.[48] Rather, he saw in the ruins a potential for a new type of historical preservation, one that cast reconstruction, rather than ruin, as a monument to the past.[49]

The documentary realist approach to portraying Warsaw's ruins in the PKF was, like any other cinematic or media treatment of "reality," an interpretation of facts. This is all the more obvious if we compare the treatment of ruins and rubble in the Varsovian-themed newsreels from the late 1940s to an eighteen-minute film from 1946 entitled *Suita warszawska* (*Varsovian Suite*), directed by Tadeusz Makarczyński and filmed by two PKF cinematographers, Adolf and Władysław Forbert.[50] Called a "poetic impression," this film evoked a prewar genre that attempted to grasp the "mood, climate, and atmosphere" of an event, rather than presenting it as "reportage" or documentary. Accordingly, the event portrayed in such poetic impressions often "became a pretext for the author-director's own statement, for a chance to share with the audience his own feelings."[51] In *Varsovian Suite*, Warsaw's ruins are melancholic, aestheticized, and romanticized.

The film is organized according to three movements representing phases in postwar Varsovian life entitled "Disaster (adagio)," "Return to Life (andante)," and "Varsovian Spring (allegro)," with each part of the film corresponding to the tempo of Witold Lutosławski's score.[52] The first refers to the ruins of Warsaw; the second to the return of Varsovians to the capital; and the final part to the normalization of life in postwar Warsaw. When described in this simple way, the themes of the film are akin to those found in the Varsovian segments of the PKF. However, the contrast between the documentary realism of the PKF and the venerative techniques used by the Forbert brothers to show Warsaw's ruins in *Varsovian Suite* demonstrate the extent to which the newsreels tried to excise ruins from the PKF screen.[53] Unlike in the newsreels, where ruins—if filmed—were filmed according to a principle of "positive" verisimilitude (i.e., made to look as good as possible), the ruins in *Varsovian Suite*, especially those portrayed in the section entitled "Disaster," are mostly filmed using low-angle shots. Illuminated with backlighting, there is a glowing effect around the buildings' skeletons and a sporadic filtration of light through holes in the ruins. Supported by Lutosławski's dissonant musical score, the contrast between light and dark created by the backlighting intensifies the ominous nature of the ruins and detracts from their architectural details. The ruins mark the Warsaw sky as scarred and populated by dark, haunting skeleton-buildings.

This sequence of ruins, which lasts about three minutes, gives the impression of an urban space emptied of human life and agency. Here Warsaw is a barren land, a ghost town. The ruins in "Disaster" are monumentalized throughout the film with the repeated use of low-angle shots. While in this poetic documentary the low-angle shot is used to aestheticize the ruins, the upward-looking angle was reserved in the PKF primarily for monumentalizing new, socialist construction projects, while the ruins of Warsaw in the news segments were most often filmed at street level or as background, if at all. For a number of shots in *Varsovian Suite*, Adolf Forbert uses filters to create a mirage effect or blurring around the edges of the screen, which sharpens the focus on the central part of the image. He also uses special effects to distort the image of such recognizable landmarks as the Prudential skyscraper, stretching the frame of the camera from a square into a rhombus. The angles and lighting heighten a sense of fragmentation and stagnation, particularly in contrast to the moving clouds captured within the camera's frame. By tapping into the history of aestheticizing ruins, Forbert's images transform the ruins from rubble that signifies the violence of war into objects worthy of veneration.[54]

In the second part of the film, "Return to Life," the repopulation of Warsaw is not presented as the mass return of Varsovians like in the newsreels (PKF 7/45:1). Instead, those who return to the capital are wounded and scarred individuals symbolized by two, lone men walking through the rubble, one on crutches and another dressed in the striped prisoner garments of the Nazi concentration camps. The contrast between lifeless rubble and solitary individuals slowly making their way among the ruins makes for a haunting portrayal of postwar Warsaw. Likewise, images of individuals clearing rubble from buildings or carrying broken furniture through an otherwise rubble-filled street, and elderly women installing door jambs, all contrast with numerous PKF segments that portrayed dozens of volunteers working in unison to clear the city of wreckage. The image of flowerpots on window sills and street musicians busking in courtyards evoke in the film an old Warsaw. They are presented as individual acts distinct from the communal effort of reconstruction promoted elsewhere. While the film features a stylized socialist realist segment with construction masons, this lasts a mere 75 seconds, in contrast to the 3 minutes and 40 seconds of individual efforts to repopulate the city.

Image, Space, Sound: Constructing Socialist Spatiality

Many Varsovian-themed news reports in the period from 1945 to 1956 focused on portraying the construction of a new Warsaw and coding this space as "socialist." Representing a concerted effort to shape Polish attitudes toward communist ideals and the reconstruction of the capital, these segments sought to redefine both the physical and discursive map of Warsaw by reporting on urban planning developments and construction activity throughout the city. Of particular interest in the PKF were major infrastructure projects that were considered symbols of socialist building practices. In the late 1940s, this meant focusing primarily on stories about Mariensztat, the newly renovated neighborhood built for workers and located on the same spot as the eighteenth-century *jurydyka* by the same name, and the Trasa W-Z that connected the left and right banks of the Vistula with a modern tunnel. In the early 1950s, the construction of the Marszałkowska Residential District (MDM) built in the center of Warsaw, on what was considered before the war a center of capitalist enterprise, was the star of the newsreel screen. But it was the Palace of Culture that was both the pinnacle of socialist construction in Warsaw, as well as the culmination of Warsaw's narrative in the PKF, a matter I return to in chapter 4. For now, suffice to say, the newsreel segments on new construction projects, particularly in the central part of the city, Śródmieście, imbued geospatial points with ideological meaning and connotations. These connotations were then reinforced by the repetition of cinematic elements throughout various PKF editions.

Representing the urban planning process on the newsreel screen was no small feat. After all, how do you dynamically present planning meetings, building plans, maps, or scale models on film? Occasional reports on urban development meetings at such places as the Office for the Reconstruction of the Capital (Biuro Odbudowy Stolicy, BOS) focused on presenting the planning process with an eye toward future construction. These reports introduced to filmgoers the architects and engineers of the reconstruction process and showed them as socialist heroes "in action" drafting buildings, planning streets, and then presenting their concepts to Bierut and other government officials. This was one of the few moments when cartography in the most traditional sense appeared in the newsreels as urban planners presented street maps of a new Warsaw (PKF 8–9/46:7). These maps, however, did not receive much screen time. Since they relied on interactive, tactile reading, maps were not productive subjects for the PKF newsreels. Instead, the PKF preferred three-dimensionality and sometimes featured small-scale architectural models that were essential in establishing a new topography of place.

With the help of the PKF, the future, socialist, Varsovian spaces were plotted onto the mental geography of viewers across Poland. Cameras creatively zoomed in on architectural models, giving the impression of life-sized buildings and spaces, and foreshadowing aerial shots of and "from" future high-rises that would exist once construction was complete. The filming of the models simulated dynamism and progress by panning around them 360°, using "long" and/or "low-angle" shots that highlighted the "monumental" size of future buildings, or showed "aerial" views of scale models that simulated the future cityscape (PKF 30/47:1–2 and 40/51:4–5). In this way, the PKF presented to audiences a more dynamic visual than flat renderings (PKF 14/48:1) and maps occasionally shown on screen or published in books or such newspapers as *Stolica: Ilustrowana Kronika Budowy Warszawy* (*The Capital: An Illustrated Chronicle of Warsaw's Construction*). These shots reminded viewers of the continued planning process and presented both what was being currently built and what was planned for the future. Thus, anticipated building projects had a dynamic screen life that predated their physical manifestation. Small-scale models of future Warsaw became a means of imagining the capital in all its socialist glory *before* construction was completed not only for the professionals designing a new capital, but for Poles countrywide. Such images shaped how newsreel audiences imagined and conceived of a new Warsaw, effectively displacing the chaos of rubble encountered on the streets and occasionally visible in other news segments and replacing it with socialist imaginings of the future.

This effect was particularly visible in news reports on May Day parades in 1952 and 1953 that filmed float-sized scale models (PKF 20/52:21 and 19–20/53:1). In addition to typical images of parade participants carrying larger-than-life portraits of Marx, Engels, Lenin, Stalin, and Bierut, these news reports spotlighted floats carrying scale models of Warsaw buildings under construction. In 1952, for example, one float displayed a large architectural rendering of the MDM, followed by moving *tableaux vivants* of various construction specialties, like plasterwork and masonry, as well as Soviet construction equipment donated for building a metro system. Another float exhibited a scale model of the Palace of Culture followed by a banner that read "We are building a socialist Warsaw" ("Budujemy socjalistyczną Warszawę"). In addition to the parades themselves, the filming of broad, Soviet-style boulevards that could accommodate mass rallies showed moviegoers one of the most conspicuous physical manifestations of socialism in Warsaw's urban planning. Such parades were made possible by topographically significant changes in the city—namely, the redesign, widening, and rerouting of Marszałkowska Street in the area of the MDM and Konstytucji Square (plac Konstytucji), and the construction of the Palace of Culture and Defilad Square (plac Defilad) in what was to become the city's new center. By parading the scale models and floats representing Warsaw's construction through the newest and most socialist areas of the city, urban planning took to the streets. The rendering of the MDM passed through the actual MDM, while the Palace claimed its place on the streets of Warsaw well before it became part of the Varsovian skyline. These scale models devoted to Warsaw's reconstruction created a multilayered metatextual narrative on screen. Not only did they represent future buildings, but by being placed on floats and paraded around the capital, even their physical presence as part of the cityscape predated their construction.

Most of the reports on new construction focused on the actual process of building and featured workers, construction equipment, the breaking of ground, and the raising of brick walls and masonry work. The layering of building activity on multiple planes within a shot was a frequently used visual composition when filming construction sites. This composition created a sense of depth, both vertical and horizontal, that gave the screen image three-dimensionality. Such a composition also intensified the literal and metaphorical appropriation of the portrayed space in the name of socialism. In construction segments, the background, middle ground, and foreground often had equal visual value and created a heightened sense of activity and progress on construction sites. Tractors moving toward the left of the screen might be foregrounded, while on the second visual plane, behind the first tractor, yet another piece of construction equipment would be moving toward the right (PKF 19/52:1–4). Cameras followed the movement of bulldozers and excavator buckets, adding vertical and circular dimensions to the screen. Such opposing movements often filled the entire screen, cutting out of the camera's view spaces on construction sites that were empty or otherwise slow-moving, idle, slothful, or even inactive.

The visual portrayal of construction alone, however, did not constitute the "socialization" of space in the PKF, which came from the superimposition of language and sound onto the image, and created a new socialist spatiality or "sense of space." Through the combination of visual, aural, and verbal elements, the newsreels explained the significance and progress of these newly constructed spaces and taught audiences how to read the meaning of future or recently completed buildings, plazas, and streets. The voice-over provided an overt socialist message that coded new construction as built for the worker by the worker, and as a culmination of Soviet brotherhood. This was done through slogans and sound bites that glorified the technology of socialist construction, denigrated prewar capitalist housing, and demonstrated progress for the future. Each phrase was attached to an image on screen, and music dictated the emotional register of a segment. The verbal, musical, and visual messages reinforced one another, working in unison to maintain visual and aural interest.

Construction sequences were often accompanied by harmonic, quick-paced music that set the rhythm of the news segment and dictated how the construction was perceived on screen. The selected music often evoked a sense of speed, positive commotion, excitement or monumentalism, power, and grace. Major keys and harmonic melodies "took control" of the often chaotic spaces being presented and marked the rhythm in which the reports were edited. The usually light, happy music used in these sequences countered the images of heavy construction equipment and made the effort of Warsaw's reconstruction seem, if not effortless, at least manageable. Some reports on new construction projects, like the *Biuletyn odbudowy Warszawy* (*Bulletin of Warsaw's Reconstruction*), had their own theme music, as did specific construction projects like the MDM or the Palace of Culture. The selected music satisfied the harmonic and melodic parameters of socialist realist aesthetics even before 1949. And most importantly, music was used to develop positive associations.[55] Tunes from popular songs reminded audiences of lyrics that imparted a propaganda message. For example, reports on the MDM were accompanied by instrumental versions of the hit song "Na prawo most, na lewo most" ("A Bridge to the Left, a Bridge to the Right"), which sang of the speed of Warsaw's construction (PKF 16/51:4–5). In one news segment reporting on the MDM, the song was even heard diegetically—that is, as part of the action on screen—even though the newsreel genre dictated that sound be limited to the voice-over and a musical soundtrack outside the action of the news report. Reports on the construction of the Palace of Culture were accompanied by sweeping, dramatic, classical pieces that evoked power, importance, seriousness, and control. As these examples show, the musical selections often mirrored the utility of these socialist spaces, providing an aural key to their spatial significance. The popular tune coincided with the MDM as a center for everyday life, a place for the proletarian to live and take care of himself and his family's needs. In contrast, the powerful music associated with the Palace reflected the skyscraper's symbolic role as an architectural representative of Moscow and Moscow's political and ideological control over the Polish capital.

Counterpoint 2: The Cutting Room Floor

To paraphrase Alfred Hitchcock, "What is news, after all, but life with the dull bits cut out." There is no better proof of this than viewing the unused footage of Warsaw filmed by PKF camera operators. Stripped of cinematic veneer—silent, unedited, sometimes of poor quality, and consisting of long shots that capture a less constructed Varsovian image than the final, edited newsreel—this unused material exposes a different reality than was presented in the "propaganda realism" of the PKF. In comparison to the final news segments that made it to the movie theater screens, this footage unmasks the power of montage, narration, and sound that are essential to any final film product. It also reveals the extent to which the PKF image of Warsaw meshed with the broader propaganda agenda. The unused footage shows the point of view of the camera operator unaltered by the editing and directorial processes, the challenges of getting usable and quality footage at a time when equipment and film stock were hard to come by, and a reminder of the amount of footage required to create a one- to two-minute news spot. And while one can argue that this raw footage creates its own discourse through framing and so forth, it nonetheless represents a less-altered image of reality than shown in final, edited PKF segments.

While the news segments sought to portray a dynamically changing, fast-paced construction zone that was being filled with socialist content, the unused footage reveals a far more prosaic image of the city space under construction. Often lacking the multidimensionality of the construction sequences shown in movie theaters, the unused footage gives the impression of a slow, sluggish reconstruction process. Raw footage from 1950 records bulldozers systematically pushing dirt and rubble aside (PKF unused footage, no. 4971) or students taking a break from the labor of building a dormitory (PKF unused footage, no. 5024). The paradigmatic, socialist realist image of the bricklayer at work, which could be found in the final versions of news segments, monumentalized both the construction site and The Worker through close-up, tight, and low-angle shots that accentuated the verticality of buildings and made everyone and everything seem larger than life. In the unused footage, however, workers and buildings are often seen in proportion to one another, filmed from neutral angles. The masons on top of a new MDM building, for example, are barely perceptible, while construction equipment moves slowly, heavily, and methodically (PKF unused footage, no. 5309). The workers are small and almost insignificant in the context of long shots, a perspective rarely seen in final news segments without immediately glorifying The Worker. In final segments prepared for the screen, quick-paced editing, music, and voice-overs compensated for the day-to-day torpidity of construction sites as seen on raw footage, and helped to present vibrant construction landscapes considered worthy of a socialist society (PKF 37/51:4).

Another, more dramatic example of Warsaw's unadulterated image is raw footage from 1948 showing the reopening of Tramline 28 on the fourth anniversary of Warsaw's "liberation." The footage begins with a shot of the ribbon-cutting ceremony, followed by shots of the streetcar filmed head-on as it travels down the track for the first time (PKF unused footage, no. 3224). The next shot is of passengers piling into the streetcar. This initial footage is filmed in the same vein as seen in final PKF segments; however, most of the unused footage adopts a rarely seen perspective. Using over-the-shoulder and point-of-view shots, Warsaw's landscape is filmed through the streetcar's windshield as it travels approximately four and a half miles north from Zbawiciela Square (plac Zbawiciela) along Marszałkowska Street through what was at the time Bankowy Square (plac Bankowy) to the district Żoliborz and back.[56] This point-of-view shot draws attention away from the purported topic (the opening of the streetcar line) and toward the city space along the route. The shots reveal the main thoroughfare as lined with nothing more than rubble on both sides, with occasional glimpses of buildings, such as the Evangelical Reformed Parish in Warsaw, in the background. Most notable are street shots along what used to be the southeast border of the Warsaw ghetto prior to 1942 and other areas on the outskirts of the ghetto that had been pulverized in 1943. While numerous still shots of ghetto devastation exist, this documentary footage gives a sense of the geographic space unlike that provided in photographs. Pedestrians walk on sidewalks lined by rubble, horse-drawn carts travel in parallel with the streetcar, and the tragedy of the ghetto's liquidation by the Germans in 1943 fills the screen. The film shows mounds and mounds of ash in which architectural remains cannot be differentiated from those of humans. Through this unused footage from 1948, we witness a city with swaths of dead, urban space that is waiting to be reclaimed by humans—an image of Warsaw that the PKF was loath to present in movie theaters.

Mediating between the Past and Present

The idea to "bring together matters of a historical-cultural [*zabytkowy*] nature with a contemporary concept of Warsaw" was already formulated in 1945 when Jan Zachwatowicz, director of the Division of Architectural History in the Office for the Reconstruction of the Capital, presented his report to Bolesław Bierut.[57] For Zachwatowicz, preserving old Warsaw was a matter of preserving Poland's past for the sake of future generations despite the fact that the authenticity of the original city could never be replicated. The debates on the exact nature of this historical reconstruction, however, continued long into the future on both preservationist and ideological grounds.[58] But the PKF did not engage in these debates. While focused on documenting and presenting socialist Warsaw, the PKF played its part in redefining the spatiality of "old" Warsaw and cinematically establishing continuity between past and present. To this end, the PKF narrowed its focus on select, historically significant areas of the city, documenting in the immediate postwar years the reconstruction of churches and monuments. It also paid close attention to the reconstruction progress of larger geospatial reference points, like the eighteenth-century Mariensztat neighborhood or the Old Town, helping to show that the communist government was not simply tossing out the "old" but rather adapting it to a new era.

The newsreels stressed a material continuity between Warsaw's past and present and gave credit to the communist authorities for preserving Poland's historical treasures. The PKF redefined the meaning and spatiality of these historic sites in order to align them with the postwar ideology. This often meant filming the physical space of a news story in such a way that would indicate historical continuity in terms of architecture and the cultural legacy or symbolism of material culture, while contextualizing these "old" symbols within a socialist framework. The PKF camera manipulated the way certain spaces were filmed in order to influence their suggested meaning and associate them with socialist values, thus appropriating spaces in the name of the authorities, and transforming or tweaking the meaning of the past. Such "historical" segments developed a new socialist spatial code through which "old" Warsaw was meant to be reread, critiqued, and understood.

Between 1945 and 1949, for example, the PKF reported on the reconstruction of important and symbolic monuments, churches, and even the reconstruction of the Royal Castle, and juxtaposed these stories with news segments that connected the postwar authorities with Poland's material past. In a 2-minute and 45-second bulletin released in September 1946, such a juxtaposition carefully (de)constructed Warsaw's spatiality by establishing a relationship between historically significant nodes of Polish identity and the prominent role of the government in the reconstruction process (PKF 30/46:5). The first half of the segment focused on the organized process of removing rubble. It showed the demolition of a building on Napoleona Square (plac Napoleona) near the Prudential building, the implosion of a city block, and Prime Minister Osóbka-Morawski with his then deputy Władysław Gomułka and volunteers—all well-dressed—shoveling rubble into the back of a pickup truck. These images were set to lighthearted music meant to counter the potential angst elicited by the destruction of yet another Warsaw building. Such a musical score coded the demolition of buildings as a happy occasion. Together, these news items demonstrated organized, official control over otherwise chaotic Varsovian space.

The following section functioned as a bridge between the first and second halves of the bulletin, showing the reconstruction of the second floor of a Warsaw city block. This news segment transitioned the bulletin away from rubble toward renovated storefronts and living quarters that stressed the normalization of everyday life in the capital. The third part of the bulletin consisted of two distinct parts and reported on the renovation of St. Stanisław Kostka Church in the Warsaw district of Żoliborz and the Jan Kiliński monument. Set to dramatic, sweeping music that underscored the importance of the news, the bulletin first showed workers installing a cross on the church tower, followed by a wide-angle shot of the Kiliński monument among Warsaw's ruins and workers placing Kiliński's sword into his left hand, the arm eternally raised and ready for battle.

Despite the postwar rhetoric of cutting ties with a prewar bourgeois Warsaw, both the church and the Kiliński monument had been raised during the interwar period. Construction on the church began in the 1930s but was interrupted by the outbreak of World War II; the monument to Jan Kiliński was unveiled in 1936 and, save for the sword, was one of the few Varsovian monuments not destroyed during the war.[59] As structures that did not require extensive postwar renovation, the church and monument were obvious Varsovian spatial markers to feature in the *Bulletin of Warsaw's Reconstruction* in 1946. Their "reconstruction," juxtaposed with the demolition of other areas, implied immediate progress being made in raising Warsaw from the ashes. At the same time, their juxtaposition possessed a symbolic value that countered the first half of the bulletin which focused on the contemporary moment, the organized removal of rubble, and the activities of the postwar government. The narrative focus on the church and monument brought Poland's past into the present and rhetorically and visually recoded the spatial meaning and historical connotations of the church and monument. As a reference to the past, the church recognizably and saliently referenced Polish Catholic notions of self and nation. Though the church is not named in the bulletin, the edifice would have been recognizable to Varsovians as the church dedicated to Stanisław Kostka (1550–1568), a Jesuit novice from Poland who was canonized by the Roman Catholic Church in 1726. The church would therefore have represented the layering of historical nodes pertinent to post-partition Poland. Through architecture, it highlighted the relationship between Poland and Catholicism, alluded to an independent Poland, and referenced the interwar period during which the church was built.

The Jan Kiliński monument functioned even more directly as a historical palimpsest, hearkening back to the final moments of Polish independence before the partitions and the Kościuszko Uprising. A master shoemaker by trade, Kiliński was known for leading the Warsaw Insurrection of 1794 against the Russian Empire. In the figure of Kiliński, the communist government could draw on Polish national consciousness in combination with the status of Kiliński as a revolutionary and as a master craftsman. The bulletin conveniently ended with the image of a revolutionary, historical artisan (i.e., a worker, laborer) who fought for Polish national sovereignty. With the final two segments possessing particularly keen historical references that had a direct relationship to traditional religious and secular nodes of Polish identity, this bulletin carefully mediated between the past and the present, appropriating material culture and Varsovian space for ideological purposes.[60]

The most significant material mediation between Poland's past and present rested in the ambitious plan to reconstruct Warsaw's Old Town and Zamkowy Square. However, the (re)construction narrative had to either account for or refute the Old Town's direct association with Poland's aristocrats, noblemen, burghers, and merchants, and the awkward fact—at least for the propaganda narrative—that the aristocracy and nobility had played important roles in the history and development of the city, as testified by the Royal Castle (Zamek Królewski). The narrative resignification of the Old Town intensified as its reconstruction was reaching completion in the late 1940s and early 1950s. In the immediate postwar years, the Old Town's reconstruction was accompanied by the language of national unity. The reinstallation of the Sigismund III Vasa Column (PKF 30/49:1), the clearing of rubble from the Old Town Market Square (Rynek Starego Miasta) (PKF 37/47:5), and references to the entire area as a burial mound (PKF 49/49:6) were interspersed with references to the trauma of war, national martyrology, and the destruction/reconstruction of Warsaw as a common, national goal.

However, with the introduction of the Six-Year Plan for Warsaw's Reconstruction and the adoption of socialist realism in 1949, this language of trauma, martyrology, and destruction gave way to rhetoric that called attention to the contemporary process of building a capital designed according to socialist principles. The reconstruction of the Old Town—despite its histori-cal, architectural characteristics that alluded to a time of aristocrats, nobles, and burghers—became the hallmark of the notion that sought to combine "socialist content with old, traditional form" (PKF 12/52:4).[61] The original "content," however, needed to be rewritten. The PKF was, of course, parrot-ing the communist dialectic of form vs. content used to talk about Old Town Warsaw, in general. This idea presented *zabytki* (here referring to architec-turally and culturally significant historical sites) as evidence of the past that had to be preserved or rebuilt.[62] The move to rewrite the "content," how-ever, meant slightly rewriting the urban palimpsest of history and revising the meaning of these buildings and spaces to adjust their prewar significance and to construct a new language that included communist newspeak.

The Old Town, while seen as representing Poland's historical legacy and civilizational achievements, was to be reconceived as a space designed, first and foremost, for the socialist worker. "Form" referred to "everything that was great and beautiful in Warsaw," such as architecture, sculpture, stone masonry, and metalwork, particularly of the gothic style (PKF 49/52:2–4). "Content" referred to emptying this physical space of such architectural con-structs as the tight and dark *oficyny* (annexes built at the back of *kamienice* for the lower classes) that symbolized poverty, degradation, and antiquated socioeconomic structures. These spaces would then be filled with "spacious, bright, and comfortable apartments, fitted with modern furnishings," such as electricity and water (PKF 7/51:3 and 9/52:3). The PKF underscored the *newness* of the Old Town by maximizing the linguistic playfulness of such phrases as the "new Old Town," which became shorthand for "old form/new content." This "old" vs. "new" dialectic served propaganda well, manifesting itself in other versions of the phrase, such as the "Young Old Town" (PKF 49/52:2–4). The linguistic and temporal incompatibility of the lexical items "old" and "new" double-coded the meaning of the Old Town's reconstruc-tion. "Old" referred to tradition and historical continuity that was coded in architectural and ornamentation styles determined to be "typical" for buildings in Poland. It also satisfied a national, communal need and acted as a testament of resilience against Nazi plans to destroy Warsaw. "New," however, coded the Old Town as a product of the postwar authorities. It grafted the abstract notions and values of the communist system onto the city's architecture. "New" separated the material expression of history in architecture from its socioeconomic meaning (i.e., as remnants of an aristo-cratic and bourgeois past). While the combination of "new old" was meant to testify to the good will of the communist authorities, it was also a selec-tively used label. For example, "new old" was very rarely used to describe the newly renovated eighteenth-century neighborhood of Mariensztat that was rebuilt after the war to house workers who were building the Trasa W-Z. On the contrary, the language defining Mariensztat was associated first and foremost with this infrastructure project and coded as "socialist," ignoring references to its historical provenance as a settlement founded by the aristo-crat Eustachy Potocki.[63]

The newsreels were able to contend with this "new-old" dialectic through a system of cinematic checks and balances. The PKF carefully constructed visual and aural reference points to ensure that historical markers were countered by direct or indirect allusions to contemporary socialist values. Often, if an image triggered a sense of the past or history, it was accompanied by language that explained its relevance to socialism.[64] In one news segment, for example, the Old Town was called the "closest neighbor of the Trasa W-Z," which rhe-torically combined the otherwise potentially anachronistic Old Town with a major urban development project that was hailed as the inauguration of socialist construction in Warsaw (PKF 49/49:6). In this news report, roughly a third of the camerawork was devoted to reconstruction that featured masonry work and scaffoldings, while two thirds was focused on the skeletal remains of Old Town buildings. The opposite, however, was also true. In shots of Old Town renovations that lacked recognizable historical reference points, the voice-over commentary emphasized the painstaking process of rebuilding the Old Town according to original plans or building methods (PKF 12/52:4).

Such a narrative ensured that the historical value of the Old Town on the PKF screen was never void of "socialist meaning." This was a particularly important aspect and contribution of the PKF to Varsovian propaganda and poetics. While the "new-old" dichotomy served as a means of constructing the contemporary meaning of Old Town's spatiality, Varsovian poetics in the PKF also capitalized on its combination of visual references with scripted commentary to reinforce the aura of the Old Town's authenticity that was seriously undercut by its actual newness. Cartographically, the aura of the authentic was determined by the geospatial coordinates of the Old Town. The PKF established these coordinates through "visual mapping"—that is, by filming extant building facades and familiar architectural elements that had survived the war. The images of Old Town rooftops with their charac-teristic shingles and decorative elements of eaves and facades affirmed and fixed the geospatial specificity. For example, one news report ended with the characteristic detail of "The Negro," a bas relief installed above the entrance to the Museum of Warsaw, which was established in 1948 (PKF 49/49:6). Such details went a long way to affirm the veracity of the geographic place, as well as a sense of authentic spatiality. In turn, filming the unearthing and reconstruction of old medieval walls, which required the participation of archeologists digging below the surface of an already shattered ground cover, testified to the layering of history and provided justification for rebuilding parts of the Old Town according to eighteenth-century documents, plans, and images. As mentioned previously, of particular importance were Ber-nardo Bellotto's paintings, while still images of prewar Warsaw served as visual reference points for a city lost to the ravages of war. Canaletto's paint-ings were cinematically animated with the use of camera pans and zooms, and photographs of interwar Warsaw were used to show Warsaw's "Old Town, the charming corner of the capital, full of memories and historical souvenirs" (PKF 9/52:3 and 49/49:6). These still images functioned similarly to the before-and-after sequences found in the photobooks. But rather than acting as a testimony to the progress made in transforming Warsaw from ruins to reconstruction, the cuts from still shots to filmed footage of present-day architectural copies imbued the edifices with the gravitas of history. Cinema was thus able to expose the essence of the urban palimpsest. Film captured the multiple temporal layers of the Old Town by presenting fast-paced sequences that anachronistically combined and mixed remnants of the past with snippets of the present. The PKF mirrored the anachronisms of the reconstruction process itself: news segments repeatedly ensured that, in addition to new socialist construction projects, reconstruction was proceeding under the supervision of conservationists and historians according to old building plans, drawings, methods, and techniques (PKF 17/50:3). "Authenticity" would not be compromised.

Post Scriptum: Gomułka's Great Rally and Beyond

A careful study of the PKF catalog at the Filmoteka Narodowa in Warsaw shows that after 1956 "Warsaw" as a topic of the newsreels disappeared from the PKF screen, save for commemorative news segments or special features focusing on specific places in the city. Newsreels on Warsaw changed from serial and episodic segments to occasional, yet longer, films made for Warsaw's anniversaries. These longer films updated what had become a tired and worn-out Varsovian plot in the PKF. Until the mid-1950s, the PKF portrayal of Warsaw's reconstruction walked hand-in-hand with the construction of a new Varsovian narrative that incorporated two very different ideas (and ideals?) of the Polish capital: one was rooted in Warsaw's historical continuity, while the other sought to create a contemporary concept of Warsaw as an exemplary socialist urban center. The basic elements and propaganda techniques were honed during the late 1940s and early 1950s to create a visual, aural, and verbal impression of the capital as a legitimate, historical, yet thoroughly innovative and new city that reflected the socialist ideology of the period. At times more dramatic than others, Warsaw's story in the newsreels unfolded according to a script with a preset cast of characters, settings, and a back-story. Sometimes "characters" were played by party leaders; directors changed; or the backdrop or scenery was modernized. For the most part, however, the narrative building blocks of Warsaw's reconstruction remained intact. By 1956 there was a worn familiarity to the Varsovian images and narrative structures which appeared on the PKF screen.

This all changed, however, with the onset of the political Thaw in 1956 that occurred in many parts of the Eastern bloc and began in Poland that

October, marking a caesura in Polish politics and thus in the Varsovian narrative. This shifting political tide was reflected in a series of documentaries filmed roughly between 1955 and 1958 and labeled "Czarna Seria" ("Black Series"); these films exposed the deficiencies of the communist regime in Poland by reporting on alcoholism, prostitution, a failing bureaucracy, and other social, political, and economic ills. However, the most symbolic event, and thus the most pertinent news segment that marked a change in the Varsovian narrative on screen, occurred on October 24, 1956, with a report featuring Władysław Gomułka's speech to a crowd of reportedly over 400,000 on Defilad Square at the foot of the Palace of Culture. On October 21, Gomułka was chosen as the first secretary of the Polish United Workers' Party, which signified a major sea change in the political order. Only a few years earlier, Gomułka had been removed from the party for exhibiting "nationalist sympathies" and was arrested. The newsreel covering Gomułka's October 1956 speech, entitled *Dodatek nadzwyczajny PKF: Wielki Wiec (Special Edition of the PKF: The Great Rally)*, focused on the major political changes at hand. While reporting on the event proper, the newsreel recorded a locus that was actively undergoing changes in its spatiality.

The camerawork in this segment departed from the tight images that had become a hallmark of the PKF style in the previous decade. The bird's-eye view and panning of the camera across the crowds of people gathered at the foot of the Palace, whose construction had been completed fifteen months earlier, marked an important visual contrast to previously focused and narrow points of view. Now the camera's lens loosened up, using wide-angle shots to film spontaneously moving and cheering crowds rather than construction sites, and it showed people climbing on the Palace's bas reliefs and shimmying up street lamps. The proportion of diegetic sound used in the segment was increased with the sound of crowds cheering, chanting, and singing "Sto lat!" (the Polish equivalent of "For He's a Jolly Good Fellow"), as well as the inclusion of a five-and-a-half minute abridged version of Gomułka's original forty-minute speech. While the obligatory message of the Soviet Union as an exemplar of socialism remained integral to the communicated message, the spatial dynamics of the camera work showed Warsaw streets controlled by the people of the city. The Palace of Culture was shown only as an establishing shot that identified the location of the mass gathering. Nonetheless, this image was integral to the reading of the event, which was described as a mass gathering that "had not been seen since Warsaw's founding" ("Takiego wiecu nie było jak Warszawa Warszawą"). Otherwise, the Palace was ignored in the news segment, while the voice-over underscored that "until now it seemed that a demonstration large enough to fill this square, the largest parade square in Europe, was impossible." Notably, however, Gomułka's speech did not necessarily satisfy the original purpose of Defilad Square, which was designed as a place for parades to showcase the military might of socialist Poland, and by extension, the Soviet Union.

In this newsreel it was a space being redefined for a post-Stalinist era. While this newsreel is not considered a part of the Black Series per se, it represents (along with the other nonfiction films of the period) a shift in PKF aesthetics away from a prescribed socialist realist aesthetic and a fundamental shift in the treatment of Warsaw on the newsreel screen.

In many of the post-1956 images of Warsaw, urban movement is filmed as spontaneous, chaotic, and even unpredictable. The images within the frame of the camera are filled with crowds rather than organized parades and demonstrations of the late 1950s. Gone is the rhythmic predictability of the socialist realist aesthetic. Gone is the carefully controlled language of Warsaw as a new-old city in which socialist ideals will be fulfilled. While still the political center, and thus a setting of political news, Warsaw was of little interest to the PKF as a topic of propaganda after 1956.

Chapter 3

Remapping Warsaw in Cinema

Geographic specificity in feature films often comes from images of well-known landmarks, which help place the setting of a film on the audience's mental map. Such cinematic mapping builds an imagined connection between moviegoers and places, making landmarks legible and decipherable whether a person has physically visited a place or not. In this way, sometimes subtly and at other times quite explicitly, film assumes a cartographic stance, transcends physical geography, and relies on a spatial iconography shared between the director, cinematographer, and audience. Through such mapping, film presupposes and contributes to a communal, abstract experience of place, and therefore participates in defining a collective identity.[1] Together moviegoers can experience New York, Paris, or London through filmic images of the Statue of Liberty, the Eiffel Tower, or Buckingham Palace, all of which function synecdochically on the level of geography, while also carrying symbolic meanings that can be supported, refuted, or mutated with each appearance of a landmark on screen. Filmmakers can assume that their audiences recognize this iconography on some level or possess the ability to unravel the meaning of the space depicted; however, these same filmmakers can also create new meanings or associations with a given locus, thus contributing to its ever-evolving spatiality.

In considering the importance of cinematic representations of space in shaping the imagination of a film audience and the power of film to participate in creating a shared (albeit imaginary) world, how was Warsaw present on the feature film screen in the decade after the war? Between 1945 and 1956, twenty of the sixty films produced in Poland were set in Warsaw and of those twenty, ten were set in the postwar period.[2] In these ten films, the contemporary Warsaw landscape was rarely featured on screen and the setting was designated primarily through language rather than image. For example, *Uczta Baltazara* (1954; *Balthazar's Feast*), directed by Jerzy Zarzycki, begins with the words "Warsaw 1947" superimposed over a shot of pickup trucks traveling down a narrow, rubble-lined street. Later in the film, Warsaw is designated by the name of the main railway station and on a license plate. Otherwise, this film does not go out of its way to represent Warsaw visually or build specific connotations with the capital.

The only drama from this period that presented Warsaw's contemporary space was Aleksander Ford's *Piątka z ulicy Barskiej* (1953; *Five from Barska Street*). The spatial organization of the movie reflects its main topic: the challenges of building a socialist society. Ford's Warsaw is a place of clashing values, where establishing socialism is threatened by prewar and wartime bourgeois mores. Courts and construction sites are coded as spaces of socialist education that support the authority of a socialist capital. These orderly spaces are contrasted with ruins, sewers, and posh interiors associated with questionable social, ethical, and moral provenance, with spaces that challenge the new system, and with loci associated with crime, hooliganism, parasitism, and the Home Army. One of the most important settings in the film is the site of Warsaw's first socialist construction project, the Trasa W-Z that was built between 1947 and 1949 to connect the east and west banks of the Vistula River (Wisła). The construction site acts as a space of rehabilitation and indoctrination. It is contrasted with the plan of the anticommunist movement to blow up the tunnel of the Trasa W-Z with the reluctant help of the Barska Street boys, and thus undermine the construction of socialism.

In addition to the diegetic role of Varsovian space in the film, the Trasa W-Z is coded extratextually. The film presents a mini-visual history of the Trasa W-Z's construction and contributes to its status as a new landmark of the Polish capital. In the film, the construction site is initially presented generically and includes a shock labor competition, as often portrayed in the newsreels.[3] The Trasa W-Z also appears in a few wide-angle shots from the upper story of a ruined building where the Barska Street boys clandestinely meet. In these wide-angle shots, however, the location remains poorly defined, lacking geographic specificity. The shots are unclear, and it is difficult to distinguish between construction and ruins. As the plot develops, however, this landscape becomes more meaningful as two of the Barska Street boys are rehabilitated from a life of deviance (i.e., potentially cooperating with the anticommunist movement) by working on the construction site. By the end of the film, the Trasa W-Z is completed and audiences are treated to one of the most often filmed and photographed views of Warsaw until today: the entrance to the Trasa W-Z tunnel that runs under the streets Krakowskie Przedmieście and Miodowa (figure 9). This paradigmatic shot, repeated hundreds of times in photography and film, reinforces a Varsovian urban iconography, melding together the message of the film with the socialist, spatial significance of the Trasa W-Z promoted elsewhere.

Four films made between 1945 and 1956, however, explicitly featured Warsaw not only as a setting but as a "main character": *Skarb* (1948; *Treasure*) and *Przygoda na Mariensztacie* (1953; *Adventure in Mariensztat*), both directed by Leonard Buczkowski with screenplays by Ludwik Starski; Jan Rybkowski and Jan Fethke's *Sprawa do załatwienia* (1953; *A Matter to Settle*); and Fethke's *Irena do domu!* (1955; *Irena, Go Home!*). Unlike other films made at this time and set in the Polish capital during the postwar

Figure 9. A view of the Trasa W-Z from *Five from Barska Street* (dir. Aleksander Ford, 1953).

period, these films were comedies that showcased Warsaw in its contemporary "glory," cinematographically exploiting well-known Varsovian vistas, building connotations with specific landmarks, and exhibiting the new, socialist city.[4] Meant to entertain, the films embraced popular genres, utilizing the conventions of romantic comedy that were well known to Polish audiences from popular films of the interwar period.[5] They featured young couples falling in love or recently married, whose relationship is threatened by external circumstances but whose story culminates in a happy ending. They also relied on the conventions of comedies of error. For example, the plot of *Treasure* is propelled by the double meaning of the word *skarb* (treasure) as either a cache of valuable objects or as a term of endearment.

In addition to their entertainment function, these movies served as vehicles for soft propaganda and pedagogy, criticizing problems encountered on the road to building socialism using lighthearted, didactic portrayals of the challenges faced. All four films use humor to exploit the clash between progressive and traditional values, particularly in the realms of class conflict and women's equality. *Treasure* critiques bourgeois mores and makes light of housing shortages and life among Warsaw's ruins. Through humor, the film teaches that patience for Warsaw's reconstruction today will lead to a better future for the heroes of the film and, by extension, the film's audiences. In *Adventure in Mariensztat*, a socialist realist romantic comedy, the romance between a hero of socialist labor and a peasant girl-turned-bricklayer takes a backseat to the capital's reconstruction and the communal effort to build a recreation center for masons. Fethke and Rybkowski's *A Matter to Settle*, while showcasing the Marszałkowska Residential District (MDM) completed in 1952, satirizes daily life in Warsaw, and denounces *bumelanci* (shirkers or malingerers) and *bikiniarze* (the equivalent of British Teddy Boys or Russian *stilyagi*) as the root of Warsaw's day-to-day tribulations. Finally, Fethke's *Irena, Go Home!* tackles misogynistic attitudes identified as a remnant of interwar bourgeois values. The film is about a stay-at-home wife who becomes a Warsaw cabbie despite her husband's protests.

The balance between entertainment and ideology in these films meant that party-minded critics were often unsatisfied by their lack of ideologically correct content. The characters were not proletarian enough. The "dramatic" conflicts between characters were interpreted as insufficiently party-minded. More subversively, in the minds of critics, these comedies acknowledged the gulf between reality and the official narratives on postwar life presented in other authorized textual forms, a fact that no one "on the ground" could ignore. As Richard Taylor points out, comedy was a double-edged sword for the propagandist, who walked a fine line between entertaining the masses and promoting comedy, which "neither took itself nor its subject matter seriously" and which ran the risk of subversion rather than indoctrination.[6] As we shall see, these films managed to walk this line successfully by striking a balance between poking fun at a society in transition and the official messages of the regime. They also revealed a shift in the authorities' confidence as the reconstruction process was carried out, a confidence that embraced humor and integrated it into propaganda. And finally, they functioned as a pressure valve by acknowledging the difficulties of daily life, turning hardship into entertainment.

While the degree of socialist or "proper" content in these movies was debated on the narrative level, critics missed the fact that the socialist message was, first and foremost, encoded in them *through the spatiality they proposed*. These comedies built an iconography of spatiality that functioned as the most ideologically imbued aspect of the movies. By cinematographically coding space according to "socialist norms," they incorporated a socialist message without sacrificing their entertainment value. Each of these comedies uses Warsaw's urban landscape not only as a setting, but also as a way of highlighting specific milestones in Warsaw's reconstruction through a visual dialogue with the Polish Film Chronicle (PKF). While the PKF newsreels that portrayed Warsaw's reconstruction were preoccupied with presenting the Polish capital as a dynamic locus of reconstruction and progress, and often deflected attention from the challenges of daily life, the comedies acknowledged the problems of building socialism well before the 1956 Thaw and the rhetorical shift that occurred in the newsreels and the Black Series as a result.

This acknowledgement of a less-than-ideal social or material context in the comedies, however, was balanced by filmic images of Warsaw that reprised, reiterated, and reinforced the spatial work taking place in the newsreels. This was no chance encounter between the newsreels and feature film. Most of the cinematographers during this period worked in both documentary and feature film genres, with documentary being their earliest encounter with camerawork. The filmic images of Warsaw in these four comedies were created by Adolf Forbert (*A Matter to Settle*), Franciszek Fuchs (*Adventure in Mariensztat*), Seweryn Kruszyński (*Treasure* and *Adventure in Mariensztat*), and Feliks Średnicki (*Irena, Go Home!*). Except for Fuchs, they had all started their work before the war and continued filming throughout the war in various capacities. Eventually, they all worked either as documentarians with the Film Studio "Czołówka" or as cameramen for the PKF.[7] Thus, for moviegoing audiences familiar with the newsreels, the images of Warsaw in these comedies evoked a documentary connotation. Viewed as a cinematic polyptych, the Warsaw comedies parallel the "official" story of a city moving from rubble to normalization, a "storyline" also present in photobooks and newsreels. These movies worked toward building new spatial and cultural connotations by outlining the material progress of Warsaw's reconstruction (albeit a bit too perfectly) and by coding Varsovian vistas for film audiences using a postwar socialist discourse. If Warsaw didn't yet have its Statue of Liberty or Eiffel Tower, film was one way to create such iconic landmarks with a socialist flair.

Postwar Polish Cinema: Between Ideology and Entertainment

Before the war, both domestic as well as Hollywood imports of the 1920s and 1930s shaped the tastes of Polish film audiences, which—like audiences in Europe and the Soviet Union—embraced commercial cinema.[8] Domestic production was dominated by melodramas, comedies, and literary adaptations, including films by Buczkowski, who was well-known for the patriotic melodrama *Gwiaździsta eskadra* (1930; *Star-Spangled Squadron*), an adaptation of Stefan Żeromski's novel *Wierna rzeka* (1936; *The Faithful River*), and the first screen version of Stanisław Moniuszko's opera *Straszny dwór* (1936; *The Haunted Manor*). Thus, through prewar domestic and imported commercial films, postwar Polish filmgoers were more than likely familiar with entertaining movies that conformed to conventional visual styles and narrative structures.

After the war, films made solely for entertainment were few and far between despite the demands of the moviegoing public. The idea of popular cinema as defined before the war ran counter to the politicization of film under communism. During the decade after World War II, Polish feature films were dominated by historical, war, or politicized dramas. Of the sixty films made between 1945 and 1956, almost fifty fell into this genre and portrayed wartime experiences. These films, however, failed to satisfy a growing desire for entertainment and distraction from the vicissitudes of postwar life.[9] Following the Soviet dictum that "cinema is for us the most important of all the arts," postwar film production was a high priority for a newly established communist regime.[10] This by no means meant that film was as important as art or entertainment. Rather, it was considered a vital tool for indoctrination and thus worthy of financial investment, despite limited resources after the war. By the time the war ended in May 1945, the prewar infrastructure of the Polish film industry had been completely destroyed. Equipment to make and screen films was scarce; there was no studio space; and there was no distribution network, with few movie theaters remaining in the country. By December 1945, however, the first film studio opened its doors in Łódź and the film industry was nationalized as Film Polski, which was responsible for producing, distributing, and exhibiting films in Poland. Over the next decade, a concerted effort was made to open movie theaters. Following the Soviet model, there was a push toward *kinofikacja* (cinefication) of the countryside, with an almost nine-fold increase of movie theaters between 1945 and 1952.[11]

Nationalized and subject to censorship, film was one of the main organs of propaganda from the start of the communist regime in Poland. Even before socialist realism was adopted, censors often demanded that screenplays be rewritten to include ideologically correct themes or that films be removed from circulation for reediting, "rehabilitation," and rerelease.[12] Thus, by the time socialist realism was adopted in film in November 1949, cinema's propaganda function was well established. Despite the seemingly programmatic nature of the aesthetic, the parameters of socialist realism were too loosely codified to provide filmmakers with specific guidelines. Film, therefore, adapted socialist realism's literary version, determined to portray reality not as it is but "as it should be." As in literature, film was to feature a positive hero victoriously overcoming struggles in a ceaseless fight for socialist ideals, illustrate the class struggle, and show the party as "organizer, mobilizer, and leader of the masses."[13] Under these general guidelines, a film's narrative (i.e., plot and screenplay) was considered the primary carrier of the socialist message and therefore the foundation of film production. This had several consequences. If screenplays were the most important aspect of film production, they would also be the most censored and controlled aspect, leaving cinematography, sound, editing, and the actors' and director's interpretation of the screenplay to some extent outside the scope of censorship and state control.[14] This became apparent in the coming decades with films from the Black Series, the Polish Film School, and the Cinema of Moral Concern that passed censorship at the script level, only to have their distribution controlled because of questionable content on other formal levels of film after production was complete.[15]

The politicization of film was also reflected in the core leadership assigned to run Film Polski with director Aleksander Ford at the helm.[16] Ford, Jerzy Bossak who was the editor-in-chief of the newsreels and the new magazine *Film*, as well as Eugeniusz Cękalski, Wanda Jakubowska, Stanisław Wohl, and Jerzy Zarzycki, were central to the mission of Film Polski and had been active in film before the war. As I mentioned in chapter 2, they were members of the left-leaning interwar avant-garde Society for the Promotion of Art Film (START) founded in 1930, and some were part of military film units with the Soviet Army and the Soviet-commanded First Polish Army during the war. Though marginal in the prewar film industry, the former START members became its gatekeepers after the war due to their political leanings.[17] They were now the ones who wielded authority in the film industry and held the power to produce or paralyze a project. Before the war, START filmmakers resisted commercial tendencies in Polish cinema and sought to inject film with a social, utilitarian mission and an aesthetic, artistic focus. This mission continued after the war in the institutionalized rejection of the prewar commercial film industry, which was derisively called *branża* or "trade" by party-minded filmmakers, scholars, and critics who accused *branża* of propagating "Hollywood-style" cinema that was "degenerate," "bourgeois," and "capitalist." Already in 1946, Jerzy Bossak wrote in the pages of the newly founded magazine *Film* that "in prewar Poland there were no good films, not just because there was no difference between the maker of films and the maker of artificial jewelry but also because we did not know how to make films or watch them . . . Today we have to create conditions in which Polish film can flourish."[18] And in 1949, the film critic and cofounder of *Film*, Zbigniew Pitera, described the interwar film industry as a capitalist creation "left to the mercy of speculators chasing after easy money and to the owners of movie theaters, who fed off the indiscriminating tastes of a disoriented public."[19] In other words, the prewar achievements of those filmmakers considered part of the interwar *branża* were simply negated and their body of work, which included popular melodramas and comedies, was seen as a remnant of interwar, capitalist culture.[20]

With such a rejection of *branża*, one would think that those film professionals of the "trade" had no place in the postwar Polish film industry. Indeed, they were officially marginalized in the early postwar years on account of their prewar body of films, which were labeled "philistine" according to socialist standards.[21] Furthermore, Polish film history written after the war by scholars and critics who were close to the former START group tended to ignore the role of *branża* in the postwar industry by suggesting that Polish film had no past or tradition of its own. However, the reality of film production in postwar Poland looked somewhat different. The leadership of Film Polski saw a need for a successful popular cinema that appealed to the masses. Moreover, it was clear that the tendency toward art cinema and the avant-garde leanings of the former START members were often unappealing to the public.[22] Thus, Film Polski had to rely not only on its "own" representatives—those members of START who now stood at the helm of the postwar film industry—but also on those prewar film professionals from *branża*, who stayed in Poland or returned after 1945.[23] In other words, Film Polski turned to the same prewar filmmakers who were being derided in theory and criticism.

Filmmakers such as Leonard Buczkowski and Jan Fethke, and the screenwriter and lyricist Ludwik Starski, had been active in interwar commercial film, making movies that focused on entertainment, rather than artistry or social intervention. Their skills, rather than the ones of the avant-gardists, were most useful for creating popular films in the postwar era. Both Fethke and Buczkowski worked during the war for the German film industry. Fethke, born in Upper Silesia into a Polish-German family, worked for the German film production company Ufa from 1928 until Hitler's rise to power and then during the war for the German film studios Film- und Propagandamittel-Vertriebsgesellschaft in Warsaw and for "Bavaria" in Munich. After the war he returned to Poland and directed several socialist realist films but eventually immigrated to West Berlin.[24] Buczkowski made short commercials and instructional films for private German companies during the war. Such wartime activity was considered collaboration with the Nazis and was often punished during the postwar period. In the case of Buczkowski, however, the need to utilize his skills and talents outweighed his wartime offenses. After the release of his first postwar film, *Zakazane piosenki* (1946, re-release 1948; *Forbidden Songs*), Buczkowski was censured by being forced to direct films under the pseudonym "Marian Leonard" for three years, a relatively mild punishment at this time considering the offense.[25]

It is thus no surprise that the first feature film released after the war was not a production of a former START member but rather Buczkowski and Starski's *Forbidden Songs*, a feature-length film whose narration was constructed around Warsaw street songs sung in defiance of the German occupation. This "*branża* rule" held true for two other postwar firsts: the first postwar comedy, *Treasure*, and the first postwar color film, *Adventure in Mariensztat*, both collaborations between Buczkowski and Starski.[26] Despite the apprehensions about *branża* filmmakers, Buczkowski was considered one of the best prewar "craftsmen" with a good reputation, well-developed talent, and the technical skill needed to create films "on order." Flexible in his craft, he could satisfy the narrative needs and desires of film audiences *and* adjust his films and screenplays to the political demands placed on film in the immediate postwar years and later to those of socialist realism. According to the film scholar Piotr Zwierzchowski, Buczkowski was one of the few filmmakers who successfully bridged Polish film production from the interwar period, through socialist realism, and past 1956. While incorporating elements of propaganda into his films out of necessity, particularly after 1949, Buczkowski placed a high premium on the entertainment value of his films and the final results were often popular, entertaining movies.[27] Thus, despite the official rejection of interwar popular cinema, *branża* filmmakers' professional experience and mastery of conventional film narrativization proved useful in the context of developing a new, socialist, popular cinema culture.[28] While this reliance on prewar models was to a large extent an inconvenient truth under socialism, some of the most successful postwar "commercial" films were the result of the cooperation between the filmmakers considered *branża* and those who toed the ideological line before, during, and after socialist realism.

Treasure: Street Views and Skylines

A romantic comedy of errors set in the late 1940s, *Treasure* (1948) is the story of newlyweds, Krysia Różycka-Konar (Danuta Szaflarska) and Witek Konar (Jerzy Duszyński).[29] They are run-of-the-mill Varsovians. She is a salesgirl, who longs for a place where she and her new husband can be alone. He is a bus driver, whose attempt to find a room where they can begin their married life in private has failed. They spend the first night of their marriage under separate roofs with roommates. Desperate to be together, Witek finds an apartment located amidst ruins on a street called "Równa."[30] Under the impression that he and Krysia will be the only tenants, Witek describes the spacious apartment to his wife and draws a floor plan, marking her "bed" with the pet-name "skarb" ("treasure"). When they move to Równa Street, however, a parade of tenants ensues. The apartment is inhabited not only by the newlyweds and the owner of the apartment, but also by her niece Basia (Alina Janowska), a waitress who loudly types the next day's menu; Alfred Ziółko (Adolf Dymsza), a sound effects man for live radio who specializes in imitating animal and nature sounds, and lives and practices his imitations in a room located behind a wardrobe; a meter reader for the electric company, who noisily calculates customers' bills on an abacus; and a prewar counselor-at-law, who puts on the airs of an aristocrat and listens "clandestinely" to the BBC.

The plot thickens when two con men, looking for a treasure purportedly hidden in the apartment walls during the war, pose as officials of the Warsaw building office. They "evict" the tenants, claiming that in just a few days the apartment, which is supporting the ruins of a four-story building, will come down to make way for the construction of the Trasa W-Z. When Ziółko overhears them discussing the location of the hidden treasure, a feverish attempt to uncover it escalates. The greedy search intensifies when Witek's floor plan with the word "treasure" is thought to confirm the location of the riches. The tenants and con men tear down the walls of the apartment, making the building collapse. Cut off from the world, they prepare for the worst. But just when all seems lost, the true heroes of the film—and of Polish socialism and its construction—save the day: a crew excavating the tunnel of the Trasa W-Z drills through the rubble and saves the tenants of Równa Street.

Poorly received by critics, *Treasure* was criticized for insufficiently highlighting socialist values by marginalizing the place of work within the narrative.[31] Neither Krysia nor Witek are paradigmatic construction workers or labor heroes as demanded by socialist realism, which was adopted the year after the film was made. And the narrative focus of the film is primarily on the problem of housing shortages. The movie was also criticized for minimizing class conflict by portraying a cross-section of Polish society rising above their differences. Furthermore, the film was considered suspect because it was an entertaining romantic comedy. As a romance, it ran the risk of suggesting that personal desire and love could be prioritized above the communal good. After all, even before socialist realism, the state film industry was supposed to teach audiences about the ideological necessity for placing the collective first.[32] What seems to have been lost on critics, however, was that the socialist value of the film came from the characters' attitude to and relationship with Warsaw and its reconstruction. As the film shows, though they complain about and are frustrated by their living situation, they are willing to make sacrifices for a future Warsaw. Though Witek and Krysia's union is threatened by construction and housing shortages, it culminates in marriage within the first ten minutes of the film.[33] The real love affair in the movie, then, is between the young couple and the new Warsaw. The happy ending comes when socialist promises are fulfilled in the form of an apartment where Krysia and Witek can kiss without people watching. According to the movie, happiness is achieved through Warsaw's socialist construction.

Socialism on the Street: From Chaos to Order

The socialist message in *Treasure* is located on the streets of Warsaw, which are presented in the contrast between ruins and (re)construction, chaos and order.[34] Such correlations are set up in the framing of the film, which begins with an aerial shot of ruins and ends with the landscape of a construction site. This framing indicates that the film is about the *process* of rebuilding Warsaw. Supporting such a reading of the film is its self-referentiality, which calls attention to the fictionality of the narrative, on the one hand, and which sets up a direct connection between the story and the audience, on the other. Warsaw is made exceptional in the opening sequence of shots that depict ruins inserted between the production logo and the opening credits. This sequence begins with an image of the destroyed Prudential skyscraper and is followed by shots of three other bombed-out buildings. During this sequence, the music, which begins melodically, turns dissonant. Superimposed over the four shots of ruins, we read:

Shot 1: Warsaw after the war was . . .

Shot 2: . . . the only city in the world, where . . .

Shot 3: . . . this authentic story, made up by the authors, . . .

Shot 4: . . . could take place.

By simultaneously stressing the historical, "authentic" aspects of the plot (i.e., war, ruins, reconstruction, housing shortages), this opening sequence forms a bridge between the fictionality of the text and the problems experienced by film viewers living in late 1940s Warsaw.

Like the opening sequence, the closing sequence of the movie is also self-referential. In the last scene, we learn that Fredek Ziółko and Basia, whose romance has been developing alongside Witek and Krysia's post-wedding tribulations, are also waiting for an apartment of their own. When in the final scene Ziółko tries to kiss Basia, she reprises one of Krysia's earlier lines: "Don't! People are watching!" After a pause, she adds, "There in the movie theater." The couple looks into the camera and Ziółko—who through the film's self-referentiality has become the real actor, Adolf Dymsza—winks at the audience (figure 10). The on-screen couple turns and walks away from the camera toward a high-rise building under construction on the horizon. As they enter the construction site, they close behind them a solid wooden gate across which is scrawled "The End." When closed, the gate blocks the lower half of the screen and the construction happening on the ground. The audience is left with an image of the scaffolding surrounding the high-rise, electric wires, and a sky that is pregnant with future possibilities.

Though the opening and closing sequences constitute a popular hook in cinema, they were outside the parameters of the coming socialist realist aesthetic that demanded a linear narrative and predetermined the ideological conversion of a story's main characters, as in the case of Ford's *Five from Barska Street*. Significantly, however, the frame of *Treasure* engages the audience as a participant in the story by consciously calling attention to the extra-diegetic level of the film, locating the narrative in a contemporary time and space with which the audience could identify. The narrative frame of *Treasure* creates a cinematic structure where the screen acts as a bridge between the audience and text. *Treasure* invites the audience to participate in poking fun at the everyday reality of life in late 1940s Warsaw, and, at the same time, invites the audience to co-create new spatial meanings for the capital as they observe the physical and rhetorical (re)construction portrayed in the movie.

Within the narrative, ruins and rubble are a source of chaos that provoke anxiety and foster deception and danger. At the same time, there is chaos on Warsaw's construction sites and in the day-to-day changes on the capital's streets. The film demonstrates how the (re)construction of the city

Figure 10. Ziółko (Adolf Dymsza) and Basia (Alina Janowska) address the audience in the final scene from *Treasure* (dir. Leonard Buczkowski, 1948).

ultimately leads to urban order that provides the characters with what they need: a roof over their heads. Chaos is contrasted in two scenes that mirror one another. These scenes portray Witek as disoriented and losing his way in the labyrinth-city. Both scenes are of comparable length, lasting between fifty and sixty seconds, and both are composed similarly: Witek stands in the foreground; ruins or construction dominate the background; a vehicle passes between these two planes. In both scenes, Witek asks for directions to his final destination. Despite these similarities, "chaos" means different things in each scene.

Witek first encounters chaos amid construction sites in the center of the city as he searches for Nowy Świat Street (ulica Nowy Świat) in downtown Warsaw and the Civil Marriage Office. His confusion and inability to merge his mental map of Warsaw with the process of reconstruction makes him late for his wedding. Humorously echoing the newsreels, which portrayed volunteers from across Poland and other newly established people's republics rebuilding Warsaw, Witek encounters a Czech, a Romanian, and a Pole from Częstochowa, none of whom can direct him toward Nowy Świat, because they do not know the city.[35] (See figure 11.) As Witek makes his way through the construction, his desperation is shown as the plight of the individual

Figure 11. Witek (Jerzy Duszyński) asks a Polish volunteer worker from Częstochowa for directions to the Civil Marriage Office in *Treasure* (dir. Leonard Buczkowski, 1948).

Figure 12. Witek (Jerzy Duszyński) searching among the ruins for the apartment on Równa Street in *Treasure* (dir. Leonard Buczkowski, 1948).

confronted with a dynamically changing landscape, an aspect of reconstruction rarely addressed in the newsreels but which made its way into popular discourses on postwar Varsovian space.[36] Witek's anxiety, however, is quickly dispelled when he makes it to the wedding bureau just moments before it closes and marries an angry bride, who thought she was about to be left at the "altar." Once he explains to her, however, that he was lost in the city searching for a place to spend their wedding night together, the bride's anger subsides. After all, Witek's delay was caused by the chaos of reconstruction, a small sacrifice in exchange for a future socialist capital.[37] As the film instructs, such construction chaos is necessary for the redevelopment of the capital, and the movie suggests that the rubble, if not a thing of the past, is being reined in, shaped, and controlled.

The second scene in which Witek is disoriented by architectural chaos occurs the first time he goes to Równa Street, which is located in an area dominated by ruins and rubble and is bereft of geographic specificity. In contrast to the disorder of construction, the film codes the rubble on Równa Street where Witek finds an apartment as dangerously "chaotic." When Witek arrives in this rubble-filled neighborhood, he can barely imagine that there is an apartment available for rent among the ruins. Wild and overgrown, the chaos-ruins directly contrast the controlled chaos of the earlier construction sequence. The next series of shots follows Witek attempting to locate the entrance to 64 Równa Street, which is hidden among the skeletons of walls, dead trees, and weeds (figure 12). Witek's foray among the ruins is accompanied by dissonant tones, descending scales, and then subsequent alternations between higher and lower octaves and scales going up, down, and back up again. The music signals adventure and the unknown, marking the ruins as dangerous and threatening.

In contrast to the chaos of ruins and construction in the film, order is represented by completed buildings, paved roads, and functioning institutions, like the Civil Registry Office or the multistory department store where Krysia works. Those areas of the city that have been renovated are bustling with people and give the street shots of the city an aura of a typical urban center. Street views are showcased on the morning after the wedding through the main characters' point of view as they travel on Witek's bus route through reconstructed parts of the city. Witek's job as a bus driver not only offers the film an opportunity to present reconstructed streets from a driver's perspective, but also helps establish a sense of control over the space. This sequence suggests that the socialist building project is a success because of functioning public transportation and the city's horizontal expansion. Though not integral to the plot, the scene is used as a mechanism for gazing upon Warsaw. The sequence begins with an aerial shot of a street without ruins, rubble, or construction. As the newlyweds continue on this urban journey that Krysia calls their honeymoon, the audience is privy to a series of shots from the shared point of view of the characters. Filmed through the windshield of the bus, the camera follows the curve of the streets, showing paved roads and people hurrying along; next is a continuous shot of the left side of the street beginning with ruins, then one of buildings in the process of reconstruction, and finally a shot of completed buildings and streets lined with trees. Reinforcing the intimate nature of these shots, the street views are rhythmically interspersed with close-ups of Witek at the wheel of the bus and Krysia looking over his shoulder and narrating or interpreting for her husband and the audience what she sees. To the sound of romantic music and the hum of the bus, Krysia describes the city as evolving from ruins to homes: "Look Witek! Everyday something new. Not long ago there were only ruins, like in this spot. And look! They are building even more. Here they are done building. Oh! Look at the curtains in the windows. People have moved in." Through image, sound, and screenplay, this sequence presents a mini-narrative of the reconstruction process, beginning with rubble and ending with inhabited buildings. Lasting about ninety seconds, the bus scene highlights reconstructed Warsaw on both diegetic and non-diegetic levels. Filmed in a tourist documentary style, it exhibits newly reconstructed areas of the city and represents intertextuality with the newsreels and photobooks. And like photobooks, the film combines the spatial representation of the city with a condensed historical narrative that summarizes different phases of Warsaw's reconstruction, showing the process of transformation from ruins to construction to completed buildings in which Varsovians make their homes.

Warsaw in the Sky: Progress and the Future

In *Treasure*, hope and a bright future are found in empty spaces that inspire dreams of new homes. These spaces are presented through aerial shots that hide and obscure the rubble and ruins and provide a "big picture" view of Warsaw. Three scenes reference an empty sky as the locus of future dwellings. The first is at Krysia's workplace. The second is on the upper story of a bombed-out building. And the last is one I have already mentioned: the closing scene of the movie that features Basia and Ziółko. Alluding to images known from the newsreels, a scale model of an apartment building is delivered to Krysia's workplace. Krysia and a lackluster colleague admire the "building" where they will eventually live. Inspecting their future homes in the form of a scale model, they daydream about their apartments on the upper floors of the building and point out "their" windows, which overlook the city of Warsaw. Krysia, however, is dismayed at the disjuncture between the finished scale model and the actual construction site where only the foundation has been poured. According to her, the building is "only air." This empty space causes a momentary crisis of faith in the reconstruction process and the newly established socialist system. She is distraught and frustrated by the empty air, which her coworker describes in idyllic terms: "Isn't it beautiful? Imagine the view from the top. And the clean air!" For the coworker, the emptiness is a space that will be filled with socialist content, where they will all live together happily. With her colleague's encouragement, Krysia's faith in reconstruction is restored and the challenges of waiting for Warsaw's renovation are placed into proper perspective. Thus, the film reinforces an official Varsovian poetics that was meant to allay fears and anxiety, provide a language of substance, and fill an empty or disordered space with order, potential, and an ideal.

The second scene that features Warsaw "in the sky" begins in the ground-floor apartment on Równa Street. Annoyed by Basia's typing, the meter reader's clicking abacus, the counselor's radio, and Ziółko's animal imitations, Krysia runs out of the apartment into the rubble-filled night. Witek frantically follows her up a rickety staircase of a bombed-out building. This mini-chase scene is scored to dissonant music, coding the ruins as dangerous just like in the scene when Witek first arrives on Równa Street. Reaching the top of the stairs, Witek and Krysia see a ray of light peeking through some shutters. Upon opening them, they reveal to the audience a bird's-eye view of Warsaw. This perspective is followed by a series of cuts that include aerial views of the city, over-the-shoulder shots of Warsaw, and eye-level shots that show the characters looking dreamily at a nighttime cityscape sprinkled with lights shining from apartment windows and cars. With romantic music playing in the background, this intimate moment between the newlyweds becomes associated with the capital and their love for Warsaw. With voices full of awe, the characters identify Warsaw as the true "treasure" of the film:

> WITEK: Look. Everywhere ruins, ruins, rubble. But it's *so* beautiful.
> KRYSIA (*whispering*): Of course it's beautiful. It's Warsaw.

These lines are short but significant. They echo the sentiments of a nation, rather than those of socialism: Warsaw is beloved despite its chaotic, postwar state. These lines, however, also serve a didactic, propaganda purpose. The bird's-eye view reminds Krysia, Witek, and the audience to distinguish the forest from the trees and to turn a blind eye to the everyday problems of living in the capital. In a reprise of the scene between Krysia and her coworker, the couple imagines their apartment house rising from the ruins, floor by floor. Their imagination fills the empty air with a building in which they occupy a sixth-floor apartment located "under that white cloud," a prospect that leads Krysia to conclude that "if you think about it like that, it doesn't seem so bad after all." (See figure 13.)

The beauty and potential that Witek and Krysia see in the Warsaw landscape is based on their memory of what the city used to be like, as well as on their faith in the reconstruction process and the future shape of the city.[38] But it is the faith in their future sixth-floor apartment that carries Krysia through the final scenes of the movie when she, Witek, and the tenants of 64 Równa Street are buried beneath ruins only to be saved by the Trasa

Figure 13. Witek (Jerzy Duszyński) and Krysia (Danuta Szaflarska) looking over Warsaw at night in *Treasure* (dir. Leonard Buczkowski, 1948).

W-Z construction crew. The broad vistas and views of the city in the film underscore the urban space as a place of future fulfillment. The individual or private desires of the newlyweds are subordinated to those of the greater good, a point expressed at the end of the film when Witek and Krysia move into their own apartment, and the comedic couple, Basia and Ziółko, are revealed as newlyweds embarking on their new life and waiting for their own apartment to rise into Warsaw's skyline. On the diegetic level of the film, when Krysia and Witek point to their apartment and later kiss in their own home, the desire for a private space is located within the frame of the main narrative. When reprised in the final scene of the film, however, Basia and Ziółko become a vehicle for unmasking the artifice of film and helping the audience identify even more closely with the story. Exploiting the potential of film, the characters and audience together gaze at a future Warsaw.

Treasure was a cinematic vehicle for the audience to see the present-day city on the streets and the future socialist city "in the air" through Witek and Krysia's gaze. While the movie does not promote any one particular urban icon, Warsaw is promoted as its own landmark in the "process of becoming." And if the couple's relationship is tested by circumstances, such as Witek being late for their wedding or a lack of an apartment in which to consummate their marriage, then these trials are minor sacrifices in light of the challenge of rebuilding the beloved capital. The film establishes a connection between external chaos, rubble, and ruins and an "old world" order that persists on Równa Street. Order, construction, progress, and a bright future on the street level and in the sky reinforce the connection between the physical reconstruction of Warsaw's space and the social and political construction of a People's Republic. As Krysia's coworker states: "Soon we will all be living together. And we will all be happy."

Mapping Warsaw in *Adventure in Mariensztat*

Musical comedy. Chick flick. Happy ending. These are not the first phrases one thinks of when thinking about communist-era Polish cinema. However, this is the combination you get in Leonard Buczkowski's *Adventure in Mariensztat* (1953). As a comedy, the movie satisfied what Boris Shumyatsky, head of Soyuzkino in the Soviet Union in the 1930s, considered comedy's most important task: the creation of a good and joyful spectacle.[39] The film is entertaining, amusing, and sentimental, even if the second half of the movie is taken over by a socialist message of communal work and social progress. At the same time, however, in the hands of Buczkowski and Starski, the propaganda tone of the movie was tempered by its commercial, *branża* style. Though considered by some scholars as too popular and thus of no importance to Polish cinematic history,[40] *Adventure in Mariensztat* was a milestone in postwar Polish cinema. Significant as an example of popular culture under socialism, it was Poland's first color film and one of the first times (if not the first) that Warsaw was portrayed on screen in color after almost a decade of black-and-white images on the newsreel screen. The Warsaw of *Adventure* is lighthearted, youthful, and a model of socialist (realist) material and social transformation. More than just the backdrop for a joyful spectacle of reconstruction, peasant migration to the city, and love between labor heroes, Warsaw is the central love interest that unites the main characters—the peasant girl, Hanka, and the hero of socialist labor, Janek. Such fictionalization of Warsaw's space represented a confidence that the socialist message had achieved a momentum strong enough to withstand comedic, romantic treatment.

Adventure in Mariensztat tells the story of Hanka Ruczajówna, a charming peasant girl who sings the lead in a provincial folk choir, and Janek Szarliński, a bricklayer who exceeds the bricklaying norm by 312 percent. The story of how they meet and fall in love is set among the frenzy of Warsaw's reconstruction. Hanka (Lidia Korsakówna, with singing by Irena Santor)[41] travels to Warsaw with a provincial choir to perform at a concert on Mariensztat Square. Donned in traditional folk dress, she breaks away from her tour group to see the capital on her own terms. Along the way, she meets Janek

(Tadeusz Schmidt) and dances away the evening with him, never learning his full name or that he is a socialist labor hero. After the concert, Hanka returns to the countryside, but not before falling in love with both Warsaw and Janek. She eventually trades in her folk dress and the fields of Złocień for worker's overalls and Warsaw's construction sites, where she becomes a bricklayer. Reunited with Janek by a chance encounter, Hanka joins his bricklayer brigade despite the protests of the misogynistic construction site manager, Leon Ciepielewski (Adam Mikołajewski). As Janek's labor productivity decreases and Ciepielewski's annoyance at women's equality increases, an intense, yet entertaining, labor competition ensues between the male and female brigades. The competition culminates with the women pledging to build, in record time, a Bricklayers' Recreation Center for the respite of all those who contribute to the construction of Warsaw. When a plumbing accident floods the center just hours before its official opening, the men—led by the former misogynist Ciepielewski—assist the women in the final hour. In the second-to-last scene, we witness a joyful renovation and cleanup where the men and women complete the center together. Only in the last scene of the movie, which occurs a year after their first kiss, do we see Hanka and Janek together again, dancing on Mariensztat Square in the company of their comrades.

Such a synopsis demonstrates the careful intertwining of romantic comedy with propaganda to create a story that satisfied the requirements of popular culture and ideology.[42] From the perspective of popular film, the movie contains such core elements as boy meets girl; boy and girl fall in love; boy and girl can't find one another; boy and girl find one another again but are at odds or argue; boy and girl are brought together again; and everyone lives happily ever after. At the same time, the movie is set in the framework of building socialism. Most obviously, it contains such elements as a focus on the construction (not reconstruction) of Warsaw; the movement from country to city; the worker, who is at the very center of the narrative; heroes of socialist labor; a labor competition; and expositions on the role of women in the communist labor force. The film is filled with happy, mostly youthful faces working cooperatively to build socialism.

Warsaw: A Uniquely Generic City

Though *Adventure in Mariensztat* incorporates parallel narrative lines that make it both popular culture and propaganda, the film's treatment of Warsaw tips the balance toward "socialist" correctness in the portrayal of the capital as both generically socialist and uniquely Varsovian. On the one hand, the cinematography casts Warsaw as a generic socialist urban space following the aesthetics of reports on Warsaw's construction in the newsreels. On the other hand, it acknowledges Warsaw's geospatial uniqueness as a product of socialist efforts and investments. This duality is incorporated into the title, with "Mariensztat" referring to the first completed postwar housing project in Warsaw located near the Trasa W-Z tunnel. Despite (or maybe because of?) its aristocratic beginnings, Mariensztat was designated after the war as a housing complex for socialist labor heroes building the Trasa W-Z. In the film, "Mariensztat" narrows the geospatial perspective to a very specific point on the city map, presuming the audience's familiarity with Warsaw and the neighborhood. And, as we shall see, for those unfamiliar with Mariensztat, the movie aims to place it on the audience's mental map and reinforce its socialist connotations by associating it with Janek the labor hero and the construction of the first major socialist infrastructure project, and by echoing a sense of spatiality promoted in newsreels.

In the months preceding its completion in 1949, the Mariensztat housing project appeared in a number of newsreel reports about the Trasa W-Z. One 1948 news segment, for example, presented a rendering of Mariensztat from a "bird's-eye view" while the voice-over referred to this image as the Trasa W-Z (PKF 7/48:1–2). A few months later, a news segment devoted to the Mariensztat housing project presented the exterior, eighteenth-century facade symbolic of the past as the epitome of the new socialist reality that was moving the city architecture away from the "annexes and tight courtyards of old Warsaw." The narrator explained that behind the old-style facades were modern, comfortable apartments with water, gas, and electricity (PKF 32/48:3). As was the case with the Old Town (Stare Miasto), here Mariensztat was promoted as a symbol of the marriage between old, material "remnants" and new, socialist values. Later updates on the progress of Mariensztat reconstruction showed the neighborhood as a quiet haven in contrast to the frenzy of the Trasa W-Z construction that was just a tenth of a mile away. The newsreels separated the two geospatial reference points with a sharp cut between images of women cleaning their Mariensztat balconies and an aerial shot of the Trasa W-Z construction site (PKF 15/49:6). While Mariensztat was represented as quaint and quiet, the images of the Trasa W-Z underscored geographic breadth. As the camera panned southwest along the thoroughfare onto an aerial shot of the street Krakowskie Przedmieście, it bypassed the edge of Mariensztat which was just out of view of the camera's frame. This filming technique effectively created two distinct spaces: one ideal for quiet and serene living, and the other for lively urban life and mass transportation. In such newsreel portrayals, Mariensztat was placed within the context of one of the most lauded construction projects of the postwar period, coded as a symbol of socialist progress and development, and promoted as an ideal place for the worker and his family to call home.

For audiences familiar with early 1950s Warsaw, the socialist connotations with Mariensztat were most likely already part of their mental maps by the time *Adventure* was released in 1953. As such, the socialist geospatial specificity of Mariensztat is adopted in the film as an assumption, and then transformed in the hands of Buczkowski and Starski into a socialist fairytale that communicates a heightened symbolic and paradigmatic value and represents as-of-yet unachieved hopes and dreams. This fairytale structure is rooted in the paradigm of the romantic comedy in the first half of the film when Hanka and Janek's romance begins on Mariensztat Square. In the second half of the movie, Hanka is reunited with her socialist "prince charming" when she runs into him on the escalator that connects the Trasa W-Z with Zamkowy Square (plac Zamkowy). Their chance encounter culminates with a visit to Mariensztat Square, where they sing the popular song "Jak przygoda to tylko w Warszawie" ("Seeking Adventure? Only Warsaw Will Do!"), a song that reinforces the relationship between Warsaw construction, women's labor, and romance. The song leads to a kiss at the stroke of midnight. Mariensztat thus becomes a space associated with Hanka's "Cinderella-like" transformation into a bricklayer-princess, as well as the socialist "fantasy" of uniting the peasant and worker in the city.[43] It is a space of romance and love, but this romance and love are predicated on Mariensztat being coded as a locus and symbol of socialist progress. The fact that Janek considers the apartment buildings on Mariensztat Square "his own" because his bricklayer brigade built them, adds to this paradigmatic, socialist quality. In the film, thus, the spatiality of Mariensztat is carefully defined as both old and new, as in the newsreels, and as a place where fairytales (and the utopia of communism?) do come true. The final scene of the film is shot in Mariensztat and shows Hanka and Janek reunited, dancing on the Mariensztat Square among their fellow bricklayers.[44] Mariensztat becomes a synecdoche for the new socialist capital as the camera zooms out from the dancing workers to an aerial shot of the city. The film ends with fireworks and the sun over the horizon, suggesting that the struggle for Warsaw and love is nearly over and that a new era is dawning.

Creating Socialist Spaces and Varsovian Specificity

Though the title *Adventure in Mariensztat* implies a cartographic specificity, the opening sequence of the film presents Warsaw as a generic space. The movie begins with a thirty-second shot of a tractor pulling down the walls of a ruined building. As the wall comes down, the screen is filled with clouds of dust. Rather than the sound of crashing bricks and mortar, the puttering of the tractor fades into music that crescendos to indicate the start of the film. As the cloud of dust fades, the image of a well-organized construction site appears. The geometric shapes of the buildings under construction contrast with the jagged, unstable wall torn down only a few moments before. In a matter of seconds, the ruins have transformed into foundations and construction scaffolding. The whirl of building activity is designated by melodic, adventurous music, rather than the sounds of roaring construction equipment. The following shots consist of repeated upward sweeps of the camera that follow the delivery of supplies to higher floors of buildings under construction. These upward sweeps are balanced by brief downward tilts of the camera that portray the construction process—a pile of bricks being lowered, the mixing and pouring of cement—only for the movement to be reversed by yet another upward motion of the camera. The non-diegetic music reflects this upward focus with ascending scales and a combination of musical articulations such as legatos and staccatos that suggest order, ease, energy, and excitement.

In this ninety-second construction sequence, "Warsaw" is presented through a typical socialist realist lens, and there are no specific geographic spatial cues to indicate where the movie is set. Instead, we see a generic urban space being constructed like any other postwar socialist city. From a spatial perspective, this opening sequence reduces Warsaw to a construction site that might just as well be Dresden, Kharkiv, or Stalingrad. Filmed from below to create a sense of monumentality, the rapid montage of construction sites, whose main subjects are workers, cement trucks, cranes, scaffolds, excavators, and bulldozers, echoes and even duplicates the countless images of bricklayers and construction workers that became iconic in the visual arts under socialism. One of the best examples of this visual intertextuality is the image of masons laying bricks on the fifth or sixth floor of a nondescript edifice. In this shot, the camera frames the workers in the same way that Aleksander Kobzdej frames the faceless bricklayers in his 1950 socialist realist painting *Podaj cegłę* (*Pass the Brick*), as already mentioned in this book's introduction. Notably, a similar scene appears in Aleksander Ford's *Five from Barska Street* (1953), while Andrzej Wajda would reconstruct and skillfully undermine the propagandist meaning of these same images in his film *Człowiek z marmuru* (1976; *Man of Marble*) almost a quarter of a century later.

If we accept the premise that "in its first shot a film establishes a geography with which every spectator is asked to contend," then the establishing sequence of *Adventure in Mariensztat* asks the audience to contend with a socialist space under construction.[45] From the first moments of the movie, *Adventure* evokes a generic spatiality that is tied less to a geographically specific locus and more to an ideological mapping of the world. In contrast to the opening sequence of *Treasure*, where a geospatial reference to Warsaw is provided in the opening title and then the construction sequence when Witek asks for directions to the well-known Nowy Świat Street, the opening sequence of *Adventure* refers to a socialist vision of space that emphasizes the ideological foundations of material and social construction, and presents a socialist universalism. Save for the title of the film, which includes the word "Mariensztat," the Polish capital is not directly present in this sequence. Rather, the opening sequence suggests that this is a film about (re)construction, about the process of filling empty spaces, and about the filling of space with socialist content. This attention paid to empty spaces is even part of the opening titles of the film, which appear on the background of an empty sky above a small strip of construction equipment, with the tops of buildings visible along the bottom edge of the screen.

Figure 14. A truck delivering supplies for Warsaw's reconstruction in *Adventure in Mariensztat* (dir. Leonard Buczkowski, 1953). The banner reads "Every Pole is building his capital."

How, thus, does Warsaw make an appearance in this film? To answer this question, we need to look at the thirty seconds that follow the opening sequence. The construction of the socialist framework continues, and like the first sequence, the second is driven by rapid movement. This time, however, the main movement is forward rather than upward. The end of the construction sequence cuts to an oncoming cargo train filled with construction supplies. Close-ups of train wheels and long shots of the railway tracks emphasize the train's length. The train shots are followed by images of flatbed trucks filled with bricks that travel along a nondescript country road strewn with red-and-white banners and flags. Steamboats float along the river. All the vehicles are clearly moving along one trajectory, implied by the diagonal movement of the vehicles from the upper-left corner to the lower-right corner of the screen. The movement is intensified by the non-diegetic music, which suggests the speed and rhythm of the train, trucks, and boats. Through this movement towards an implied single point, the opening sequence narrows the cartographic viewpoint of the film: the vehicles move toward one final destination. Furthermore, the sequence invites the viewer to follow along to what the banners indicate is "Warsaw." The emblem "ZMP," which stands for "Związek Młodzieży

Polskiej" or "Union of Polish Youth" (the Polish equivalent of the Soviet Kom-
somol), can be seen on the engine of the train and the trucks. The banners read:
"Every Pole builds their capital" ("Każdy Polak buduje swoją stolicę"), "We
are building our capital" ("Budujemy naszą stolicę"), and "We greet Warsaw
with song and dance" ("Pieśnią i tańcem witamy Warszawę"). (See figure 14.)
Specially highlighted in this sequence is a train traveling from the Soviet Union
to Warsaw carrying crates marked in Cyrillic "City of Warsaw, Poland," material evidence of the Soviet contribution to Warsaw's reconstruction.

Following these shots is a two-minute musical interlude performed by a
youth choir traveling on one of the trucks. The choir is coming from the countryside, dressed in peasant costumes from Opoczno in south-central Poland,
and singing the Stalinist-era propaganda song "To idzie młodość" ("Here
comes youth"). This is the first diegetic sound of the film, save for the initial
puttering of the tractor that tears down the ruins a few minutes prior. In tune
with socialist realism, the song glorifies the joy and strength of youthful hands
from city and countryside storming the capital in order to build and defend
both socialism and the city, and lead to the rebirth of the world under socialism.
Warsaw is thus designated by song and banners, and associated with peasant
youth migrating, or at least traveling, to the city accompanied by Soviet trains,
the ZMP, and volunteer brigades ready to aid in the building of Warsaw. The
caravan of ZMP trucks shows the nationwide contribution to (re)building the
city, the love of all citizens for the capital is expressed by the banners, and the
devotion of the masses to Warsaw is expressed in song. The scene ends with the
heroine of the film affectionately proclaiming to her peasant friend: "Maryśka!
Warsaw!" The opening sequence ends with a medium close-up of Hanka and
Maryśka staring into the horizon that we presume is Warsaw, though it is a
horizon that is never shown on screen. The film audience is not privy to this
magnificent Warsaw skyline that greets them. Instead, as viewers of the film,
we observe Hanka being overwhelmed by her first sight of the capital.

Thus, the opening sequence of a film that announces itself as an adventure
in Warsaw is not actually filmed in Warsaw. Instead, Varsovian spatiality is
first articulated linguistically by citing propaganda slogans and through song
lyrics. This verbal articulation of Warsaw space is, in turn, associated with
socialist imagery such as construction, vehicles symbolizing industrialization,
the forward march of the proletariat designated by the "forward" movement
of the opening sequence, and peasant migration to the city. The musical score
unifies these elements, creating a visceral experience. The music culminates in
a popular mass song that encourages audience participation through its easy-
to-sing composition and marching rhythm. From a perspective of mapping or
cartography, the associations triggered here are not reliant on the actual city
space, but rather on the ideas and concepts related to Warsaw at the height of
socialist realism and Bierut's Six-Year Plan for Warsaw's Reconstruction. In
this film there is no history or war, save for the occasional ruin barely visible
in the background of the film. More importantly, the opening sequence, which

establishes the setting of the film as "Warsaw," has little to do with specific geospatial points, and more to do with the movement toward imbuing the geographic space with socialist meaning. This three-minute-and-forty-second introduction to the film sets the stage for the audience's perception of the film as simultaneously exemplifying the specificity of Warsaw, while underscoring the generic quality of the socialist city that is to be everything for everyone. Determined by nonspatial cinematic and narrative means, urban space does not define Warsaw at the start of the film, and neither do iconic or symbolic images of the city. Rather, socialist ideas shape how the audience is directed to contend with the geography of the film, a geography that is more specifically defined in the following scenes where iconic Varsovian sites are presented in what is best described as a tourist sequence.

A Walking Tour of Warsaw, or How Best to Visit a Socialist Capital

For centuries, media in all its popular forms—from literature and poetry to music and visual arts—have been an inspiration for tourism and sightseeing by "constructing or reinforcing particular images of . . . destinations and acting as 'markers.' "[46] Countering the generic, universalist characterization of Warsaw established in the opening sequence, *Adventure in Mariensztat* reinforces certain Varsovian places as "tourist spaces" in a two-minute sequence that maps the city for visitors from all over Poland. The tourist sequence in *Adventure in Mariensztat*, however, was not just a fictional concoction created for the film. It had its parallel in PKF segments that promoted Warsaw as a tourist destination. For example, a 1953 segment entitled "Na wczasach w Warszawie" ("Vacationing in Warsaw") (PKF 8/53:4) advertised the capital as an excellent place to visit even in winter. It publicized the transformation of a card club for landowners into a newly built Warsaw Vacation Center for "workers, peasants, people of labor from all over Poland." It also showcased the street Krakowskie Przedmieście as the "new old Warsaw" and the 1952 socialist realist Marszałkowska Residential District (MDM) as a sign of the "completely new Warsaw." The winter tour of Warsaw ends with a visit to the construction site of the Palace of Culture and Science (Pałac Kultury i Nauki) and an outing to the theater.

A similar segment from 1949 entitled "Zwiedzamy Warszawę" ("We Are Visiting Warsaw") (PKF 48/49:5) encouraged tourism in the newly revived capital. It featured Poles from across the country—some dressed in contemporary clothes and others in traditional folk dress—traveling to Warsaw on weekend excursions to tour the capital in its newest, socialist form. As the shot analysis in figure 15 shows, the segment developed a socialist tourist discourse around specific, reconstructed or newly constructed Warsaw places. It created destination markers through cinematic cartography by promoting the Trasa W-Z, Mariensztat, and other socialist sites as tourist destinations. It also mapped out a proposed tour path that could be cartographically

	Description of Camera Shots	Voice-over
Shots 1-3	*Tourists in contemporary clothes dis-embark from a train. A guide from Orbis (the state-owned travel agency) leads tourists down the train platform. Sequence ends with a close-up of the guide's Orbis armband.*	Every Sunday hundreds of trips are taken to Warsaw from around the country. Everyone is hoping to see the rebuilding effort to which they have contributed by donating money to the Fund for the Reconstruction of the Capital.
Shot 4	*Over-the-shoulder shot showing tour-ists walking toward the Trasa W-Z and Mariensztat.*	The first steps lead to the **Trasa W-Z**.
Shot 5	*Group of tourists look at a fountain.*	This is the new square of the housing settlement at **Mariensztat**.
Shot 6	*Close-up of a young boy smiling.*	[music]
Shot 7	*Group of tourists face camera and play at the fountain.*	
Shot 8	*Close-up of female guide speaking to three women in folk dress.*	
Shot 9	*A shot of the clock located on Marien-sztat Square.*	This **clock** is a gift from the watchmak-ers of the capital.
Shot 10	*Close-up of tour guide looking up.*	
Shot 11	*Low-angle shot of the Sigismund III Vasa Column.*	Ladies and Gentlemen! Look! **King Sigismund** once again stands in his usual place.
Shot 12	*Shot of a downward escalator crowded with tourists in folk dress from the Lublin region.*	And the greatest excitement comes from the first trip down an **escalator**.
Shot 13	*Extreme long shot showing the Łazienki Palace and pond.*	It is a pleasure to rest next to the recon-structed **palace in Łazienki Park**.
Shot 14	*Shot showing visitors feeding swans in the pond in front of Łazienki Palace.*	[music]
Shots 15-17	*Shot of tourists—highlanders in folk dress from the Zakopane region—as they pose for a photograph in front of the monument to King Jan III Sobieski located in Łazienki Park.*	As a token of their time in Warsaw-reborn, the highlanders will return home with a photo taken at the **monu-ment to Jan Sobieski**.

Figure 15. Shot analysis of PKF 48/49: "We Are Visiting Warsaw." Bolded text indicates places that are promoted as destination markers in the newsreel segment.

A Statue of the Mermaid of Warsaw on Wybrzeże Kościuszkowskie Street

B Mariensztat

C Sigismund III Vasa Column

D Krakowskie Przedmieście

E Łazienki Park

F The fountain in front of Kino Muranów

Figure 16. Map of the Złocień choir's walking tour from *Adventure in Mariensztat* (dir. Leonard Buczkowski, 1953). Visualization by Lorin Bruckner.

	Description of Camera Shots	Tour Guide's Script
Shot 1	*Camera zooms out from the statue of the Warsaw Mermaid to show the Złocień choir and their tour guide standing on Wybrzeże Kościuszkowskie Street on the bank of the Vistula River.*	Before us stands the **statue of the Mermaid,** which—as we know—has been on Warsaw's coat of arms since time immemorial. It constitutes an ornament of **Wybrzeże Kościuszkowskie Street** where we currently stand.
Shot 2	*The guide indicates various points of interest with his arms while standing in one place. The choir members turn to look toward each point of interest as it is mentioned.*	The **Śląsko-Dąbrowski Bridge,** a gift from Silesia to Warsaw. **Praga**—a suburb of Warsaw. **The Railway Bridge. The Poniatowski Bridge. The Vistula**—the queen of Polish rivers.
Shot 3	*Wide-angle shot of the group as they walk along the embankment of the Vistula River.*	Moving on.
Shot 4	*Camera cuts to the staircase leading to Mariensztat. The group walks up a few steps toward Mariensztat Square and stops. The guide directs them to look at various points of interest.*	Stop! What are we looking at? <u>**Mariensztat.**</u> A housing development with new *kamienice* in the eighteenth-century style. <u>**The market square.**</u> <u>**The fountain.**</u> <u>**The clock.**</u>
Shot 5	*Close-up of guide. The choir members look over their shoulders as the guide indicates more points of interest.*	**An escalator. The Copper-Roof Palace. A statue of a market woman. A view of Praga.** Moving on.
Shot 6	*The camera follows the group, which moves up the staircase only a few more steps.*	[music] Stop!
Shot 7	*Wide-angle shot of Sigismund III Vasa Column and Old Town. Camera tilts downward from the top of the column to its base, where the choir and tour guide are standing.*	Before us stands the <u>**Sigismund Column,**</u> a symbol of old Warsaw. Here it is. It owes its name . . .
Shots 8-12	*The guide lists and points to more places of interest. Heads of the choir members rapidly turn in the direction indicated by the guide.*	. . . indeed—as we can see—to the fact that it is in the shape of a column, and indeed at the top stands King Sigismund. Charming, **little bourgeois** *kamienice.* **Old Town** in its reconstruction phase. **A historic bell tower**—fifteenth century. Moving on.
Shots 13-26	*Guide leads group along the Royal Route. They stop at the **monument to Copernicus,** race down **Krakowskie Przedmieście** and **Ujazdowskie Avenue** to <u>**Łazienki Park and Palace**</u>. They stop at the **fountain in Muranów.** The choir is clearly exhausted.*	[music]
Shots 27-30	*The choir rests on the steps of the Muranów fountain.*	Attention! Attention! Moving on!

Figure 17. Shot analysis of the Złocień choir's walking tour from *Adventure in Mariensztat* (dir. Leonard Buczkowski, 1953). Bolded text indicates sites that are treated as destination markers in the sequence. Underlined text indicates destination markers that also appear or are mentioned in PKF 48/49: "We Are Visiting Warsaw" (compare figure 15).

re-created. Finally, the peasants in regional folk dress provided an additional cartographic element, creating a bridge between the capital and other parts of Poland. In the guise of reporting on "hundreds of excursions," the segment functioned as an advertisement that encouraged travel to the capital and showed how visiting Warsaw provided the chance to build memories. The final shots of the segment show a group of *górale*, or highlanders, in traditional dress taking photographs at the statue of Jan III Sobieski in Łazienki Park.[47] While not explicitly speaking of socialism, the segment connoted socialist content with images of the peasant in the city, its focus on the Trasa W-Z, and references to the Mariensztat settlement—all particularly strong socialist symbols in November 1949, just five months after Bierut had presented his Six-Year Plan for Warsaw's Reconstruction.[48]

Other segments outlined tourist paths and activities, presented "socialist" spaces as noteworthy tourist stops, or publicized the Vistula River and its banks as an alternative beach, sailing, or vacation destination (PKF 32/51:10, 34/52:2–3, 33/49:6). The MDM and Konstytucji Square (plac Konstytucji) were hailed as the first *truly* socialist spaces of Warsaw and as sites worth photographing (PKF 34/52:2–3), while the area around the Trasa W-Z was presented as a place to take evening strolls (PKF 33/49:6). The newsreel camera zoomed in on socialist sculptures and framed new construction or vistas of the city using static shots, which alluded to the composition of paintings, photobooks, or a museum setting. In this way, the PKF aestheticized newly constructed spaces and taught audiences how to see and read them as socialist tourist attractions that should be leisurely enjoyed and contemplated like art.

Such PKF segments suggest that the two-minute tourist sequence of *Adventure in Mariensztat* should be read intertextually as a comedic pastiche of the destination tourism promoted in the newsreels. I say "pastiche" and not "parody," for the tourist sequence in the movie goes out of its way to celebrate, rather than deride, the new Warsaw by showing a giddy, exhausting, guided tour of the capital. In contrast to the leisurely tours portrayed in "We Are Visiting Warsaw," *Adventure in Mariensztat* portrays the Złocień choir in folk costumes running after a tour guide as he points to and names the new-old sites of Warsaw. The walking tour starts at the statue of the Warsaw Mermaid located on the bank of the Vistula River,[49] continues to Mariensztat near the tunnel of the Trasa W-Z, stops at the Sigismund III Vasa Column on Zamkowy Square, travels part of the Royal Route (Trakt Królewski) along Krakowskie Przedmieście and Ujazdowskie Avenue (Aleje Ujazdowskie) to Łazienki Park, only to zigzag up through Warsaw's central district, Śródmieście, for a moment of respite at the fountain in front of the movie theater in Muranów, resulting in a six-and-a-half mile hike through the capital city that can be mapped according to the cues given by the guide (figure 16). The mapping in this sequence, however, is not created by visual cues captured by the camera. Rather, it is outlined by the tour guide, who lists and points to places that are mostly outside the camera's frame (figure 17).

Figure 18. The guide (Edward Dziewoński) leading the Złocień choir on a walking tour of Warsaw in *Adventure in Mariensztat* (dir. Leonard Buczkowski, 1953).

The comedy of the sequence results from the guide's rapid listing of Warsaw's sites and the heads of the members of the choir quickly turning to and fro, following the guide's arm as he points now left, now right, now behind. The rapidity of the sequence comes from its editing, with the two minutes consisting of twenty-six shots, or an average of one shot per four or five seconds. The sense of speed is also intensified by the exhausted Złocień choir, who are out of breath and barely able to keep up with the guide (figure 18).

In the film, mapping functions within the narrative not only as a means of giving the choir a tour but also as an invitation to the audience to visit the capital. When mapped, the path of the tourist sequence flaunts the main sites of Śródmieście, from the left bank of the Vistula River to Marszałkowska Street (ulica Marszałkowska), and from Łazienki Park in the south to Muranów in the north. This sequence quickly and efficiently incorporates into the narrative a view of central Warsaw as a completely (re)constructed space. With the camera focusing on the members of the choir as they become more and more tired from the pace set by the tour guide, the audience is left with an image of the central part of Warsaw as a zone free of ruins and construction. Despite the focus of the camera on the choir, the movie calls attention to "seeing" and "visiting" Warsaw.

While calling attention to specific places, however, the film ignores others. For example, missing from the landscape of the film is the construction site of the Palace of Culture on which ground was broken in 1952, and which is located on the western edge of Śródmieście between Marszałkowska Street and what was then called Juliana Marchlewskiego Avenue (aleja Juliana Marchlewskiego, today Jana Pawła II Avenue). Likewise, during the filming of *Adventure in Mariensztat* the central neighborhoods of Mirów and Muranów were in mid-construction. Largely located within the borders of the Warsaw ghetto and destroyed during the Warsaw Ghetto Uprising in 1943, the complete lack of reference to their reconstruction (other than the movie theater where the choir rests during their tour) demonstrates how spatiality can be constructed to selectively exclude entire areas from its discourse. In this way, the tourist sequence of *Adventure in Mariensztat* becomes complicit in a narrative disfigurement of historical reality, bypassing unrenovated areas or major construction zones, and embracing a selectively defined narrative of space. Thus, the film is yet another example of what Bożena Karwowska describes as narratives about Warsaw's reconstruction that erase from communal memory that which no longer exists in architecture and which no one has any intention of physically reconstructing.[50] As regards both the Palace and the construction of postwar Muranów, both spaces were not only meant to be imbued with ideological meaning, but also triggered controversial, and—in the case of Muranów—traumatic, historical and cultural connotations. As such, they had no place in a *branża*-style soft propaganda film; and, like in the newsreels, the camera successfully selected its particular viewpoint, which ignored ruins for the sake of a propagandized Varsovian spatiality.

Cinematically, the tourist sequence quickly summarizes and reminds the audience of the successful reconstruction of the city for which the authorities took credit in newspapers and the PKF, and also constitutes one of the funniest moments in the film. It sets the lighthearted tone of the film and relies on poking fun at the tropes developed around the rebuilding of the capital, in particular listing the successes of reconstruction. This element of humor, however, specifically targets those iconic and symbolic elements of Warsaw that were associated with the "old" city. The tour highlights the most historically iconic elements of Warsaw: the Warsaw Mermaid, Zamkowy Square, the Sigismund III Vasa Column, Mariensztat, Łazienki Park, and the iconic buildings located along the Royal Route. It acts as a counterbalance to the socialist sequences at the start of the film, providing historical specificity.

At the same time, the comedic element of the sequence associates humor, and to some extent derision, with this old Warsaw. The exhausting pace set by the guide ends with Hanka breaking away from the tour and setting off on her own excursion through Warsaw. Though her desire to break away from the tour is precipitated by the guide's speed, it is equally motivated by his focus on the *wrong* Warsaw. When Hanka visits the city on her own terms, she rejects the "old" narrative and tourist path presented by the guide

Figure 19. Hanka's walking tour of Warsaw in *Adventure in Mariensztat* (dir. Leonard Buczkowski, 1953). Above: Hanka (Lidia Korsakówna) sees the Marszałkowska Residential District for the first time. Below: Architectural details of the Marszałkowska Residential District.

and not only searches for—but embraces—the new city. The Warsaw that she visits is not the capital of newly renovated historical monuments and reconstructions. Rather, Hanka is enchanted by a Warsaw of socialist symbols, workers, and construction sites. Her first stop is Dzierżyńskiego Square (plac Dzierżyńskiego) with a monument to Feliks Dzierżyński, a Bolshevik revolutionary and head of the Soviet Cheka.[51] She next visits the MDM, where she "soaks up" the new Warsaw and the audience sees close-ups of socialist-style facades and ornamentation (figure 19). The film's foray into old Warsaw ends when Hanka begins her own tour of what the movie states is the "real" Warsaw. For the remainder of the film, the "unique" Warsaw (as defined in the PKF) is relegated to the background. The socialist Warsaw becomes the movie's setting, save for Hanka and Janek's first date, which is a walk along the embankment of the Vistula River, past the headquarters of the Civic Fund for the Reconstruction of the Capital located on the corner of Jerozolimskie Avenue (Aleje Jerozolimskie) and Nowy Świat, toward Trzech Krzyży Square (plac Trzech Krzyży) and Łazienki Park, only to return to Mariensztat where they kiss at midnight. But the focus of these scenes is not on the city itself or on highlighting the reconstruction process. Rather, the city is normalized and serves as the backdrop for a budding romance. The rest of *Adventure in Mariensztat* is set on construction sites, in building or government construction offices, in homes, or at the Bricklayers' Recreation Center.

In comparison to the Warsaw of *Treasure*, or to the Warsaw of early postwar photobooks and newsreels, the Warsaw of *Adventure in Mariensztat* is no longer a space filled with angst about coming to terms with the debates and contradictions of Warsaw as a new socialist city with undertones of a bourgeois and aristocratic past. Instead, Mariensztat is used in the film as a bridge between old and new, aristocratic and socialist, past and future. In *Adventure*, Warsaw is a new city with undeniably old roots, foundations, street plans, and traditions. It is firmly rooted in these contradictions and seamlessly embraces them. But the film takes a firm stance as to where the "real" and "true" Warsaw is located: on construction sites and in the world of the peasant-worker. By the end of the film, Warsaw's importance as a reconstructed postwar capital becomes secondary to the socialist message of communal work or the ability of the system to provide workers with new housing and recreation spaces.

In both *Treasure* and *Adventure in Mariensztat*, touring Warsaw takes center stage as a clever if not obvious means of highlighting Warsaw, not only as the setting of the film but as a socialist success story. In *Treasure*, the bird's-eye view presents Warsaw as full of hope, while the bus and walking tours in *Treasure* and *Adventure in Mariensztat* highlight new-old historical monuments and sites, shops, office buildings, and housing complexes. The Warsaw scenes in these two films not only outline the success of reconstruction but also cast the city as a tourist destination, a place that embraces migration from country to city, and a place for professional and personal fulfillment.

In both films, however, Warsaw is a work in progress. As a primary catalyst in the films, the cityscape drives the narratives and motivates the characters to act. The city thwarts and challenges the characters, though it also inspires affection, hope, and joy. Ultimately, the new-old Warsaw can be admired, but socialist Warsaw represents a "better," "brighter" future.

Normalized Urban Space

While Buczkowski and Starski's movies *Treasure* and *Adventure in Marien-sztat* defined Warsaw's spatiality as a dynamic process, Jan Fethke and Jan Rybkowski's *A Matter to Settle* (1953) and Fethke's *Irena, Go Home!* (1955) primarily showcased a "normally" functioning urban space. The early 1950s was a time when Warsaw's (re)construction had indeed reached a turning point in its urban development, and the city's representation in these two films reflected this very phase. The exciting days of rapidly changing urban vistas are marginal to these movies. Construction sites briefly appear in the beginning of *A Matter to Settle*; otherwise, they are mere asides and are never shown again in the movie. In these films, Warsaw is not a historical or even marginally historicized place. Rather, the Polish capital is cinematically "normalized" and represented as a contemporary socialist city.

A Matter to Settle begins with a bird's-eye view of Warsaw filmed from the seventeenth floor of the recently renovated Prudential building, the tallest building in Warsaw at that time. Giving a 180° perspective filmed from the top of the skyscraper, this establishing shot consists of two long takes reminiscent of newsreel cinematography. The camera pans in an arc from left to right facing the Vistula River and showcases the rooftops of Warsaw's mostly reconstructed Śródmieście, beginning just north of the Prudential building (figure 20). Superimposed over the image of the city is a prologue to the film presented in static text and read by Andrzej Łapicki, whose voice was familiar to viewers as the PKF narrator until 1956. The first lines of the film are as follows:

> The view from the seventeenth floor of a Warsaw building is beautiful, isn't it? Let's take advantage of the rare moment when we can look at the city from on high, because walking everyday down there, down below, we constantly have to watch out for holes in the torn up streets, piles of bricks, and bulldozers and diggers that block our path. People say that the wind brings clouds of dust. And sometimes, even a tiny bit of dust in your eye can obscure the most beautiful view.

This opening sequence achieves a number of narrative goals. By identifying Warsaw and its (re)construction in the voice-over, it locates the film unmistakably in a specific time and place. By visually citing the cinematographic

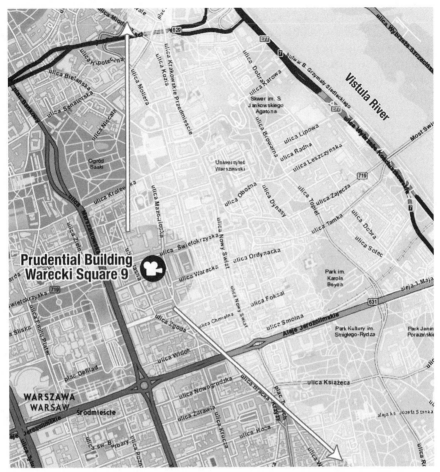

Figure 20. Mapping of opening shot from *A Matter to Settle* (dir. Jan Fethke and Jan Rybkowski, 1953). Visualization by Lorin Bruckner.

style of the newsreels and by casting Łapicki as the narrator, it provides this feature film with a degree of veracity suggesting that despite its fictionality, it is grounded in reality. With humor, the narration reminds viewers of the challenges and frustrations of the troublesome reconstruction process on the ground, details of which are notably ignored by the camera in the first moments of the film and which were rarely openly and critically acknowledged in other information sources, such as the newsreels. At the same time, the visual power of the panoramic shot of Warsaw, which lasts almost a minute and half, draws the audience's attention away from the construction suggested by the prologue, and supplants images of a rubble Warsaw in the audience's imagination with a beautiful city vista. This panoramic shot is followed by tracking shots through the streets of a fully functioning urban space, where buildings, streets, and bridges are filled with automobiles, pedestrians, and shops. From the very start, the film announces its geographic setting and shapes the meaning of this space with intention, emphasizing the best of this newly constructed socialist capital, and ignoring the areas still under construction. The first moments of the movie didactically predispose the audience toward focusing on the forest, not the trees. They remind the moviegoer to forget about the dust in one's eye, and they brandish the beauty of Warsaw in its most recent form.

The movie thus begins by cartographically communicating to the audience a specific geography and articulating the space of Warsaw both visually and verbally. The cartographic information comes from the panoramic and tracking shots in which we can orient ourselves using the most recognizable elements of the landscape: the scaffolding-bound Holy Trinity Evangelical Church, the Church of the Holy Cross located on Krakowskie Przedmieście, and the view of the Vistula River and its bridges. And in case the audience is unfamiliar with these architectural clues found among Warsaw's rooftops, the setting of A Matter to Settle is further confirmed by the voice-over, with Warsaw identified in the very first sentence. In this way, the opening shots of the movie function as a topographic projection that "can be understood as an image that locates and patterns the imagination of its spectators." Furthermore, the spatial strategy in the film "encourages its public to think of the world in concert with its own articulation of space."[52] It announces from the start that the film will teach Varsovians on the ground how to contend with spatial (if not social and/or socialist) construction by encouraging a mental mapping of reconstructed Warsaw, rather than one of Warsaw as a work in progress.

A Matter to Settle was released in 1953, a year after the MDM was completed and at the halfway point of Bierut's Six-Year Plan for Warsaw's Reconstruction. By this time, Mariensztat and the Trasa W-Z were already integrated into the everyday functioning of the city; the first phase of the Old Town's reconstruction was nearing completion; Łazienki Palace was under renovation; and ground had been broken on the construction of the Palace of Culture a year earlier. As the newest accomplishment in the socialist realist architectural plan for the city, the MDM was specially featured in the film, with the camera granting it significant screen time.[53] When Zosia (Gizela Piotrowska), a hero of socialist labor in a provincial shoe factory, comes to Warsaw, her first destination is a piano warehouse in the MDM where she has the titular "matter to settle": based on the promise of Stefan Wiśniewski (Bogdan Niewinowski), a reporter for Telewizja Polska, she is supposed to collect a new piano for the factory recreation room. She wanders the construction-filled streets from the train station to the MDM, and—despite the convoluted directions of a construction worker—quickly finds her way to Konstytucji Square. As she turns from a side street filled with scaffolding, construction equipment, and mud, the MDM is dramatically unveiled and the screen is filled with the image of an open, bright, clean, paved, and inviting square built in a monumental, neoclassical style. The filming of the MDM is presented as a "great reveal," an impression underscored by the crescendo of non-diegetic music from the popular song "Chcecie to wierzcie" ("Believe it or not") about falling in love with the MDM. As Zosia walks through Konstytucji Square looking for the piano warehouse, the camera follows her. Instead of our heroine being the object of the camera's attention, however, the lens admiringly focuses on the MDM, using wide-angle shots to display Konstytucji Square. These shots build iconographic connotations with the vistas of the MDM, placing them on the mental map of the filmgoer. At the end of the film, when all bureaucratic matters have been settled and the delivery of the piano has been secured, the MDM makes another important appearance in the movie, constituting its very last images. Here, the new construction is displayed for its own sake. There is little attempt to integrate this view of the MDM, or other images of the city, into the storyline. At the end of the film, the cityscapes function more like photos in a photobook and claim a documentary-like perspective, like that of the newsreels. Despite the construction on the side streets shown on Zosia's walk from the train station to the MDM, the focus of the film is not on Varsovian space being built, but rather on a city that exists as an "objective," "documentary" reality.

Such normalization of the cityscape is also apparent in Fethke's *Irena, Go Home!* In 1955 when the movie was made, ruins remained a part of Warsaw's landscape; in the movie, however, they are nonexistent within the frame of the camera. Warsaw in 1955 is presented as a backdrop, free of the scars of war. And more importantly, in this last Warsaw comedy before the onset of the Thaw the following year, the capital is not made unique. The main conflict in the film is the final frontier of communist-era social reconstruction, namely the equality of women in the workplace. Zygmunt (Adolf Dymsza), an engineer in a factory, refuses to allow his wife Irena (Lidia Wysocka) to work. Nonetheless, she signs up for driving lessons and becomes a cabdriver. To keep her secret safe, she masterfully balances her domestic responsibilities with her driver's training course until Zygmunt announces that the family will be leaving for vacation the following day, the day that she is to begin her new job. A series of misadventures leads to Irena's exceptional driving skills being showcased in a chase scene near the end of the movie as her boss and husband follow Irena's cab through Warsaw's streets in a pickup truck filled with geese. The chase scene would seem to offer another chance to showcase the city, as in *Treasure* or *Adventure in Mariensztat*. However, the camera does not take advantage of this opportunity. Instead, the viewer's attention is directed toward the chase and Zygmunt's growing pride in his wife's driving skills.

The path of the chase is secondary to the buildings blurred by rapidly moving tracking shots that feature rotating tires and screeching vehicles, all

Figure 21. Final "chase" scene through the streets of Warsaw from
Irena, Go Home! (dir. Jan Fethke, 1955).

set to the rhythm of fast-paced music (figure 21). *Irena, Go Home!* shifts
the camera's attention from characters gazing in awe at Warsaw, as is the
case in *Treasure* and *Adventure*, to showcasing a city of lively avenues filled
with cars and pedestrians, crowded housing complexes, playing children,
and comfortably accommodated workers and their families. While the audience is gazing at Warsaw's spatiality on screen, the characters are engaged in
the quotidian of their everyday lives. Twenty minutes into the film, there is
little focus on Varsovian icons and no attempt to define the setting as specific to the capital, other than a single shot when the pickup truck stops in
front of the Church of the Holy Cross on Krakowskie Przedmieście. Many of
the scenes in which Irena or her colleagues are driving show the chauffeurs
behind the steering wheel, while the surrounding streets are of little interest to the camera. Zygmunt's factory, his family's apartment, parks, the taxi
depot, and children's playgrounds define daily life in Warsaw. The capital in
Irena, Go Home! is even a place of leisure, where families spend their week-
ends entertaining themselves at amusement parks and restaurants. Gone are
the trials and tribulations of construction, chaos, ruins, and rubble—at least
in Fethke's comedic, fictionalized world. Instead, the panorama of Warsaw
and its environs has been successfully integrated into the background and
simply represents Warsaw as a city like any other. Such fictionalization of the
city space was, of course, motivated by the goal of creating an entertaining,
popular movie. At the same time, however, *Irena* was part of a broader normalizing narrative, toeing an ideological line about the success of Warsaw's
socialist reconstruction and co-creating Warsaw's image and spatiality on the
cusp of the 1956 Thaw.

By exploiting the cartographic potential of film in combination with the gaze of the camera via the characters, mapping occurs on multiple levels in the Varsovian comedies of the late 1940s and early 1950s. The films directly interact with their audiences' preconceived notions about Warsaw, as well as the narrative and socialist appropriation of Varsovian space promoted in the years after the war. Though Warsaw carries its own, non-cinematic history, these films attempted to re-create Warsaw's spatiality through the point of view of the films' characters, as well as by integrating the city space into storylines that promoted socialist values. These films thus contributed to the creation of a spatiality that helped read postwar Warsaw within a "proper" socialist context. In addition to the cartographic mapping that occurs on screen, the Warsaw comedies also provide an ideological map that was deemed vital to the building of socialism during this period.

Bridging the short-lived period of socialist realism in Poland, all four films represent the conflation between spatial and social (re)construction. As comedies they engaged the practical and social challenges that had been largely ignored in the PKF and other feature films: housing shortages and problems of communal living; the maze of construction throughout the capital; and the relationship between building a new capital and a new society shaped by communist ideology, particularly in the sphere of women's equality. These concerns may have appeared in other areas of official cultural production, but they were rarely tackled head-on. This critical task was left to the Warsaw comedies, which performed a jester-like function by openly and humorously acknowledging the difficulty of living in a capital with an underdeveloped urban and institutional infrastructure.[54] They extended the appropriation of the capital in official discourse beyond the urban development projects, which reflected socialist spatial concepts, and bolstered the meaning of the city as a place of socialist progress on all fronts. At the same time that these films fulfill a propaganda function, they possess a quality that remains enticing to viewers even today; they are pleasant romantic comedies or comedies of error that follow a prescribed narrative arc, humorously and formulaically treating courtship, gender relations, and the vicissitudes of everyday life.

As I indicated at the start of this chapter, the cinematography of the Varsovian comedies built an iconography of spatiality by featuring images of newly renovated, constructed, or reconstructed spaces of Warsaw. By cinematographically coding both new and "old" Varsovian spaces according to socialist norms, these movies participated in a broader project of socializing the capital by highlighting specific milestones in Warsaw's reconstruction and reducing the spatial reference points of the films to building and infrastructure projects most closely associated with socialist initiatives. As with the newsreels and photobooks, narrowing the geo-specificity to a handful of landmarks effectively silenced the urban spaces in between. At the same time, these movies aestheticized and objectified Warsaw's space, creating

destination markers and defining architectural landmarks. While not promoting one iconic locus, these films co-created communal imaginings of the
Trasa W-Z, Mariensztat, Old Town, Łazienki Park, and MDM, among others, that remain a part of Warsaw's spatiality to this day.

Chapter 4

✦

Reappropriating Warsaw and
the Palace of Culture

New York's Empire State Building. The Tower of London. Paris's Arc de Triomphe. Berlin's Brandenburg Gate. Warsaw's Palace of Culture and Science? Is it possible that for Poland's capital this "gift from the Soviet peoples [*narody*] to the Polish people [*naród*]" belongs on the list of internationally recognizable architectural symbols? According to polls taken in 2013 by *Gazeta Stołeczna* (*The Capital Newspaper*), the Palace of Culture and Science (Pałac Kultury i Nauki) is the architectural object most recognized and most likely to be remembered by foreign tourists visiting Warsaw.[1] Despite its prominence in the city center, however, some insist that the Palace of Culture is far from the most appropriate symbol of the Polish capital—architecturally or otherwise—because of its Soviet provenance. They point to other, more politically or culturally "appropriate" icons, such as the Warsaw Mermaid, the Sigismund III Vasa Column, the colorful new Old Town (Stare Miasto), or Łazienki Park, which evoke legends of Warsaw's founding and Polish history rooted in a distant past. Yet none of Warsaw's material artifacts has generated the same complex sense of spatiality as the Palace of Culture and Science, whose discursive meaning has been written, rewritten, adapted, and transformed from the very moment it was handed over for public use on July 21, 1955.[2]

Those who know little about the history of the Palace may remember it for its size and "unusual" style. Located in the central district Śródmieście, it is integrated into Warsaw's built environment. Though new skyscrapers surround the Palace, its pinnacle continues to rise above all the other buildings, and it is one of the first buildings you see when exiting from the main railway station Warszawa Centralna or from the Centrum metro station (figure 22). It stands out from among the numerous new glass skyscrapers because of its height (777.6 feet), 42 floors (with two more underground), 141-foot spire, welded steel frame filled with poured concrete and hollow bricks, and the characteristic facade made of beige ceramic tiles manufactured in a remote Soviet factory in the Urals. The total square footage of the Palace is 1.12 million, while its footprint in the center of Warsaw is 380,000 square feet

Figure 22. The Palace of Culture and Science as
seen from the exit of the Centrum metro station,
June 2015. Photo by the author.

or almost nine acres.[3] According to the Palace of Culture's website, it was
the second tallest building in Europe when completed in 1953, and as of
2017 it is the tallest building in Poland and the nineteenth tallest in Europe.[4]
In addition to its current architectural and geographic centrality to the city,
the Palace possesses a practical value. Located in the Palace is the 2,880-
seat Congress Hall (Sala Kongresowa), which once hosted communist party
congresses and today serves as a concert and event venue. There are four
theaters, four museums, a movie theater, seven educational institutions, restaurants and cafes, bars and nightclubs, a post office, shops, and prime office
space.[5] It is a mini-city unto itself.

The statistics about the Palace of Culture say little, however, about the
discourses inscribed onto the edifice that make this "gift from Stalin" a
quintessential example of architectural palimpsestuousness. One of the most
popular riddles about the Polish capital asks, "Where can you see the best
view of Warsaw?" The answer: from the thirtieth-floor viewing terrace of
the Palace of Culture, because from there you can't see the Palace itself. This
is such a simple riddle, yet it reveals so much about the multifarious meanings of the skyscraper. On the one hand, the Palace is just "a pile of stones

glued together with cement."[6] On the other hand, the Palace demonstrates the power of architecture and the built environment to generate historical, political, and aesthetic debates that reflect and shape the lived experience of place. After the fall of communism there were campaigns to tear down the Palace, calling it an ulcer on the cityscape. These campaigns focused on the Palace as a symbol of Soviet oppression that should be erased from Warsaw's material and metaphorical skyline. Others waged campaigns to preserve the Palace as one of the best examples of Polish socialist realism, seeing it as an indispensable monument to Poland's past, a valuable historical symbol of twentieth-century totalitarianism.[7] In the end, the "preservationists" won the debate, with the Palace of Culture being declared a *zabytek* (historical landmark) in 2007. Despite conflicting opinions about the building, one thing remains certain: the Palace of Culture and Science is one of the most eloquent urban palimpsests of the Polish capital that, according to the historian and journalist Beata Chomątowska, has absorbed over sixty years of Poland's history. As she aptly notes, the Palace of Culture may be "a pile of stones glued together with cement," but the "rest is all in our heads."[8]

While in the previous chapters I have sought to understand how the official, communist-era narrative of Warsaw's spatiality was shaped across genres by focusing on modes of expression that combine image and text, this chapter aims to expose the competing narratives superimposed on one another and attached to one specific object of Warsaw's landscape, the Palace of Culture and Science, which was originally named "Pałac Kultury i Nauki im. Józefa Stalina." By focusing on a particular object of the built environment as a case study, we can get a deeper understanding of how the layers of the urban palimpsest are created. As Daniel Cooper Alarcón has demonstrated, narratives of a palimpsest simultaneously work together and compete against one another. These competing narratives are integrated and interlock—that is, they rely on one another to create a larger discursive environment in which the competition between narratives prevents a "dominant voice from completely silencing" others.[9] Alarcón's notion of the urban palimpsest coincides with Yuri Lotman's model of the semiosphere as discussed in the introduction. Both concepts—"palimpsest" and "semiosphere"—provide us with models of relationality between competing or counter-discourses, and show how a dominant narrative rarely eradicates or silences alternative narratives but rather displaces them. In this chapter, I study a selection of these interlocked narratives about the Palace of Culture to show the interdependence between official and counter-discourses. Such an approach demonstrates how narratives dynamically react to one another and rely on one another for their continued evolution. To get at the core of this process, this chapter engages four layers of the Palace's narrative: (1) the original intentions underpinning its construction and design; (2) the officially promoted narrative as constructed in newsreels called the Polish Film Chronicle (PKF); (3) the 1956 counter-narrative developed in the nonfiction short film *Warszawa*

1956 (*Warsaw 1956*); and (4) the textualization of the Palace of Culture and its surrounding environs in the literary and cinematic works of Tadeusz Konwicki, whose fascination with the edifice has shaped an entire generation's perception of its meaning and symbolism.[10]

Original Intentions, Unexpected Appropriations

The Palace of Culture and Science was the most eloquent architectural expression of communist ideology in postwar Poland. Symbolizing Poland's communist future and the idea of socialist "brotherhood among nations," the Palace's construction was part of the socialist plan to rebuild Warsaw as an antidote to a prewar capitalist city that was presented in official discourse "as a fragmented, socially alienated and poverty-stricken environment."[11] In addition to the ideological foundation of the design, the Palace was meant to "socialize" postwar cultural and political Varsovian life by providing spaces for activities that would forge the new socialist Pole, and turn peasants into proletarians. The building was to provide a place to educate Polish youth in the ways of socialism and hold communist party congresses, as well as be a place from which to witness military parades that would pass through Defilad Square (plac Defilad) at the foot of the building. Many of the decorative details of the building were created to express basic tenets of ideology through their design. Allegorical sculptures representing socialist versions of poetry, philosophy, literature, music, history, and theater were designed to adorn the edifice and grace its niches. Other niches were filled with statues representing youth from around the world (Africa, China, India, the Middle East, and the Soviet Union) and workers of various industries (a mechanic, a miner, an agricultural worker, and a construction worker). Included in the building's exterior décor was a statue of a young man holding a book by Marx, Lenin, Engels, and Stalin, as well as a ribbon-like bas relief on the portico, which represents socialist authority. It portrays "peace-loving workers holding hands . . . a dove, and a banner, together forging a bright future."[12]

Desiring to fulfill the socialist dictum "national in form," the Palace's Soviet architect, Lev Rudnev, traveled with his team to such cities as Kraków, Toruń, and Chełm to identify traditional elements of Polish architecture and incorporate them into the final design.[13] But the primary requirement—that the building be "socialist in content"—would be purportedly satisfied by the Palace's Soviet design, labor, construction, architectural intertextuality, and intended practical value that would "fill" the Palace with ideological meaning from its very inception. The official narrative about the Palace of Culture, which was carefully controlled from the moment the project was unveiled, "indisputably" promoted the building's "Soviet origin." This narrative located the genesis of its design in the *stalinskie vysotki* or "Seven Sisters" of

Moscow, skyscrapers built in the late 1940s through the mid-1950s.[14] In particular, the new Moscow State University building, also designed by Rudnev, was promoted in propaganda as a precursor to the Polish skyscraper and underscored Soviet innovation and technical advancement.

This narrative of the Polish Palace and the Soviet *vysotki*, however, remained silent about one inopportune fact: the construction techniques and designs used to erect these Stalinist-era skyscrapers were based on technical advances in the United States and the turn-of-the-century Renaissance Revival in American architecture. The Soviet versions were thus modeled on such edifices as the Municipal Building in New York and the City Hall in Oakland, California (both built in 1914), the Wrigley Building in Chicago (completed in 1924), and New York's Savoy-Plaza Hotel (built in 1927 and demolished in 1965).[15] Important to note is that the Soviet and American skyscrapers were different in one important respect: the footprint of the buildings. American advances in the construction of skyscrapers were propelled by market factors, namely the rising cost of real estate in large cities, which led to taller buildings that took up less ground space. From the Soviet perspective, such market-driven parameters were of no concern, nor were the construction costs of any supposed consequence. Rather, the Soviet skyscrapers, including Warsaw's Palace of Culture, were meant to project power and status, looming high over their respective cities and taking up significant square footage within their landscapes.[16]

The Palace had its detractors from early on.[17] The Stalinist building clashed with Warsaw's "traditional" architecture being reconstructed in other areas of the city, distracted attention from the reconstruction of Warsaw's Old Town that was occurring at this time, and took resources—especially labor—from other building sites in the city. In a Warsaw rising from ruins, every construction worker was valuable and, despite Soviet promises to provide materials and labor for the Palace's construction, the Polish side of the equation had to supply a significant amount of both. This was particularly true in the early stages of construction when the Poles were building housing for Soviet workers, the construction zone still needed to be cleared of rubble, and foundations were being laid.[18] Furthermore, the work environment on the construction site of the Palace developed a reputation that refuted the ideals of peace and harmony attached to the edifice's construction in official discourse. Wages for Polish workers on the Palace were considerably lower than on other construction sites in Warsaw; workers were supervised not only by technical engineers but also by the state Security Apparatus; and exaggerated rumors regarding unsafe working conditions circulated broadly.[19] Negative attitudes toward the Palace were intensified by the impact of its construction on Varsovians' everyday lives, especially those who were forcibly resettled in order to make room for the "Friendship" housing development built for Soviet workers in Jelonki, a neighborhood five and a half miles west of the future Palace. More disruptive, however, was the size of the Palace's construction site in Śródmieście, the very center of Warsaw, which resulted in the demolition of extant prewar buildings and streets, the elimination of residential areas, and the displacement of over 4,000 people from their homes at a time of housing shortages.[20]

Despite the negative impact on many Varsovians, the Palace continued to be promoted in official discourse as a "didactic symbol of Communism's imminence."[21] Called "Stalin's Palace," it was considered a physical manifestation of the Soviet leader's authority over the Polish communists and, by extension, Poland. Jakub Berman, who was largely responsible for Stalinist-era repressions in Poland, recollected that Stalin "wanted his gift to be something great, splendid, symbolic and unrepeatable . . . a palace that would be visible from any point in the city."[22] This prominence was meant to change the shape of Warsaw's streets and skyline and to call attention to the connection between postwar Poland and the Soviet Union. The Palace was not only designed as the new center of Warsaw, but it was meant as a symbol of socialist order that would build a bridge between the communist government and its people, and that would help establish a "supranational" order constructed by the Soviets with Stalin at the center.

The Palace was also seen as an important pedagogical tool that would teach Poles the basics of socialist realist architecture, a sort of SocReal 101. As the prominent architect Szymon Syrkus stated:[23]

> There may be some doubt as to whether the Palace of Culture and Science, this first-born child of communism, is not being built too early in our country that is still in the stormy process of building socialism. But such doubts are completely unnecessary, since this edifice will be more than an immovable guiding star on our road to transforming the old, princely, royal, magnate, bourgeois, capitalist Warsaw into a socialist Warsaw. The construction of this edifice will be a great dialectical school of the socialist building industry. It will be a mighty stimulus for our architecture, for our art, for the construction of our cities and for our building techniques.[24]

Considering that two of the first major socialist infrastructure projects had been completed by the time ground broke on the Palace, calling the skyscraper the "first-born child of communism" was telling. For some, the Palace was, indeed, the first truly communist edifice untainted by the remnants of old Warsaw city plans. Unlike the Trasa W-Z or the Marszałkowska Residential District (MDM), both of which were more or less built *into* Warsaw's landscape, the Palace was built to transform it. Furthermore, as a Moscow-inspired project, it moved the scope of Warsaw's construction and spatial considerations away from the local and toward the East.[25] As such, this also meant that the Palace was as much a pedagogical tool as it was a practical, material manifestation of socialist principles. This lesson plan was based on showing how the Palace fit into Warsaw's landscape, a task perfectly suited for visual propaganda like photobooks or newsreels.

In this context, the official narrative about the Palace of Culture overlapped with the narrative developed around Warsaw's reconstructed historical areas, even though the Palace was a *new* architectural project. As with the language devoted to promoting the Old Town, the dictum "socialist in content, national in form" was used to describe "Stalin's building." As I have already mentioned, "socialist content" referred to the intended practical value of the building as a place for the socialist worker, while "national in form" meant that the architect Lev Rudnev incorporated decorative elements from historical buildings across Poland into the design.[26] Nonetheless, the "national form" of the Palace, manifesting itself in baroque stucco ornamentation and those elements borrowed from what had been identified as traditional Polish architecture, remained compromised at best.[27] The palatial quality of the interior ornamentation that purportedly cited Polish design was seen by some as out of place in contrast with the socialist values it was meant to represent, while others failed to see its connection with national tradition. For still others, the reference to the edifice as a "palace" seemed ironic in the context of rejecting the aristocratic aspects of Poland's history and architecture, while for others the word "palace," grafted onto a socialist construct, consigned to the proletariat their rightful material legacy.

The location of the monumental Palace of Culture on an enormous square was considered an important refutation of interwar "bourgeois urban development" which, according to the official narrative, had filled this area of prewar Warsaw with crowded housing resulting from capitalist exploitation.[28] Furthermore, this central location satisfied socialist urban planning ideals, which required that traditional city centers, with town squares, plazas, or churches, be replaced by factories or presidia. In the case of Warsaw, this meant shifting attention from prewar areas considered central to the city, such as Saski Square (plac Saski), and constructing the Palace as the new center of the capital marked by its soaring silhouette.[29] The Palace's prominence, opulence, and size denoted it as a secular-sacred center akin to the role of a cathedral within the urban landscape.[30] And like the organizational relationship of a cathedral to its smaller churches, the Palace of Culture was a central manifestation of *domy kultury* (literally, houses of culture) that proliferated throughout the communist period and which functioned as spatial conduits for propaganda, ideology, and indoctrination. In fact, in early planning stages for Warsaw's reconstruction, a version of a Stalinist-style skyscraper was referred to as "Centralny Dom Kultury" (Central House of Culture).[31] Once completed, the Palace of Culture stood as the epitome of these humble, local spaces found in large cities and small villages alike. In its final conception, the Palace was to extend in multiple directions, connecting ideology and people with the surrounding space. It reached horizontally across Poland ("locally" or "nationally") while vertically exerting pressure from above, both literally and figuratively.

Figure 23. Socialist realist sculpture on the Palace of Culture. A trace of the name "Stalin" is visible below the names "Marx, Engels, Lenin." Stalin's surname was removed in the wake of the 1956 Thaw. Photo by Paweł Moszyński, used under GNU Free Documentation License and available at https://pl.wikipedia.org/wiki/Pa%C5%82ac_Kultury_i _Nauki#/media/File:Removed_Stalin.jpg.

In addition to the Soviet and ideological origins of its design, the timing of the Palace's construction contributed to its historical and symbolic meaning. Ground broke on the construction of the Palace of Culture and Science on May 2, 1952, when Warsaw was in its third year of the six-year plan for the capital's reconstruction and Poland was in its third year of its six-year centralized economic plan.[32] Over the next three years, the skyscraper would become part of the Varsovian skyline, while the streets in its vicinity would be taken over by a construction site that would eventually become Defilad Square. At one point, this square was to boast a monument to Stalin, but such plans never came to fruition for lack of a politically correct design.[33] As the Palace of Culture transformed day-by-day over the next three years, so too did the Soviet world. The Palace's completion in 1955 coincided with Stalinism's denouement. By the time Nikita Khrushchev gave his 1956 "Secret Speech" denouncing Stalin and the following period of de-Stalinization ensued, the Palace of Culture's official, intended ideological message had weakened, if not altogether lost its raison d'être, not only as a monument to Stalin but as a central symbol of communist ideology and politics. These changes created a discursive vacuum that was ripe for palimpsestic erasures and the surfacing of other narratives that competed with those originally inscribed onto, and intended for, the Palace. Most literally, Stalin's name was removed from the building's entrance, as well as from a sculpture adorning the building (figure 23). And after the start of the Polish Thaw in October 1956, the intense focus of propaganda on the Palace disappeared from official discourse.[34] Ever practical and useful, however, it did not disappear from peoples' everyday lives. By being centrally located and fitted with sports facilities, museums, cinemas, and theaters, the practical value of the building remained its primary asset. And in many respects it truly served as a cultural center, housing the theaters that remain there today, as well as such institutions as the Polish Academy of Sciences (Polska Akademia Nauk).

The (re)appropriations of the Palace of Culture were not limited to the building's socialist or practical everyday use value. From popular films to serious literature, the Palace made numerous "appearances" that were well outside the parameters of a carefully controlled official discourse about the edifice during the Stalinist era. In the early stages of its construction, negative assessments of the Palace of Culture were not allowed to appear in print or otherwise.[35] Nonetheless, there were cracks in the propaganda foundation that made it into the pages of at least one novel as early as 1955: Leopold Tyrmand's *Zły* (translated as *The Man with the White Eyes*). Writing about the Palace from the perspective of the character, Kuba Wirus, Tyrmand described it using language that was far from the optimistic phraseology of official discourse. More nuanced and subtle than the panegyrics on the Palace appearing officially, the Palace of Culture in Tyrmand's novel is part of a nostalgically perceived postwar Varsovian cityscape. In this description, Tyrmand writes about the "permanence" of a city that is being reconstructed, a permanence marked by the centrally located "cream-colored, gigantic obelisk." At the same time, this edifice triggers in the character a sense of mourning for a past to which he cannot return, to the passing of the "pioneer-like atmosphere" of the immediate postwar years.[36] For Tyrmand/Wirus, the Palace is a sign of change, but not a change that anticipates the brighter, better, socialist future. Rather, it sheds light on the past through its monumental immovability. In actuality, Tyrmand's opinion about the Palace was harsher, a sentiment he recorded on the pages of his *Dziennik 1954 (Diary 1954)*.

> Some see it as the Russki fist, others are speechless with delight. . . . I was one of its most implacable enemies . . . I spat knowingly on the proportions, an un-Warsaw-like scale, the pompous style . . . If it had been covered with glass and left alone, we'd have been happy enough . . . The horror socrealism has materialized in the very center of the city is like a blooming growth on a drunkard's nose.[37]

While some, like Tyrmand, characterized the Palace of Culture as a blight on the cityscape, others eventually adapted it humorously. For example, it was a favorite setting of the director Stanisław Bareja, who used the Palace in his movies of the 1970s and 1980s as a means of heightening the irony of his comedies.[38] In *Co mi zrobisz, jak mnie złapiesz* (1978; *What Will You Do When You Catch Me?*), Bareja undermines the Palace's ideological intentions by using it as the setting for a game show based on labor competitions between teams of surgeons racing to finish an operation. In his cult classic *Miś* (1980; *Teddy Bear*), an infirm government minister spends his days on the thirtieth-floor viewing terrace as a cure for what ails him. And what Polish film aficionado can forget Andrzej Wajda's cinematic re-signification of the edifice in the political classic *Man of Marble* (1976), when his heroine goes to the strip club located next to Congress Hall in order to interview a former agent of the Security Apparatus who is now the club's manager. And the Palace was featured in a number of other movies under the direction of Krzysztof Kieślowski, Janusz Kondratiuk, and Andrzej Munk,[39] each time adding to the building's palimpsestuous layering, each time engaging the ideological discourse on some level, only to counter, reject, and rewrite it. In the end, the Palace symbolized not so much socialist dominance, but rather the historical and political tensions of an entire era.

As a symbol of Soviet oppression and the imposition of communism, the Palace might have easily suffered from discursive neglect, as did many imperial Russian structures ignored by nineteenth-century Polish authors who carefully described a "Polish" Warsaw while avoiding references or descriptions of anything "tsarist."[40] But unlike its nineteenth-century architectural predecessors, the Palace did not disappear from photographs, films, music, or literature, fueled by its palimpsestuousness. Like its official narrative that was reshaped by the political and ideological changes of the mid-1950s, the competing discourses associated with the Palace stemmed from its time, place, and practical value. As the journalist and satirist Michał Ogórek observed, "there were many events that tried to drown out the [Palace's] ideological nature."[41] It was in the Palace of Culture where Western publications not vetted by censors could be bought at international book fairs and exhibits or in the bookstore of the Polish Academy of Sciences. With time, the size of Congress Hall made it a popular venue not only for obligatory party meetings, but for events that directly or indirectly challenged the ideological meaning of the space. This included performances of popular Western artists, such as the Rolling Stones in 1967, the first major Western rock band to perform behind the Iron Curtain; Miles Davis (1988) and Ray Charles (1984), who performed in the annual Jazz Jamboree; and Leonard Cohen, whose *Various Positions* tour came to Poland in 1988. By "filling" the Palace with cultural or intellectual encounters with the West, such events rewrote the purported "socialist content" of the building and textualized the Palace with lived experiences that countered its ideological symbolism.[42]

Visualizing the Palace of Culture

Tucked away amid 367 pages of photographs, statistics, renderings, maps, and quotes presenting Bolesław Bierut's Six-Year Plan for Warsaw's Reconstruction is a folded plate with a small photograph of Marszałkowska Street (ulica Marszałkowska) in 1949. In the foreground is a bus followed by a car. In the background are buildings, tall and erect, next to architectural skeletons that will be torn down in the coming years. The ruins are barely discernible because the image is only 4.75 by 3.5 inches. The focus of the photograph as framed is empty space cleared of rubble waiting to be filled. Unfold the 13-by-18-inch page and you reveal an early rendering of what we know today as Warsaw's Palace of Culture. In 1949 it was labeled "Centralny Dom Kultury" (Central House of Culture). Fast forward to April 15, 1952. The first news segment of the PKF in the movie theater that week was entitled "Dar przyjaźni" ("A Gift of Friendship"). It reported on the newest socialist project of Warsaw's six-year reconstruction plan. Though the segment lasted only seventy-seven seconds and had a seven-sentence voice-over, it was packed with four references to the Soviet Union. It underscored that the Soviet Union "takes upon itself the responsibility of building the monumental Palace of Culture and Science in Warsaw." It stated that this building was a gift, "a new, beautiful symbol of assistance, the kind that Poland continues to experience from the Soviet Union." And it stressed that the "Palace of Culture and Science will be a magnificent monument and symbol of the eternal friendship that joins the Polish nation with the Soviet one." According to this segment, the Palace was a "symbol of new, socialist relations that unite our two countries" (PKF 17/52:1).

This PKF segment communicated a typical message about the Palace of Culture propagated during the period of its construction. Throughout this time, information about the building was broadly circulated, though also carefully controlled and coordinated by the Information Department of the Government Plenipotentiary's Office (Biuro Pełnomocnika Rządu). Between 1952 and 1955, there were almost 5,000 articles published about the building or in which it was mentioned, and another 291 radio broadcasts that reported on it. The broadcasts and articles—geared towards eliciting the emotional engagement of the audience—informed listeners and readers about the progress of construction, technical innovations in building skyscrapers, the cooperation between Soviet and Polish urban planners, and the superiority of Soviet laborers.[43] The newsreel coverage of the Palace's construction followed this propaganda program, incorporating discursive points outlined by the Information Department into its choice and presentation of topics. Between April 1952 and December 1953 alone, the newsreels featured at least a dozen reports related to the Palace. These segments covered everything from the planning process to the groundbreaking. They recorded the construction process step by step, scaffold-by-scaffold, floor-by-floor. Featured in the PKF were the signing of the agreement between Poland and the Soviet

Union to construct the building (PKF 17/52:1); the planning process, which portrayed cooperation between Polish delegates and Soviet planners, as well as a scale model of the future Palace of Culture and footage of demolition work that made room for the structure (PKF 19/52:1–4); the pouring of the foundation (PKF 33/52:1); regular updates on the progress of construction; and the final mounting of the spire (PKF 49/53:1–4).

The verbal message about the Palace of Culture and Science in the newsreels echoed and condensed propaganda phrases found in other media. "Socialist content" was underscored through references to the building as a "gift" or "palace" of friendship symbolizing brotherhood and Soviet generosity (PKF 17/52:1, 33/52:1, and 47/52:2–9). The construction of the skyscraper was hailed as a demonstration of highly skilled and superior construction methods developed by the Soviets. While the voice-over toed the ideological line, the visual power of the film camera was unsurpassed by anything found in newspapers or radio. What the newsreels did, which articles, radio reports, or grainy photographs in newspapers could not, was show how empty urban space was being dynamically transformed from rubble into a socialist skyscraper. The PKF adopted a socialist realist aesthetic with which viewers were familiar from other editions of Varsovian-themed news segments. Like other construction sequences in the PKF, those filmed about the Palace of Culture focused on construction equipment, the process of construction, and workers. The camera dynamically panned from left to right and back, or followed the 360° circle of excavator buckets, cranes, and other equipment. Likewise, the layering of construction activity on multiple planes within a shot—an aesthetic developed to ensure that construction sites seemed eternally active— was an integral element of the presentation of the Palace on screen.

Unlike "generic" construction sites, however, the large scale of this construction project intensified the socialist propaganda message and provided an opportunity for hitherto uncharted territory in the world of Polish newsreel cinematography. Pouring the building's foundation and erecting the steel structure of the building were colossal feats of engineering, even without the official propaganda glorifying the Palace's construction (PKF 47/52:2–9). But filming the construction of a skyscraper was the ultimate challenge for PKF cinematographers like Karol Szczeciński, who became known for his daring camera work that recorded construction workers from precarious angles and positions.[44] By sitting on a crane or steel beams, he captured the final stages of construction up close and intimately, bringing the higher levels of the skyscraper's construction to PKF audiences (PKF 47/53:4–6 and 49/53:1–4). Camera angles that emphasized the height of the building increased the sense of danger associated with construction, while close-up shots of workers provided audiences with a sense of "being there" and relating to this colossus on a human level. This was all done in the hopes of bringing the building closer to the people and inserting the Palace of Culture not only into the Warsaw skyline, but also into the city's spatiality and map. Each segment included numerous long shots that contextualized the building in Warsaw's broader landscape. These segments also presented a contrast between the size of the structure and those working on it. The steel framework of the Palace was often filmed from low or high angles, while workers themselves were filmed at eye level. The segments relied on the contrast between close-up, intimate portraits of workers, long shots showing Warsaw from a bird's-eye view, and intermediate shots focusing on the height of the Palace. The PKF showed the workers not only as heroes but as daredevils "who know no fear and don't suffer from vertigo" (PKF 47/53:4–6). Welders were filmed sitting on beams and harnessed to the building's steel frame with Warsaw's landscape in the background. Such a composition demonstrated the vertical appropriation of Varsovian space, the courage required for executing such a project, and the human element involved in building the Palace, and by extension, socialism. The atypical cinematography underscored the structure's exceptionality and iconicity, reinforced its incongruity with the rest of Warsaw, and accentuated its interference with Warsaw's panorama.

Nonetheless, attempts were made to present the Palace of Culture as a natural part of the cityscape. For example, a news segment that was purportedly about the Warsaw Fotoplastikon as a source of archival information about "backwards" Warsaw ended with a shot of the Palace's reflection in the display window of the gate at 51 Jerozolimskie Avenue, the entrance to the courtyard where the Fotoplastikon is located.[45] Though the voice-over does not name the Palace of Culture, it associates this image with the words "today's life is faster than in old Warsaw. Faster and more beautiful!" emphasizing the Palace of Culture as a ubiquitous part of the contemporary city (PKF 51/53:11). Another image of the Palace integrated into Warsaw's landscape can be seen in Szczeciński's filming of the installation of the spire, which is constructed of hundreds of mirrors. The newsreel shows a reflection of the entire building, reduced on the one hand to the frame of a mirror, and on the other, gaining status as having permeated even the smallest corner of the city (PKF 47/53:4–6). This cinematic integration of the Palace into Warsaw's landscape through reflections had a potential double meaning, suggesting that the Palace could be seen not only from all angles, but—like a specter—could omnisciently see all.

As the PKF cinematically integrated the image of the Palace into the urban landscape, it also established the Palace as an urban icon and as a cartographic reference point. In order to achieve this, cinematographers used wide-angle shots, like in the opening of "Iglica w górę!" ("Spire Going Up!"), to locate the skyscraper in the center of socialist Warsaw by filming it from the newly constructed Marszałkowska Residential District (MDM) about one and a half miles away (PKF 47/53:4–6). From that perspective, the camera avoided filming rubble that existed in the vicinity of the Palace, and visually relocated the city center to the area of the skyscraper by showing it protruding above the MDM. Such a shot provided a *socialist* Varsovian landscape that

Figure 24. Bernardo "Canaletto" Bellotto, *A View of Warsaw from Praga*, 1770. The Royal Castle in Warsaw—Museum, inv. no. ZKW438. Photo by Andrzej Ring, Lech Sandzewicz. Reproduced by permission from Zamek Królewski w Warszawie—Muzeum.

remapped Warsaw for audiences and created a new iconography of the city. This socialist framing of the skyscraper from the point of view of the MDM countered and displaced well-known panoramic views that gave preference to such geospatial reference points as the Royal Castle located on Zamkowy Square (literally, "castle square"), or other similar loci, and competed with Bernardo "Canaletto" Bellotto's paintings of the capital that portray views of Warsaw from across the Vistula River (Wisła). (See figure 24.)

Regardless of the PKF's attempts to present the Palace as an integrated part of the Varsovian landscape, there remains in the newsreels a sense of the edifice's otherness. This otherness was underscored in the newsreels by building a visual connection with the design of the Moscow State University (MGU) building. As early as 1951, before ground had been broken on the Palace of Culture, the PKF introduced to Polish audiences the Palace of Science that was being built for MGU, and in 1952 it reported on the final moments of the MGU building's construction (PKF 13/51:11 and 42/52:12). Such segments acted as a preview of the future Polish Palace. Shown on the PKF screen during the first months of the Polish skyscraper's construction, the almost-completed MGU building was presented as the gold standard of Soviet construction and architecture. The segments were filmed by a Soviet newsreel crew, and their cinematographic techniques also set standards for the way in which Polish crews filmed the Palace of Culture a year later.

The Palace's Soviet connection was part of the PKF in other ways as well. A 1953 segment commemorating the eighth anniversary of Warsaw's "liberation" by the Soviets featured two memorials or monuments:[46] the Monument to Brotherhood in Arms (Pomnik Braterstwa Broni), erected in 1945 and described in the segment as a memorial to honor Soviet heroes and the soldiers of victorious armies; and the Palace of Culture and Science, described as a "monument to the brotherhood of labor and to the friendship between our nations" (PKF 4/53:3–8).[47] Of the three-minute segment, thirty seconds were devoted to the 1945 monument, while the remaining two-and-a-half minutes focused on the Palace of Culture. The segment focused on the speed at which the skyscraper's construction surpassed that of other Warsaw buildings, the skill of Moscow-raised construction crews, and the contribution of special construction elements that came from the "steel mills of Magnitogorsk, factories in the Urals, and plants of the Donbas." The fact that Poland also contributed labor and materials to the building of the Palace was completely cut out of the report, as were the economic problems associated with the construction of the building, the aforementioned dissatisfaction of Polish construction workers on the job, and the displacement of thousands of people to make room for the building and its surrounding parade grounds. This failure to acknowledge problems associated with the Palace's construction, as well as the focus on its non-Polish genesis, whether in the PKF or elsewhere in official discourse, contributed greatly to the notion that the Palace was an "imported creature" imposed on Warsaw's skyline.[48]

Unlike other projects, like the MDM or the Trasa W-Z, the Palace remained tainted by a veneer of foreignness. While the Palace was embraced for its practical value, propaganda failed to justify the form and aesthetics of the building within Warsaw's spatiality. Though the PKF's presentation of the Palace reinforced the meaning of the building as a socialist symbol and integrated it into the spatial iconography of Warsaw, the otherness of the structure dominated the PKF screen. The monumental scale of the building was a creative boon for cinematography, but this cinematography reinforced the distinction of the Palace within Warsaw's postwar spatiality. The PKF connected the Palace with communist ideology, marked it as a foreign import and ideological imposition, and added a palimpsestic narrative layer to the Palace that destabilized the official discourse proposed by propaganda.

Already after Stalin's death in 1953, newsreel attention to the Palace of Culture and Science began to taper off, and with the 1956 Thaw it became "strangely invisible" if not physically in the skyline, then at least rhetorically.[49] In both photobooks and newsreels, direct verbal attention was not given to the Palace of Culture, though it remained ever-present, either in the background or as part of the cityscape. In photobooks, the Palace was shown as a central point of Warsaw's skyline but was barely referenced or described in accompanying text. A similar phenomenon occurred in newsreels. For example, in the first color newsreel, which reported on the military parade commemorating the 1,000th anniversary of Poland's statehood and the twenty-second anniversary of establishing the People's Republic of Poland, the Palace of Culture is physically present but aesthetically and rhetorically absent (PKF 31A/66). It is the background for politicians and dignitaries sitting in the reviewing stand on Defilad Square, but the building is filmed only from the street level at its base. Gone are the metatextual days of scale models of the Palace being paraded through the streets, as shown in PKF reports featuring the 1952 and 1953 May Day parades (see chapter 2). The most important contrast, however, is that the wide-angle shots of Warsaw in the film capture newer, less palimpsestic architectural objects, as do numerous shots of Warsaw from the sky, showing flyovers displaying military aircraft. Yet there is little cinematographic attention granted the Palace itself.

Occasional commemorative news segments, such as one entitled "Trzydziestolatek" ("The Thirty-Year-Old"), would bring the Stalinist structure back to the PKF screens. By that time, however, the images of the Palace of Culture would be read through almost two decades of aesthetic strategies that played with and against socialist realism (PKF 29/85:3). The soundtrack of "The Thirty-Year-Old," for example, set the socialist realist camera work and outtakes from the 1950s to disco music, following Andrzej Wajda's stylization of the building in the opening shots of *Man of Marble*, while the voice-over focused not on the building's ideological value, but rather on its practical value as a venue for sports events, international conferences, and political gatherings. Shots of the Palace showed the skyscraper from various angles only a few blocks away from Defilad Square, and the voice-over called the edifice "a new topographical sign visible from afar," explaining that for many years it had been surrounded by ruins and was referred to as "the wild west." The segment ended with before shots taken from the thirtieth-floor viewing terrace in 1956 contrasted with after shots from the mid-1980s. This news segment was not focused on constructing a narrative about a socialist city. Rather, it deconstructed and even abandoned the previous, official narrative and used socialist images of Warsaw's space against the ideology that had originally inspired them.

Warsaw 1956: Rewriting Ruins and the Palace of Culture

The effect of the 1956 Thaw on Varsovian poetics in nonfiction film is exemplified by a six-minute PKF segment entitled *Warsaw 1956* (directed by Jerzy Bossak and Jarosław Brzozowski) that became part of the Black Series. The film begins with a meta-socialist realist representation of Warsaw: a 45-second series of wide-angle shots that cite a decade of the PKF's aestheticization of the capital, summarize Warsaw's reconstruction progress, and showcase newly constructed streets, housing projects, playgrounds, and palaces. The wide-angle perspective, shot at eye level and showing the horizontal breadth of the capital, presents a well-ordered urban space constructed for the proletariat. This sequence ends with a vertical view of the most illustrious socialist edifice in Warsaw, the Palace of Culture and Science. In *Warsaw 1956*, the Palace of Culture is filmed from the base of the building to its pinnacle in one continuous shot that monumentalizes the edifice as in earlier PKF segments reporting on everything from the groundbreaking in 1952 to the finishing touches in 1955.

This monumentalizing shot is followed by a sudden cut to a long shot of the Palace from about 1.3 miles south of the city center that counters the visual discourse developed in previous PKF segments. It pushes the skyscraper into the background and places it in the context of rubble and a still-decimated, postwar landscape that fills the foreground of the screen. This image is in direct contrast to the pre-1956 PKF image of the Palace, which located it amid construction sites and a reconstructed landscape. The image is accompanied by a voice-over announcing that the Warsaw traditionally shown on the newsreel screen is not the focus of this segment. Rather, the narrator informs audiences that "the year 1956 is different from previous years. The chronicler looks carefully and sees that which in the past he tried not to notice." In contrast to the representation of Warsaw during the previous decade, the proximity of the Palace of Culture to the rubble and ruins shown in this segment shrinks the horizontal and vertical reach of the newly (re)built city, underscoring the ironic deployment of the preceding montage, which focused on clean, new, sleek, expansive spaces and buildings. Cunningly placed as the transitional image between the first and second part of the film, the vertical image of the Palace of Culture unifies the seemingly incompatible horizontal planes presented on screen by underscoring the simultaneous presence of rubble and renovation. Furthermore, the following sequence of images and the voice-over cut the monumentalism of the Palace of Culture down to size, beginning with the first image of "real life" represented by a woman hanging laundry in the foreground as the Palace of Culture looms insignificantly in the back.

In a symbolic move, the woman pulls a bedsheet across the laundry line, a move that draws a curtain between the Palace of Culture and the gaze of the audience, further underscoring the irony of the film. After all, the film claims that the previous PKF segments about Warsaw were pulling the wool over the eyes of viewers; in a reverse motion (meaning the *covering up* of the Palace), this bedsheet acts as a curtain, announcing a series of "true" revelations. As the film historian Paul Coates observed, this sudden re-contextualization of the Palace of Culture in the film "triggers the awareness that there are facades in Polish reality . . . [even] though [the Palace of Culture] is presented as if it were the crowning instance of the 'Warsaw palaces' mentioned on the soundtrack."[50] The remainder of the film shows Varsovians living in dangerous, unsanitary ruins converted to dwelling places and presents close-ups of bug-infested garbage and soup. The living quarters are filmed using worm's-eye shots of a four- or five-story courtyard in ruins, a filming technique that simultaneously cites and rejects the Palace of Culture's monumentalization. These dissonant images are accompanied by an equally disquieting soundtrack, culminating in the final two-and-a-half minutes during which the camera follows a toddler roaming along the edge of the ruins. As the child walks toward the precipice, the soundtrack falls quiet except for the sound of the toddler's feet shuffling toward the perilous edge. About to fall into the chasm, the child trips and loud cries echo among the ruins. This echoing cry serves as the soundtrack to a montage of Warsaw's ruins, calling to mind images of the capital in the immediate aftermath of the war. The child's haunting cry lingers through the entire final minute of the film.

On the most obvious level, *Warsaw 1956* worked as an exposé. While adopting a stance of self-criticism and taking the blame for trying "not to notice" this "other" Warsaw, the film's sudden attention to the unpolished and unidealized side of Varsovian space was an obvious critique of the authorities. The irony of the commentary cannot be lost even on those unfamiliar with the era. The film's juxtaposition of renovation and ruin acknowledged on screen the presence of two Warsaws, whose existence was more than obvious to the residents of the capital, the "real" one being written out of the official Warsaw narrative until the 1956 Thaw. On one level, the juxtaposition of ruins with renovated or new construction that celebrates the Palace of Culture as the crowning glory of Bierut's Six-Year Plan for Warsaw's Reconstruction could be construed as a typical before-and-after sequence creating linear or diachronic representations of the city and underscoring the progress achieved in reconstruction. On another level of the film, however, images of ruins undermined the visual harmony of the first minute of the film and introduced a sense of simultaneity between the ideal and the real that had not been present in official Varsovian poetics up to that time. Clearly rejecting the socialist aesthetic that required the PKF to focus selectively on the "new" and "better" Warsaw, the film marginalized the Palace of Culture by presenting a stark contrast between the geometric, standardized socialist and socialist realist portrayals of the capital, and a realistic, gritty, naturalist aesthetic that showcased the squalor of Varsovian life only a few blocks from the city center.[51]

Tadeusz Konwicki's Palace of Culture

In a 1952 poem called "Palace of Culture," Jan Brzechwa, an author and poet best known for his contributions to children's literature, compared the edifice to a palace in a fairytale that reaches into the clouds where birds fly. The second half of this seventeen-line poem, however, moves out of the realm of fairytale and into that of official narrative: the Palace is described as a generous gift from the Soviet Union, and the poetic "I" declares that Polish-Soviet friendship will last "like faith in man" and "love for a child." Such socialist realist literary representations of the Palace were not uncommon in the early 1950s. Often structured as odes otherwise reserved for the likes of Stalin, they almost always fixated on the height of the Palace and its dominance in the skyline. The fashion for creating such idyllic panegyrics on the Palace of Culture did not last long, however, and they barely circulate in Polish culture today. Nonetheless, while the Palace of Culture in official discourse was displaced as a meaningful ideological "text" after the Thaw, it remained present in almost all other areas of culture, such as literature, feature film, and music. Rather than expounding on its socialist value, however, portrayals of the Palace after 1956 tended to critique, resist, and reconfigure the narrative nodes originally delimited by propaganda.

In fact, dystopian images of the Palace of Culture are more common today. In the realm of popular music, for example, the punk band Dezerter recorded a song named after the building. Written in 1985, the lyrics sing of the Palace as a symbol of "communism's fist" crushing Central Europe and tell of a man standing at the foot of the Palace ready to blow himself and the building up. Later, in 2001, Dezerter band member and drummer Krzysztof Grabowski designed an album cover depicting Godzilla breaking off the spire of the Palace (figure 25). According to Grabowski, the Palace was built in Warsaw "to remind everyone who was in charge. To show the little ones, how the [communist] authorities were great and powerful."[52] In contemporary literature, the Palace of Culture also continues to make an appearance. In Michał Łukasiewicz's novel *Warszawska Atlantyda* (1997; *Varsovian Atlantis*), the skyscraper serves as a penal colony. Such contemporary dystopian visions of the Palace of Culture, however, are preceded by the complex and palimpsestically layered imaginings that appear in the works of the author-director Tadeusz Konwicki (1926–2015). In 1986, Konwicki said that he tried "to make the Palace of Culture stand for something more than it really does," to "inspire [his] world [with it]," "to rescue it as best [he] can." He concluded, however, that his efforts were all for nothing.[53] But what did Konwicki mean when he stated that he tried to make the Palace of Culture "stand for something else"? How and why does one "rescue" a building, poetically, rhetorically, or discursively, as in Konwicki's case?

At the core of Konwicki's statement is a clue about the Palace of Culture and its palimpsestic nature. While Konwicki himself considered his attempts to "rescue" the Palace as failed, he nonetheless inscribed onto it meaning and symbolism that extend far beyond a "pile of stones glued together with cement." Few readers of such novels as *Wniebowstąpienie* (1967; *Ascension*) and *Mała apokalipsa* (1979; *A Minor Apocalypse*), or viewers of the films *Jak daleko stąd, jak blisko* (1972; *How Far Away, How Near*) or *Lawa: Opowieść o "Dziadach"* (1989; *Lava: A Story about "Forefathers' Eve"*) can forget the vivid literary and cinematic images of the Palace of Culture presented in these texts. From the description of the Palace as an "obelisk" or

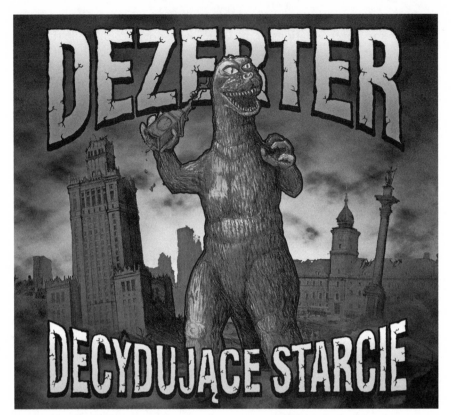

Figure 25. Album cover for the CD *Decydujące Starcie* (2001) by the punk band Dezerter. Artwork by Krzysztof Grabowski. Courtesy of Krzysztof Grabowski.

"lit-up pyramid" that incessantly towers over the Warsaw skyline in *Ascension*, to the representation of the edifice as the shoddy architectural work of Soviet construction in *A Minor Apocalypse*, to the twentieth-century image of the Palace of Culture presented in conjunction with Adam Mickiewicz's nineteenth-century *Dziady* (*Forefathers' Eve*), Konwicki actively created new layers of meaning for the Palace and grafted them onto both the building and Warsaw, using the city space as a cathartic conduit for what Katarzyna Zechenter calls a process of "coming to terms with postwar Polish history and politics."[54]

But what are the textual layers that Konwicki brings to the rhetorical facade of the palimpsest-Palace? What lies at the root of his inscriptions onto Warsaw's and the Palace's spatiality? To understand the answers to these questions, we need to understand that Konwicki's artistic oeuvre—whether we consider its literary or cinematic manifestation—was shaped by a continual artistic reassessment of the wartime experiences of his youth as they related to the establishment of the communist regime in Poland.[55] Born in 1926, he was a teenager during World War II.[56] He finished high school during this time in a system of underground education that promoted a patriotic ethos shaped by nineteenth-century notions of romantic nationalism. Inspired by the idea of self-sacrifice for a nation oppressed by foreign powers, he joined the Home Army in 1944, fought against the Nazis and then Soviets in what is now Lithuania, and in 1945 escaped to a new Poland whose territory was redrawn according to agreements reached at the Yalta Conference earlier that year. Having witnessed what he considered the moral and ethical failures of the wartime partisan movement, Konwicki became disillusioned by the patriotic spirit on which he was raised and, after the war, turned to socialism and the socialist realist aesthetic. He joined the communist party in 1951, a decision not uncommon among intellectuals of his generation who were called *pryszczaci* or "the pimpled ones."[57]

The trauma of the war years described in his novel *Rojsty* (1956; *Marshes*) precipitated his rejection of the Polish cultural paradigm of patriotic martyrology (i.e., messianism) and his embrace of socialism. After 1956, however, Konwicki entered a period of ideological skepticism, reassessing his personal and professional relationship to the communist regime. Disenchanted by the unfulfilled promises of communism and his comrades' ideological turnabout, Konwicki reevaluated his commitment to the communist regime, eventually rejecting it as well. This was a turning point in his career. Shedding himself of all belief systems, he felt liberated from the shackles of ideologies and freed from the demands of a higher authority. This would be the start of his most productive and creative period. Beginning in 1966, Konwicki lost favor with the regime after he signed a letter of support for the philosopher Leszek Kołakowski, who had been expelled from the Polish United Workers' Party. By the mid-1970s, Konwicki was publishing in *drugi obieg* ("second circulation" or the alternative press), starting with *Kompleks polski* (1977; *The Polish Complex*).[58] In the mid-1980s he once again published in the official press, though in his texts he openly derided the censorship office.[59] For the rest of his career, his reassessment and critique of the ideological systems around him—be they "socialism" or "messianism"—are important reference points for understanding his literary and cinematic oeuvre, and they provide the context in which he textualizes Varsovian space, in particular the Palace of Culture and its environs.

In some of Konwicki's Warsaw narratives, like *Zwierzoczłekoupiór* (1969; *The Anthropos-Specter-Beast*) and *The Polish Complex*, the Palace appears to exude its political implications but not structure the space in the novels.[60] In these texts, Konwicki does not explicitly develop a poetics of the Palace. For example, in *Nowy Świat i okolice* (1986; *New World Avenue and Vicinity*)[61] the Palace does not appear, despite its relative proximity to the main spatial concept suggested in the title ("Nowy Świat Street") and the Palace's looming (though textually invisible) presence in the Warsaw skyline. In

Ascension, *A Minor Apocalypse*, and *Lava*, however, Konwicki appropriates the Palace as the foundation of his Varsovian poetics, calling attention to the edifice's height and monumentalism, to its role as a symbol of totalitarianism, and to its potential as a counter-ideological space. Through his portrayal of the Palace in these texts, Konwicki redefined and appropriated the meaning of the Palace by playing on the tension between the intended original signification of the building and its function as a dynamic edifice that could be redefined in a localized (Polish), urban (Varsovian), and historical context, while simultaneously grappling with the legacy of the Polish romantic paradigm that was so influential on Konwicki's generation. In *Ascension* and *A Minor Apocalypse*, Konwicki critiques communist ideology by applying a Christian discourse to the Palace. In turn, this invokes and places into question the Polish romantic messianic and martyrological tradition in popular (not literary) culture. In *Lava*, however, the symbolic power of the Palace of Culture visually peaks and explodes into what seems to be Konwicki's final statement on the process of re-signifying (i.e., "rescuing") the skyscraper, and it results in what may seem like a surprising and naive embracing of Mickiewicz's messianic message.

While the Konwicki texts analyzed here are from the 1960s and 1970s and take this project beyond 1956, they provide an important reference point for *Mapping Warsaw* and demonstrate that despite the changes in politics and propaganda surrounding both Warsaw and the Palace of Culture after 1956, the "official" discourses deployed in the decade after World War II continued to appear and reappear in various cultural contexts. A witness to the establishment of the communist regime in Poland and the struggles of "patriots" and "socialists" alike, Konwicki was deeply attuned to the political and ideological environment around him. He was also deeply attuned to the language and imagery of the regime and actively played with the discourses it created. Like the films of the Black Series, he appropriated the socialist aesthetic to reveal its weaknesses, textualizing postwar Warsaw, and in particular, the Palace of Culture. At the same time, the process of rewriting and reappropriating Warsaw's space relied on the interlocking of his narrative with that of the communist regime. Without one, the other could not exist.

The Palace of Ascension

Konwicki's novel *Ascension* (1967) is set in Warsaw on the eve of the Harvest Festival (*dożynki*) being celebrated at the Tenth Anniversary Stadium (Stadion Dziesięciolecia) located east of the Palace, across the Vistula River.[62] The main character of the novel, Charon (named after the mythological figure who accompanies the dead across the River Styx into Hades), awakens under a bridge with amnesia and a fist-sized hole at the back of his head. The novel follows him through the city, accompanied by criminals, prostitutes, homosexuals, and peasants, as he searches (albeit half-heartedly) for his identity.

This realist description of the text, however, does not take into account the fact that Charon is half-dead. He wanders through Warsaw in a purgatory-like state, existing in the space between life and death.

In *Ascension*, the Palace of Culture is present as the central, vertical axis of the city. Its force is so strong that even the amnesiac has a preexisting memory of the structure: it is the only building in Warsaw that he remembers by name. The force exerted by the Palace, however, does not come from its ideological power but rather from the building's verticality. From the perspective of Stalinist architecture, the vertical axis of the Palace and similar buildings was to represent the power of the state and the successful abolishment of the pre-communist past. Konwicki, however, reinterprets this vertical axis in religious terms. He inscribes onto the Palace a tension between upward and downward forces and recasts the edifice as a cathedral-like conduit between heaven and earth (with certain hellish aspects). This is implied, of course, by the title of the novel, *Ascension*, which indicates an internal, divine function of the Palace and dynamic upward motion, in contrast to the quasi-divine function of the Palace in socialist terms (i.e., the verticality of the building as representing the "New Faith," to borrow Czesław Miłosz's phrase).[63] This vertical, religious imagery is further exploited when Konwicki describes the Palace's elevators as "cathedral-like confessionals" ("katedralne konfesjonały") that go up but not down (173, 180–84).

In opposition to the upward movement indicated by the title of the novel, Konwicki further undermines the originally intended significance of the Palace by describing the bowels of the building through which Charon enters on two occasions. The most detailed descriptions of the building's interior are of a fictional, secret underground passage that begins in the Śródmieście Train Station (located on the northwest corner of Defilad Square) and leads to the basement of the Palace. It is only in relation to this passage created by Konwicki's imagination that the "great donor" of the Palace of Culture, "Józef Wissarionowicz," or in other words Stalin, is mentioned (31). Charon enters the Palace through this passage, making his way into "a bathroom, full of fancy baroque stucco" with "a layer of black dust"; he passes through a dark and defunct engine room with only one light bulb; and walks past a room of convoluted pipes "shining with dew like rime" and rhythmically dripping water that smells of rust (32). This decrepit image of the Palace and its mechanical systems also works in opposition to the title of the novel by introducing an earthly and even downward focus (i.e., a focus on hell), and indicates that the Palace is neglected and deteriorating at its core.

The re-signification of the building is further underscored by Konwicki's use of a religious discourse to describe the areas around the Palace. Charon compares Defilad Square to the valley of Josaphat, the site of the Last Judgment in the book of Joel (25). He also experiences a baptism of sorts in the fountain located at the foot of the Palace, which brings him a sense of health and wholeness. As he enters the pool, stepping "deeper and deeper into this

Figure 26. View from the thirtieth-floor terrace of the Palace of Culture, looking east toward Praga, a district of Warsaw, June 2015. Photo by the author.

rain full of light," he realizes that "the inconceivable state in which I found myself the previous afternoon had passed. I waited for the moment when my memory, locked by a sudden cramp, would reopen" (169–70). Charon's cleansing and renewal are, unfortunately, short-lived. At the end of the novel, Charon and his companions gather on the thirtieth-floor viewing terrace of the Palace hoping to catch an eastward glimpse of the Harvest Festival taking place across the river; however, a monotonous gray sky obscures their view (181). (See figure 26.) Because the elevators do not work, the thirtieth floor of the Palace becomes their eternal purgatory from where they look upon a city that is scarred by the vagaries of history (177, 180). From the viewing terrace, Charon sees a city that suffers in perpetual ruins and is covered by wounds and ulcers. The aerial view of Warsaw provided by the Palace of Culture reveals (rather than masks) the lack of "healing" and progress promised by the communist system. From the viewing terrace, Warsaw looks like a city experiencing the final agony of life with no hope of resurrection (177, 180). At the end of the novel, the cathedral-Palace is defunct as both an ideological symbol and a religious one, for despite the height of the building, the view towards Moscow (and ideological salvation?) is obscured and the viewing distance is limited by the contingencies of weather. Any hope of ascension is dashed.

The Road to Golgotha: A Minor Apocalypse

Written in 1979, *A Minor Apocalypse* is the first-person narrative of a second-rate dissident writer chosen by members of the dissident movement to self-immolate as a political protest in front of the Palace of Culture.[64] The condemned man spends his final day circling the edifice and narrating the events leading up to his self-immolation. Like Charon in *Ascension*, the narrator encounters people from all walks of life along his journey. He meets a young Russian woman, who is a specialist in the technology of self-immolation and the granddaughter of Lenin's lover; a paralyzed soldier of the Home Army; dissidents, whose motivations and opposition to the communist regime are called into question; party officials and Security Apparatus agents, who beat and interrogate the narrator; and a group of women sitting around a bonfire in downtown Warsaw. In addition, the writer is followed throughout the novel by a young fan, Tadzio Skórko, who carries a blue gas canister filled with the deadly liquid and a book of matches. Near the end of the novel, Tadzio reveals himself as a Security Apparatus agent.

The novel is set on July 22 during a party congress held in honor of an unnamed anniversary of the People's Republic of Poland. Called the National Holiday of Poland's Rebirth (Narodowe Święto Odrodzenia Polski), July 22 was a holiday designated by the communist government to commemorate the 1944 Manifesto of the Polish Committee of National Liberation (PKWN), which asserted the legitimacy of a communist, Moscow-backed leadership in Poland. This was a date reserved for unveilings of particular import to the authorities: elaborate anniversary parades, the 1952 adoption of the name "People's Republic of Poland" and a new constitution, and the anniversaries of numerous "openings" associated with the rebuilding of Warsaw. On or around July 22 the following projects were handed over to public use or completed: the new Poniatowski Bridge (1946), the Trasa W-Z (1949), the Tenth Anniversary Stadium (1955), and the Palace of Culture (1955). Thus July 22 was closely associated with commemorating multiple stages of the "rebirth" of Warsaw and the communist endeavor to claim the capital.

As in *Ascension*, the poetics of *A Minor Apocalypse* appropriates the space around the Palace of Culture by deploying religious imagery. Like Charon, the narrator of *A Minor Apocalypse* compares Defilad Square to the Valley of Josaphat (114). Furthermore, the Palace of Culture is assigned the role of a sacrificial site or a communist-era "Golgotha." While the term "Golgotha" is not used in the text, it is implied by the narrator's reference to the streets that circle around the Palace and the events that take place in the novel as his "stations of the cross" ("stacje męki"; 39, 180, 189). The parallel between the events of the novel and the Christian narrative of Jesus Christ's persecution (particularly the Roman Catholic version as portrayed by the Stations of the Cross) is direct, though distorted. The gas canister stands in for the crucifix;[65] Tadzio Skórko, who carries the canister for most of the novel and betrays the narrator to the secret police, represents a merging of the figures of Simon of Cyrene (Station 5: Simon of Cyrene helps Jesus carry the Cross) and Judas. Other perverted parallels between *A Minor Apocalypse* and the Stations of the Cross include the fact that the narrator is chosen by his colleagues to die (Station 1: Jesus is condemned to death); Tadzio Skórko says to the narrator: "I should wipe your face. But I don't have a kerchief" (Station 6: Veronica wipes the face of Jesus) (189); the narrator meets a group of women (who all happen to be former girlfriends) around a bonfire (Station 8: Jesus meets the women of Jerusalem) (171–78); and the narrator is mugged on the streets of Warsaw (Station 10: Jesus is stripped of his garments) (166–67). The novel ends with the narrator walking toward the Palace of Culture, just before self-immolation. Though the parallel with the Christian narrative of the Passion ends before crucifixion, death, and resurrection, we can see that Konwicki is engaging a redemptive-like discourse, with the Palace of Culture cartographically and conceptually in the center of the text. Through narration, Konwicki endows the edifice with the *potential* of becoming a sacred site, though not in the sense of communist ideology. But this martyrological discourse—according to Konwicki's story—is highly unstable.

The rewriting of Warsaw's streets as a Via Dolorosa counter-narrates the communist discourse represented by the Palace and its surrounding environs. It rhetorically pushes against the numerous July 22 demonstrations, mini-parades, and commemorative banners that the narrator encounters along the path from his apartment to the Palace's Congress Hall where the party congress is being held. Despite the importance of the communist holiday, each banner that the narrator reads indicates a different anniversary year: one reads "30th"; another "40th"; yet another "50th." Most importantly, however, almost all the banners read: "We have built socialism!" ("Zbudowaliśmy socjalizm!"), a paraphrase of the 1950s propaganda slogan "We are building socialism!" ("Budujemy socjalizm!"). By changing the phrase from the imperfective, present tense "budować" (to build) to the perfective past "zbudować" (to finish building or to complete the building process), Konwicki pulls together the abstract concept of building socialism on the level of ideology with the concrete act of building state enterprises and rebuilding Warsaw—both considered to be physical manifestations of socialism. By changing the aspect and tense of this common propaganda phrase, Konwicki attacks the communist regime on multiple levels. He points out its failures vis-à-vis its own ideology and presents "new" "socialist" Poles on the streets of a city that, when seen from the thirtieth-floor viewing terrace of the Palace in *Ascension*, is scarred and broken. At the same time, the narrator's experience of the propaganda-filled streets as a personal road to martyrdom shows how the meaning and symbolization of space is fluid and malleable, and reveals the limits of the effectiveness of propaganda.

Note that the narrator's potential act of suicide works on an abstract, ideological level (as political protest), while Konwicki's use of a religious metaphor to narrate his character's final hours rewrites the Varsovian space around the Palace, rhetorically claiming it away from a communist discourse. In *A Minor Apocalypse*, the space that was rebuilt purportedly according to the language of socialism is now recast according to Christian, martyrological language, evoking in the Polish context the civic martyrology of Polish romanticism. On the one hand, Konwicki engages this religious discourse to rescue the Palace of Culture by giving it a "redemptive" meaning, but because the religious discourse is so closely associated with the nineteenth-century Polish romantic, messianic tradition, à la Mickiewicz, his attempts are thwarted. Thus, the narrator's self-immolation constitutes a *potentially* significant and secularly redemptive act of protest against the communist party that will *hopefully* "liberate" Poland. But such a result is doubtful.

The value of the narrator's self-sacrifice is wrought with uncertainty not only because he recognizes the futility of his act, but because he also recognizes the complicity of his fellow dissidents in the perpetuation of the communist regime. Furthermore, the code of civic messianism no longer holds credence in the postwar era. When the narrator asks the paralyzed soldier of the Home Army, who spent a decade in Soviet gulags and is the embodiment of the messianic imperative, whether or not he should self-immolate, the soldier cannot give him an answer: "Then we knew everything, and now we know nothing. The world was simple then. Now it's deformed. It either deformed itself or it was deformed by that long draft of ideology that came through like a hurricane" (45). The soldier's non-answer suggests that in a new age, the cultural legacy of the revolutionary romantic spirit is no longer valid. Konwicki similarly undermines this cultural paradigm in *The Polish Complex*, where a flashback to the 1863 January Uprising ends with the question "Was it worth it?"—a question that interrogates the value of personal sacrifice for the cause of Polish independence (67).[66] The communal messianic sacrifice as defined by Mickiewicz and which led to generations of Poles culturally indoctrinated to sacrifice themselves for the cause of Poland becomes diluted in *A Minor Apocalypse* as the personal sacrifice of a second-rate dissident, who is uncertain whether or not he can go through with the act of self-immolation; who questions the value of the sacrificial act; and who recognizes that his self-sacrifice will have little or no redemptive impact on Polish history.

In *A Minor Apocalypse*, therefore, the narrator's pending self-immolation is simultaneously a protest against communism, as well as a rejection and refutation of the enactment of the Polish romantic paradigm and its directive. After all, the narrator neither willingly nor heroically walks to his death. He is not eager to redeem his countrymen. And the value of his death to the dissident movement is questionable. I should also mention that from a historical and intertextual perspective, the act of self-immolation in *A Minor Apocalypse* alludes directly to the suicide of Ryszard Siwiec, who set himself on fire during the 1968 Harvest Festival at the Tenth Anniversary Stadium.

Though *Ascension* was written prior to Siwiec's act, the gaze of Charon and his companions from the viewing terrace of the Palace toward the stadium where the Harvest Festival is being held becomes an extra-textual historical reference in *A Minor Apocalypse*, in which the self-immolation of the narrator, like Siwiec's own act, will be suppressed by the authorities and thus fail in its impact. In sum, the Palace of Culture as a vertical conduit between heaven and earth in *Ascension*, and as Golgotha in *A Minor Apocalypse*, calls attention to the martyrological narrative of Polish romantic messianism, while at the same time employing a Christian discourse (sullied by Mickiewicz's messianic message) to "rescue" the Palace from its socialist signification. But redemption never arrives.

Rescuing the Palace: Lava

In 1989 Konwicki filmed *Lava: The Story of "Forefathers' Eve,"* an adaptation of the nineteenth-century romantic drama *Forefathers' Eve* by Adam Mickiewicz.[67] In the film, Konwicki combines a traditional interpretation of the play using period costumes and settings with brief street shots and panoramic views of contemporary Warsaw and a focus on the Palace of Culture. As the subtitle of the film suggests, *Lava* demands to be read as a layering of interpretations and historical events associated with *Forefathers' Eve* from its creation to the 1989 film adaptation. The image of the Palace rests at the center of Konwicki's reinterpretation and, through his camera lens, the skyscraper reaches a new level of signification.

Considered the greatest work of Polish romantic drama, *Forefathers' Eve* consists of four parts written between 1820 and 1832. Loosely connected by the old Slavic pagan custom of *dziady* (communicating with the dead), the four parts of the play explore such romantic themes as the exaltation of folk tradition and the cult of death, and the individualism of the heroic poet-bard. Most influential on the romantic legacy in Polish culture is part 3, written in 1832. It is based on Mickiewicz's arrest in 1823 and depicts Polish revolutionary romanticism through the story of a young man and his schoolmates arrested under conspiracy charges by the government of Tsar Alexander I. Part 3 famously contains the "Improvisation," during which the main character, Konrad (formerly Gustaw), rails against God for his silence and indifference to humanity, and—as a self-proclaimed poet-bard—demands from God "mastery over souls" (*rząd dusz*).[68] It is in part 3 that Mickiewicz expressed in dramatic form his concept of messianism: the Polish romantic paradigm of self-sacrifice for the service of one's country. In combination with the rise of nationalism and romantic revolutionary ideas, Mickiewicz's messianism, which sought to alleviate the scars left by the failed November Uprising (1830–31), contributed to a cult of individual martyrdom for the sake of the Polish (and therefore, European) collective. This cultural paradigm, highly popularized by the end of the nineteenth century, became engrained in Polish

collective consciousness during the January Uprising (1863), and again during World War II (especially during the Warsaw Uprising of 1944).[69]

By creating a film version of this quintessentially messianic drama, Konwicki seems to abandon his critique of the martyrological imperative which
occurs on the pages of such novels as *Marshes, The Polish Complex,* and *A
Minor Apocalypse.* However, in an interview about the making of the film,
Konwicki explained that he made it in part due to his impatience with the
Polish messianic paradigm. He stated that "even if throughout history we
have yielded to deformity, we can't constantly say that we were distorted
by history. We must stand on our own two feet."[70] Furthermore, in a con-
versation with the film critic Tadeusz Sobolewski, Konwicki described his
adaptation of *Forefathers' Eve* as an insolent project that does not end tragi-
cally with a vision of Konrad as a wounded exile in Siberia, but rather as a
project with a "happy ending."[71]

While it is always important in the case of Konwicki to question the
author's self-effacing and ironic assessment of his work, the above statements
are consistent with Konwicki's general rejection of the Polish martyr complex. As such, what could be misconstrued as a wholehearted embracing of
the romantic paradigm (i.e., making a film based on *Forefathers' Eve*) must
be interrogated more deeply. Like in *Ascension* and *A Minor Apocalypse,*
Konwicki's critique of the messianic paradigm overlaps with his critique of
communism, precisely in the image of the Palace of Culture. Through skillful
incorporation of the Palace into the diegetic structure of the film, Konwicki
sets out on a multipronged, expansive mission of cultural and political critique: (1) to create a film that is a historical vessel by presenting Poland of the
partitions, World War II, and the People's Republic as one continuum; (2) to
put an end to ideology—"socialist" and "messianic"; and (3) to "rescue" the
Palace of Culture, which is a synecdoche for "Warsaw" and thus a synecdoche for "Poland," in the service of achieving points 1 and 2.

To accomplish these goals, Konwicki masterfully merges the four dispa-
rate parts of the drama, reordering the acts and lines of the original. He
also emphasizes the play's continued relevance through a historical reading
that juxtaposes the nineteenth-century text with images from World War II.
For example, Konrad's debate with God over his silence and inhumanity is
visually punctuated by documentary footage from the war, including images
from Auschwitz, the Warsaw Uprising of 1944, executions, and emaciated
corpses.[72] By integrating these images into the film, Konwicki reinterprets
and adapts Mickiewicz's drama for a new era. And here is where Konwicki's
Palace of Culture makes an appearance. Konwicki relies on the viewer of
Lava to read the Palace as a palimpsest. The edifice appears in the film three
times, with the first image reprised at the end of the film. Presented during
the opening credits, the Palace is shown from a distance in the center of
Warsaw's skyline, while the Guardian Angel (Grażyna Szapołowska) rushes
toward the city. The angel's trajectory and gaze is on a linear, diagonal path

directly toward the Palace. This shot comes immediately after the Poet (Gustaw Holoubek) recites the first lines from the preface to part 3 of the play, which tell of Poland's martyrdom at the hands of Tsar Alexander I and N. N. Novosiltsev.[73]

The next shot shows the Guardian Angel on a crowded street in Warsaw, followed by a sequence of images presenting Jewish, Muslim, Roman Catholic, and Russian Orthodox cemeteries in Warsaw and Vilnius. These first shots and sequences use the Palace as a signal to the viewer that the film transgresses historical periods. Furthermore, the presence of the angel on the contemporary streets of the Polish capital acts as a symbol of Mickiewicz's continued "presence" in Polish culture even during the communist period.[74] Juxtaposed with the cemetery images, the view of the Palace of Culture also calls our attention to Warsaw not as a capital rebuilt under the watch of the communist authorities, but as both a symbolic and real cemetery.[75] In this way, Konwicki integrates into his film Poland's prewar multiethnic and multi-denominational population. The second image of the Palace of Culture appears in a long shot taken through the window of Gustaw's prison cell. This shot underscores the importance of the edifice to Konwicki's reading of *Forefathers' Eve* as a text that is dynamically present in and relevant to contemporary Polish culture.[76] After all, in Mickiewicz's version of the play, a view of Warsaw (let alone the Palace of Culture) from the prison cell is impossible; in the play, Gustaw/Konrad is imprisoned in Vilnius. In Konwicki's rendition, the visual contrast between nineteenth-century Vilnius and twentieth-century Warsaw establishes the cinematic text as a distillation of two centuries of Polish history read through the messianic paradigm. Furthermore, both Vilnius and Warsaw become supra-territorial, defying physical space and time. Konwicki adds to the layering of the Palace's re-signification, which he begins in *Ascension* and *A Minor Apocalypse*, by explicitly integrating into his film an overt reference to the events of 1968, when the production of *Forefathers' Eve* at the National Theater (Teatr Narodowy) was shut down for its anti-Russian/anti-Soviet sentiments.[77] Konwicki no doubt counted on his audience to make the connection between the 1989 production of the film and 1968 by casting Gustaw Holoubek (1923–2008), who played the young Gustaw/Konrad in the 1968 production, as an older Gustaw/Konrad, as well as the Hermit and Poet, once again building a bridge between the events of the nineteenth and twentieth centuries, and equating the Soviet regime with tsarist Russia.

The final image of the Palace in *Lava* presents a four-part sequence of documentary shots from the mass celebrated by Pope John Paul II during his 1987 pilgrimage to Poland.[78] Held on Defilad Square at the foot of the Palace of Culture, this mass presented the unforgettable image of the "Polish Pope's" (and, by extension, the "Polish Nation's") victory over the communist authorities. In 1989, the images of the papal mass with the Palace of Culture looming in the background inserted into Mickiewicz's *Forefathers' Eve*

Figure 27. The 1987 papal mass held on Defilad Square at the foot of the Palace of Culture in *Lava* (dir. Tadeusz Konwicki, 1989).

simultaneously evoked and rejected the memory of the many socialist/communist events that took place in and around the Palace of Culture, beginning with the opening of the Palace in 1955 and Władysław Gomułka's October 1956 speech that announced the Polish Thaw. The first shot of this final "Palace" sequence depicts a crowd of people during an International Workers' Day demonstration on Defilad Square; next we see a close-up of priests in gold vestments processing up the steps of an outdoor altar; the third shot is a close-up of this altar clearly located on a city square; the final shot of the sequence reveals the full view of the altar built for the papal mass against the backdrop of the Palace of Culture (figure 27). During this sequence, we hear the following words from the preface to part 3 of *Forefathers' Eve*: "What are all the past cruelties in comparison with that which the Polish nation now suffers and upon which Europe looks indifferently! The author wanted only to preserve for the nation a faithful souvenir of Lithuania's history from recent years."[79] The martyrological tone of Mickiewicz's text contrasts distinctly with the hopeful and powerful image of the Palace of Culture as the background to the papal altar. At the same time, it designates the cinematic text as a historical vessel. And it is this final apposition of official discourse (the Palace of Culture) and counter-discourse (the papal mass) that negates both the paradigm of Polish suffering and communist ideology. According to Sobolewski, this is, no doubt, the "happy ending" to which Konwicki refers, for the message of suffering expounded by the greatest Polish romantic poet is incongruous with the redemptive image of a Stalinist edifice being used as an altar prop.[80]

This crescendo toward the last view of the Palace in *Lava* represents the apotheosis of Konwicki's discursive redefinition of the Stalinist edifice. The altar and cross set against the facade of the Palace of Culture in combination with Mickiewicz's text provided Konwicki with the discursive, visual power to "kill" three birds with one stone: the messianic paradigm, communist ideology, and the socialist symbolism of the Palace. While in hindsight the crowds gathered on Defilad Square in 1987 were a sign of the approaching end of communism,[81] this composite image becomes Konwicki's symbolic, cinematic end of the "Polish screenplay of defeat."[82]

Konwicki's literary and cinematic representations of the Palace of Culture undoubtedly had a lasting effect on how the skyscraper was understood and viewed. In *Ascension, A Minor Apocalypse*, and *Lava*, he used the Palace as a synecdoche for postwar history and politics, exploiting its socialist signification to comment on communism, messianism, and ideology (in general). To achieve this, Konwicki exploited the Palace's palimpsestuousness in *Ascension* and *A Minor Apocalypse* by placing on it a veneer of Christian discourse and undermining its communist connotations. In *Ascension*, the potential for "ascension," portrayed on the vertical axis as the tension between heaven and earth, is limited by the horizon and the cloudy landscape as seen from the viewing terrace of the Palace. In *A Minor Apocalypse*, the discursive power of the Christian narrative, portrayed on the horizontal axis as the symbiosis between the Palace (Golgotha) and the streets surrounding it (Via Dolorosa), also fails. The process of self-immolation is not portrayed in the text, and the reader is left with some certainty that the sacrifice of the narrator is of little value. In *Lava*, however, Konwicki indulges in a redemptive act by presenting the Palace of Culture in the context of the 1987 papal mass, with all its historical, political, discursive, ideological, and anti-ideological implications, creating a discursive end point in the redefinition of the Palace of Culture and a cinematic farewell to communism and Mickiewicz's messianic tradition. Here, Konwicki did not need to fabricate a veneer of Christian discourse; history handed it to him on a plate.

Almost a quarter of a century after the fall of communism, the Palace of Culture and Science continues to act as a dynamic discursive space, generating new meanings in the context of post-communist democratization and economic transition. In 2015 the Palace celebrated its sixtieth anniversary, which generated a flurry of books and articles devoted to unpacking the significance of this edifice originally dedicated to Joseph Stalin.[83] Still dominating the center of Warsaw, the skyscraper's socialist realist facade testifies to the intersection of space and spatiality, to the phenomenon of spatiality becoming part of the material content of space. Adorned with socialist realist sculptures, the building was *meant* to be the physical manifestation of socialism (i.e., communism). Today, however, the meaning of the names Marx, Engels, and Lenin etched upon a book held by a statue of a young worker have a markedly different place in the cultural, political, and historical discourse than they did in the early 1950s when the 42-story building was erected. The removal of Stalin's name from this "book cover" after 1956 was one of the earliest physical signs of this discursive change, which preceded the removal of Stalin monuments across the Eastern bloc in the aftermath of communism's fall.[84] Yet, despite the socialist architectural elements of the Palace of Culture, the building today serves a practical value that overrides the controversial, symbolic meaning of the edifice and the connotations originally attached to it. Nonetheless, the textual elements of the building, those elements that demand "literacy," remain intact. The discourse of socialist realism remains a part of the Palace of Culture even if that discourse represents a negative value and even if subsequent generations must be taught to read it.

AFTERWORD

After 1989, questions of how to contend with space as textualized by social-ism abounded. Whether it was the names of buildings, streets, or plazas, monuments to brotherhood and Soviet victories, or the facades of Stalinist-era architecture and the 1970s Gierek-era *bloki* (housing complexes made up of geometric blocks with little to no adornment), verbal and visual remnants of socialism had permeated the built environment not only in Warsaw, but in all of Poland. Some forms of textualization were quickly removed in an attempt to erase communist reference points from daily life. For example, streets honoring Marx, Engels, Lenin, Stalin, and other heroes of communism were swiftly renamed. In 1990, two of Warsaw's main avenues that intersect a mile north of the Palace of Culture and Science went from marking central areas of the city as appropriated by communism, to inscribing onto these streets a new narrative that honored those who had fought against com-munism. Juliana Marchlewskiego Avenue, named after Julian Marchlewski, a Polish communist who lived at the turn of the nineteenth and twentieth centuries, was changed to Jana Pawła II Avenue (aleja Jana Pawła II) after the Polish pope, John Paul II, who was elected in 1978 and helped bring an end to communism in Poland and the region. Karola Świerczewskiego Avenue (aleja Karola Świerczewskiego), named after Karol Świerczewski, a communist activist and a general in the Soviet Army and the Polish People's Army, was changed to Solidarności Avenue (aleja Solidarności) after the Soli-darity movement that hastened communism's end in the Eastern bloc. And let's not forget Feliksa Dzierżyńskiego Square featured in the film *Adventure in Mariensztat*, which was renamed Bankowy Square, as it had once been called. Such de-socialization of the landscape abounded in the region after 1989, reflecting a return to national narratives that had been suppressed by the language of communist ideology and propaganda, or reflecting a new economic reality. In the early 1990s, unsuspecting tourists bought maps printed before the fall of communism, only to find the cartographic nomen-clature of the city on their paper Warsaws reflecting a "completely different" reality than was indicated by street signs. Without the textual connection between the actual streets and the lines on the map, the city was not navi-gable and was in some ways illegible. But this state of affairs represented its own truth. While the paper Warsaws seemed out of sync with the real ver-sion of the streets, the cartographic and material spaces together reflected the reality of political, economic, and social transition. Changing names of streets was a relatively easy, albeit potentially confusing, way to de-socialize the urban text. Other actions required more effort, like the removal of statues and monuments celebrating communist-era heroes. And still other socialist-era remnants, like the Palace of Culture, will most likely never disappear save for a natural cataclysm or another war. As a result, Warsaw's palimpsestuousness persists, on the one hand embracing new forms of textualization on the streets and in cultural texts, and on the other resisting the erasure of a complex twentieth-century history that has left an indelible mark on its stones and streets.

Such a layering of meaning inevitably leads to discursive contradictions, which were the inspiration and genesis of this project. My line of inquiry has been driven, first and foremost, by a desire to understand and resolve the palpable conflicts that are part of Varsovian spatiality and that persist within the city's cultural discourse up to today. As such, *Mapping Warsaw* is a discursive, cartographic project that traces the ways in which Warsaw's postwar narrative was crafted and shaped by the parameters of an official, socialist narrative promoted in visual and written texts during the communist period. It also signals ways in which counter-narratives developed even within the limits of censorship and ideology. In particular, I have explored the mechanisms employed by postwar propaganda and the historical and artistic processes that wrote these narratives, some of which supported the communist regime's ideological agenda and some of which seemed contradictory to its overarching purpose. The focus of this book has been primarily on official discourses of the communist period, through which I have demonstrated how images-texts shaped a socialist imagining of space. This study thus "maps" some of the central themes in the discursive semiosphere we call "Warsaw" by following geo-specific points that surface time and again in the primary sources. In addition to shedding light on Warsaw's postwar spatiality, my analysis signals the extent to which our impressions of place, based on narrativized visual and visualized narrative representations, shape our understanding and reading of the world in which we live.

As a reader will note, there are specific loci that recur throughout this book. They reflect the delimiting of space as defined by the sources themselves. As we move through the version of Warsaw created between these pages, we return to places like the Trasa W-Z, Mariensztat, the Marszałkowska Residential District (MDM), the Palace of Culture and Science, Łazienki Park, the Old Town, and the Sigismund III Vasa Column on Zamkowy Square. This is a map of Warsaw dictated to a large extent by propaganda's fixation on its largest socialist infrastructure projects, as well as a narrowing of historical reference points within the city to provide authenticity to the socialist narrative, while minimally compromising its ideological underpinnings. While certainly other parts of Warsaw were textualized in official publications, these points of reference tended to receive the most attention and provide the strongest points of intersection between the materials studied.

After 1956 Warsaw was a silent presence within the framework of social-ist propaganda. It was a functioning urban center and the capital of an internationally recognized People's Republic, despite its many shortcomings. Warsaw's *stołeczność* or "capital status" was unquestioned, the new "historic" sites of the city were already earning the aged patina of authenticity, and the communist regime of the People's Republic of Poland was less concerned with legitimizing its authority through the symbolic appropriation of space than with addressing the new political challenges introduced by the 1956 Thaw and later by protests against the communist regime in 1968, 1970, 1976, and the Solidarity movement of the 1980s. While Warsaw remained an important place, the regime's efforts to control its spatiality were no longer of primary concern.

But 1956 was far from the end of Warsaw's spatiality, which became dominated by both material and textual reconsiderations, reappropriations, and rewritings of the city's symbolic importance. As the novels and films of Tadeusz Konwicki show, the textualization of Warsaw space continued and does so to this day. While throughout *Mapping Warsaw*, I have tried to highlight moments of intersection between the narratives that ran counter to the official discourses discussed in the previous pages, there are numerous points of reference which I would still like to reach and incorporate in an attempt to grasp the whole of "Warsaw." But as the theoretical models I have relied on teach us, the spatiality of place is ever-changing, always greater than itself, never static, and inherently ungraspable. With each new textualiza-tion or articulation of space, spatiality grows and transforms. Delving more deeply into these counter-discourses suggests another, future line of inquiry that I may map one day in the future. This future map would include literary manifestations of Warsaw in the works of Sylwia Chutnik, Andrzej Stasiuk, or Krzysztof Varga, whose contemporary textualizations of the Polish capital unearth hidden stories of the city, as well as add numerous new layers to its palimpsest.

I should also mention that there is an inherent danger in any textualization of space, including my own: namely the risk of marginalizing, or worse yet, silencing narratives and stories that are not just worth telling, but should be told. Throughout this project, I have focused on the image-text expressions of the Polish capital in an official discourse, but there are many alternate ways of studying and approaching the textualization of Warsaw, whether it is through the eyes of contemporary Varsovians, the lens of partisans traveling through the sewers during the Warsaw Uprising, or through the perspective of men, women, and children forcibly moved to the Warsaw ghetto that was more than likely their last "home." At no point during this project did the lived experience of place not accompany me on this journey to better under-stand Warsaw. While some of these stories were "silent" in the materials I studied, they have the potential to resurface and reinsert themselves on the cityscape. We just need to stop, listen, look, and read between the lines.

Book epigraph: Quoted according to Esther Leslie, "Siegfried Kracauer and Walter Benjamin: Memory from Weimar to Hitler," in *Histories, Theories, Debates*, eds. Susannah Radstone and Bill Schwarz (New York: Fordham University Press, 2010), 123.

Prologue

1. The term *"kamienica"* (*kamienice,* plural) is often translated into English as "tenement house" or "row house." There are, however, significant differences between the Polish *"kamienica"* and these English-language equivalents. *Kamienica* refers to a brick or stone single- or multifamily dwelling of several stories, sometimes with a shop or office on the ground floor. *Kamienice* are built adjacent to one another, sharing side walls like row houses or brownstones; however, unlike row houses, each individual *kamienica* has its own style and façade, giving the frontage of historical streets in Polish cities their unique and recognizable architectural character.

Introduction

Epigraph: Stanisław Jankowski and Adolf Ciborowski, *Warszawa 1945 i dziś* (Warsaw: Interpress, 1971), 6. Available in English as Stanisław Jankowski and Adolf Ciborowski, *Warsaw 1945 and Today* (Warsaw: Interpress, 1971). Unless otherwise noted, translations throughout are my own.

1. The phrase "discursive topography" is an adaptation of Svetlana Boym's "rhetorical *topos*." See Svetlana Boym, *The Future of Nostalgia* (New York: Basic Books, 2001), 77.

2. My thinking on this topic owes much to Franco Moretti's pioneering use of literary and cultural mapping in *Atlas of the European Novel, 1800–1900* (London: Verso, 1998). See also Franco Moretti, *Graphs, Maps, Trees: Abstract Models for a Literary History* (London: Verso, 2005).

3. The terms "communism" and "socialism" have been problematized with distance from the Cold War and the fall of communism in 1989. Throughout this study, "communism" refers to the particular Soviet brand of communism, the politics of various communist political entities that existed in communist Poland, and the final goal that was ostensibly sought by the authorities of what was eventually called the People's Republic of Poland. "Socialism" was the term used by the regimes of the Eastern bloc in reference to the governments of the period and was defined as a stepping-stone towards achieving "communism." Throughout, I tend to use the term "communism" diachronically when focusing on broader political or social agendas expressed by the material presented, and "socialism"

when presenting a synchronic moment. Admittedly, this distinction is not always possible, and at times the terms are used synonymously.

4. In this context, "official" refers to sources that were published or produced by state-owned enterprises during the communist period. Thus, I treat the discourse of the communist authorities as the dominant discourse of the postwar era until 1989 based on the power dynamics established under totalitarianism. This means that popular paradigms of Polish national identity, such as "Polish romantic heroism," the "patriotic partisan," or "Pole-Catholic," among others, are treated here as counter-discourses, even though at other times in history they may be considered dominant narratives.

5. I define "ideology" as the political and social agendas of the postwar Soviet-imposed communist regime and "propaganda" as the "pedagogical" means through which this ideology was promoted.

6. Such texts include Antoni Słonimski's *Wspomnienia warszawskie* (Warsaw: Czytelnik, 1957); Miron Białoszewski's 1970 *Pamiętnik Powstania Warszawskiego,* published in English as *A Memoir of the Warsaw Uprising,* trans. Madeline G. Levine (New York: New York Review of Books Classics, 2015); and Andrzej Wajda's films *Pokolenie* (1954) and *Kanał* (1956). On the role of Warsaw in Czesław Miłosz's ouevre, see Marek Zaleski, ed. *Warszawa Miłosza* (Warsaw: Stowarzyszenie "Pro Cultura Litteraria," Wydawnictwo PAN, 2013).

7. Karl Schlögel, *W przestrzeni czas czytamy: O historii cywilizacji i geopolityce,* trans. Łukasz Musiał and Izabela Drozdowska (Poznań: Wydawnictwo Poznańskie, 2009), 58. Numerous literary and cultural studies have been devoted to the representation of space in the post-World War II period. See Gaston Bachelard, *The Poetics of Space* (New York: Orion, 1964); and Raymond Williams, *The Country and the City* (New York: Oxford University Press, 1973). See also Anne Fuchs, *After the Dresden Bombing: Pathways of Memory, 1945 to the Present* (Houndmills, Eng.: Palgrave Macmillan, 2012); Katharina Gerstenberger, *Writing the New Berlin: The German Capital in Post-Wall Literature* (Rochester, N.Y., and Woodbridge, Eng.: Camden House and Boydell and Brewer, 2008); Paul Melo e Castro, *Shades of Grey: 1960s Lisbon in Novel, Film and Photobook* (London: Maney Publishing for the MHRA, 2011); and Silvia M. Ross, *Tuscan Spaces: Literary Constructions of Place* (Toronto: University of Toronto Press, 2010). For an interdisciplinary perspective, see Santa Arias and Barney Warf, eds., *The Spatial Turn: Interdisciplinary Perspectives* (London: Routledge, 2009). See also Jaimey Fisher and Barbara Mennel, eds., *Spatial Turns: Space, Place, and Mobility in German Literary and Visual Culture* (Amsterdam: Rodopi, 2010).

8. In reading each text at its word, I follow J. Hillis Miller in his *Topographies* (Stanford, Calif.: Stanford University Press, 1995), 5.

9. Maurice Merleau-Ponty, *Phenomenology of Perception,* trans. Donald A. Landes (London: Routledge, 2012).

10. De Certeau's "place" and "space" are the equivalents of Merleau-Ponty's "geometrical space" and "spatiality," respectively.

11. Michel de Certeau, *The Practice of Everyday Life,* trans. Steven Rendall (Berkeley: University of California Press, 1984), 115. See especially the chapters "Walking in the City" and "Spatial Stories."

12. Miller, *Topographies.*

13. Ibid., 3.

14. Boym, *Future of Nostalgia*, 77.

15. See Ernest W. B. Hess-Lüttich, "*Spatial Turn*: On the Concept of Space in Cultural Geography and Literary Theory," *meta-carto-semiotics: Journal for Theoretical Cartography* 5 (2012): 3. Here, Hess-Lüttich refers to Benno Werlen's *Sozialgeographie: Eine Einführung* (Bern: Haupt, 2000).

16. Schlögel, *W przestrzeni czas czytamy*, 21.

17. Biblioteka Uniwersytecka w Warszawie, "O Bibliotece / Historia / 1915–1999: Biblioteka Uniwersytecka w Warszawie," www.buw.uw.edu.pl. Tadeusz Mazowiecki was the first prime minister of Poland after the fall of communism.

18. For more on "palimpsest," see Sarah Dillon, *The Palimpsest: Literature, Criticism, Theory* (London: Continuum, 2007).

19. Niedenthal's photograph was published as part of the feature article by Harry Andreson et al., "Poland Under the Heel," *Newsweek*, December 28, 1981.

20. In the version published in *Newsweek*, the photograph was cropped, cutting off the name of the movie theater.

21. Bożena Karwowska, "Metamorfozy pamięci—odbudowa Warszawy w narracji Poli Gojawiczyńskiej," in *Kobieta—Historia—Literatura* (Warsaw: Instytut Badań Literackich, 2016), 181.

22. Adolf Rudnicki, "Czysty nurt," in *Sto jeden* (Kraków: Wydawnictwo Literackie, 1984), 68–69. English translation from "The Crystal Stream," in *Art from the Ashes: A Holocaust Anthology*, ed. Lawrence L. Langer (New York: Oxford University Press, 1995), 380.

23. The extent to which Jewish Warsaw was erased from Polish cultural memory during the communist period can be attested to by the fact that Singer's novels were almost completely unavailable in Poland prior to 1989, with only selective releases around the time Singer won the Nobel Prize in 1978. I would like to thank an anonymous reviewer for pointing this out.

24. See Marek Steedman, "State Power, Hegemony, and Memory: Lotman and Gramsci," in *Lotman and Cultural Studies: Encounters and Extensions*, ed. Andreas Schönle (Madison: University of Wisconsin Press, 2006), 136–58. While Lotman associated his work with structuralism, his later engagement with the concept of the semiosphere indicates a move away from structuralist, binary paradigms toward a more complex, three-dimensional model of culture associated with post-structuralism and cultural studies. For more on the evolution of Lotman's theory, see Amy Mandelker, "Logosphere and Semiosphere: Bakhtin, Russian Organicism, and the Semiotics of Culture," in *Bakhtin in Contexts: Across the Disciplines*, ed. Amy Mandelker (Evanston, Ill.: Northwestern University Press, 1995), 177–90.

25. On the relationship between Lotman's theory and the spatial turn, see Winfried Nöth, "The Topography of Yuri Lotman's Semiosphere," *International Journal of Cultural Studies* 18, no. 1 (2015): 11–26.

26. Jurij M. Lotman and Boris A. Uspenskij, Authors' Introduction to *The Semiotics of Russian Culture*, eds. Ann Shukman and Boris Andreevich Uspenskij (Ann Arbor: Department of Slavic Languages and Literatures, University of Michigan, 1984), xii.

27. Ibid.

28. Jonathan Bolton makes a similar point: "one function of the semiosphere concept for Lotman is to explain how different languages can exist in continuous

conflict and dialogue within a culture, along many different axes, forming an organic whole that never stops evolving." See Jonathan Bolton, "Writing in a Polluted Semiosphere: Everyday Life in Lotman, Foucault, and de Certeau," in *Lotman and Cultural Studies: Encounters and Extensions*, ed. Andreas Schönle (Madison: University of Wisconsin Press, 2006), 320–44.

29. Hess-Lüttich, "*Spatial Turn*," 6.

30. Note that this concept does not eliminate fantastical representations of the city. Warsaw as a setting becomes determined by the way recognizable (though not necessarily symbolic) spatial signifiers are deployed in a narrative. See Igor Ostachowicz's novel *Noc żywych Żydów* (Warsaw: Wydawnictwo W.A.B., 2012). See also Dariusz Gajewski's movie *Warszawa* (Poland: Gutek Film, 2003). In both cases, fantastical narrative elements are countered by the realistic portrayal of the city, which is determined by well-known landmarks—that is, by geospatial specificity.

31. See Bolesław Prus, *The Doll*, trans. David Welsh and revised by Dariusz Tołczyk and Anna Zaranko (Budapest: Central European University Press, 1996); Isaac Bashevis Singer, *The Family Moskat* (New York: Farrar, Straus and Giroux, 1950); and Zbigniew Uniłowski, *Wspólny pokój i inne utwory* (Wrocław: Zakład Narodowy im. Ossolińskich, 1976). I reference Prus and Uniłowski, who include Jews within their Varsovian cityscape, as a contrast to Polish narratives of the 1950s and 1960s in which Jews are, for the most part, absent. Singer's work is an important reference point in this respect since it defines Warsaw's prewar Jewish spatiality in a post-Holocaust context.

32. For an analysis of Jewish Warsaw after the war, see Karen Auerbach, *The House at Ujazdowskie 16: Jewish Families in Warsaw after the Holocaust* (Bloomington: Indiana University Press, 2013). See also Michael Meng, *Shattered Spaces: Encountering Jewish Ruins in Postwar Germany and Poland* (Cambridge, Mass.: Harvard University Press, 2011).

33. See Stanisław Jankowski, "Warsaw: Destruction, Secret Town Planning, 1939–44, and Postwar Reconstruction," in *Rebuilding Europe's Bombed Cities*, ed. Jeffry M. Diefendorf (New York: St. Martin's, 1990), 78.

34. Until the creation of the Warsaw ghetto by the Nazis, there was no Jewish ghetto in Warsaw per se. Before World War II Jews were not allowed to settle in certain areas of Warsaw, but they were also not limited to a closed section of the city. This resulted in certain neighborhoods having higher concentrations of Jewish households. One such area was the Dzielnica Północna (Northern Neighborhood), which—for the most part—became enclosed within the Nazi-established ghetto during World War II.

35. Zbigniew Grzybowski, Hubert Hilscher, and Leszek Wysznacki, *Warszawa 1945–1970*, trans. Regina Gorzkowska et al. (Warsaw: Wydawnictwo "Sport i Turystyka," 1970), 8.

36. On capital cities as related to national identity, see Lawrence J. Vale, *Architecture, Power, and National Identity* (New Haven, Conn.: Yale University Press, 1992), 15.

37. The Polish-Lithuanian commonwealth was partitioned by the Austro-Hungarian, Prussian, and Russian empires in 1772, 1793, and 1795.

38. Stephen D. Corrsin, *Warsaw before the First World War: Poles and Jews in the Third City of the Russian Empire, 1880–1914* (New York: Columbia University Press, 1989), 1.

39. On the strategic importance of Warsaw's location, see Edward D. Wynot's "Introduction" in *Warsaw between the World Wars: Profile of the Capital City in a Developing Land, 1918–1939* (New York: Columbia University Press, 1983).

40. On the international perception of Warsaw in the interwar period, see Martin Kohlrausch, "*Warszawa Funkcjonalna*: Radical Urbanism and the International Discourse on Planning in the Interwar Period," in *Races to Modernity: Metropolitan Aspirations in Eastern Europe, 1890–1940*, eds. Jan C. Behrends and Martin Kohlrausch (Budapest: Central European University Press, 2014), 208–9. According to statistical predictions from 1912, Warsaw's population was to quintuple by the mid-twentieth century. Ibid., 209.

41. Corrsin, *Warsaw before the First World War*, 21.

42. On the Citadel, see David Crowley, *Warsaw* (London: Reaktion, 2003), 12. See also Wynot, *Warsaw between the World Wars*. On Russified Warsaw in the late nineteenth century, see Józef Bachórz's introduction to *Lalka*, Bolesław Prus (Wrocław: Zakład Narodowy im. Ossolińskich, 1991), lxxxvii–xciii.

43. Crowley, *Warsaw*, 12.

44. Wojciech Tomasik, "Warsaw in 1945–55: The Emergence of a New Chronotope," in *The Phoney Peace: Power and Culture in Central Europe, 1945–49*, ed. Robert B. Pynsent (London: School of Slavonic and East European Studies, University of London, 2000), 328–36.

45. The partisan Home Army was the largest independent noncommunist resistance formation in Europe throughout the war. See Norman Davies, *God's Playground: A History of Poland*, vol. 2, *1795 to the Present* (New York: Columbia University Press, 1982), 272, 464, 66.

46. Ibid., 467.

47. Tomasz Markiewicz, "Prywatna odbudowa Warszawy," in *Zbudować Warszawę piękną: O nowy krajobraz stolicy (1944–1956)*, ed. Jerzy Kochanowski (Warsaw: Wydawnictwo "Trio," 2003), 217.

48. Bronisława Skrzeszewska, "O pomocy Związku Radzieckiego dla Warszawy w pierwszym okresie po jej wyzwoleniu," in *Warszawa: Stolica Polski Ludowej*, no. 1, ed. Jan Górski, vol. 5, *Studia Warszawskie* (Warsaw: PWN, 1970), 211. See also Władysław Gomułka, *Pamiętniki*, vol. 2, ed. Andrzej Werblan (Warsaw: Polska Oficyna Wydawnicza "BGW," 1994), 502–3; and Piotr Majewski, "Jak zbudować 'Zamek socjalistyczny'?: Polityczne konteksty odbudowy Zamku Królewskiego w Warszawie w latach 1944–1956," in *Zbudować Warszawę piękną: O nowy krajobraz stolicy (1944–1956)*, ed. Jerzy Kochanowski (Warsaw: Wydawnictwo "Trio," 2003), 29.

49. Refer to Sejm of the Republic of Poland, Ustawa z dnia 3 lipca 1947 r. o odbudowie m. st. Warszawy (Dz.U. 1947 nr 52 poz. 268). See also Józef Jakubowski, *Dekret o odbudowie Warszawy* (Lublin: Wydawnictwo Lubelskie, 1980).

50. David Crowley, "Paris or Moscow? Warsaw Architects and the Image of the Modern City in the 1950s," in *Imagining the West in Eastern Europe and the Soviet Union*, ed. György Péteri (Pittsburgh, Pa.: University of Pittsburgh Press, 2010), 105–30.

51. See Grażyna Stachówna, "Socjalistyczne romanse, czyli gorzko-słodkie losy melodramatu w Peerelu," *Kino* 41, no. 476 (2007): 52.

52. For a discussion of the debates surrounding Warsaw's reconstruction, see Stanisław Tołwiński, "Czy były wątpliwości co do budowy nowej Warszawy na dawnym miejscu?" in *Warszawa: Stolica Polski Ludowej*, no. 2, ed. Jan Górski, vol. 11, *Studia Warszawskie* (Warsaw: PWN, 1972). See also Jan Górski, "Dyskusje o odbudowie Warszawy w latach 1945–1946," in *Warszawa: Stolica Polski Ludowej*, no. 1, ed. Jan Górski, vol. 5, *Studia Warszawskie* (Warsaw: PWN, 1970), 75–140.

53. On the Cathedral of Christ the Savior in Moscow, see Boym, *Future of Nostalgia*, 100–108. See also Ryszard Kapuściński, *Imperium* (New York: Alfred A. Knopf, 1994), 95–108.

54. The Royal Route is an old communication route that begins at Zamkowy Square (plac Zamkowy) and travels southeast along Krakowskie Przedmieście, Nowy Świat Street, Ujazdowskie Avenue, Belwederska and Sobieskiego streets (ulica Belwederska and ulica Sobieskiego), and ends at the seventeenth-century Wilanowski Palace.

55. Bernardo Bellotto and Mieczysław Wallis, *Canaletto, malarz Warszawy*, 5th ed. (Warsaw: Auriga, 1961), 5. Bernardo "Canaletto" Bellotto (1722–1780) was the nephew of the Venetian *vedutista* Giovanni Antonio Canal (1697–1768), known as "Canaletto."

56. Grzegorz Piątek, "Koniec, który stał się początkiem / An End and a Beginning," in *Kronikarki / The Chroniclers (Zofia Chomętowska i Maria Chrząszczowa): Fotografie Warszawy 1945–1946 / Photographs of Warsaw 1945–1946*, ed. Karolina Lewandowska (Warsaw: Archeologia Fotografii, 2011), 284–85.

57. Crowley, *Warsaw*, 28.

58. As Emma Widdis's research on the Soviet Union demonstrates, the conflation between spatial representation and identity politics was not unique to the Polish case. In the first two decades of the Soviet Union, newly Sovietized spaces were part of an extensive propaganda campaign that used cartography in film, print media, literature, and visual arts "to propagate appropriate images of the new world," a campaign that relied on both traditional cartography and discursive mapping. See Emma Widdis, *Visions of a New Land: Soviet Film from the Revolution to the Second World War* (New Haven, Conn.: Yale University Press, 2003), 3. While in the Soviet case this mapping stressed a unification of the Soviet Union's expansive geographic space, the Polish cartographic identity project narrowed its focus on Warsaw as the symbolic point of unification between Poles of conflicting political and ideological factions.

59. "Warszawski wrzesień," *Stolica: Warszawski Tygodnik Ilustrowany*, September 18, 1949. *Stolica* was published from 1949 to 1989.

60. "Piękno Warszawy, której już nie ma, a którą wskrzesimy," *Stolica: Warszawski Tygodnik Ilustrowany*, November 3, 1946, 6.

61. Ibid., 7.

62. Boym, *Future of Nostalgia*, 77. On the idea of aura as it relates to authenticity, see Walter Benjamin, "The Work of Art in the Age of Mechanical Reproduction," in *Illuminations*, ed. Hannah Arendt (New York: Schocken, 2007), 217–51. Warsaw might be considered the ultimate example of the connection between reproducibility, politics, and authenticity. When in 1936 Benjamin wrote "The presence of the original is the prerequisite to the concept of authenticity . . ." (220), the trajectory of the coming war and its devastation to European

life could not have been predicted. In his essay, Benjamin demonstrated that the function of photography and film in Western society challenged notions of artistic authenticity through technical reproducibility and reproduction. Through reproducibility, he argued, photographs and other reproducible images forgo their "aura" and ritualistic or cult value, giving way to a new type of exhibition value and a politicization of art that was unprecedented in history. In the case of Warsaw, the large-scale reproduction of the city according to images (themselves endlessly reproduced in the following decades) was driven by a highly mechanized and industrialized ideology that sought political control over an entire nation.

63. The Six-Year Plan for Warsaw's Reconstruction coincided with (but should not be confused with) the second centralized plan for economic and industrial development called the "Six-Year Plan, 1950–1955." See Bolesław Bierut and Hilary Minc, *Plan sześcioletni* (Warsaw: Książka i Wiedza, 1950).

64. Bolesław Bierut, *Sześcioletni plan odbudowy Warszawy* (Warsaw: Książka i Wiedza, 1950), 11, 39.

65. Crowley, *Warsaw*, 32–33.

66. Bierut, *Sześcioletni plan*, 11, 65.

67. Ibid., 69.

68. Socialist realism was first adopted in November 1948 at the IV General Assembly of the Union of Polish Composers and at the Convention of Satirists. See Jerzy Smulski, *Od Szczecina do . . . Października: Studia o literaturze polskiej lat pięćdziesiątych* (Toruń: Wydawnictwo Uniwersytetu Mikołaja Kopernika, 2002), 16. For a report on the proceedings of the Convention of Satirists, see PKF 47/48:8, "Kongres satyryków" (November 17, 1948). Throughout 1949, socialist realism was officially adopted in literature (January); theater, architecture, and art and sculpture (June); music (August); art schools (October); and film (November). See Alina Madej, "Zjazd filmowy w Wiśle, czyli dla każdego coś przykrego," *Kwartalnik Filmowy* no. 18 (1997): 207.

69. Departures from socialist realism began as early as 1954, when the publishing house Czytelnik commissioned Leopold Tyrmand to write a novel about *bikiniarze* (hooligans and beatniks). The result was Tyrmand's 1955 best-selling crime novel *Zły*, which is considered an early harbinger of the end of socialist realism and Stalinism. Also in 1955, Adam Ważyk published his reckoning with Stalinism, called "Poemat dla dorosłych" ("A Poem for Adults"), in *Nowa Kultura* (*New Culture*), the official organ of the Polish Writers' Association (Stowarzyszenie Pisarzy Polskich). See *Nowa Kultura*, no. 34 (1955).

70. Zbigniew Jarosiński writes that socialist realism was "a cancerous transplant from a foreign organism." See Zbigniew Jarosiński, *Nadwiślański socrealizm* (Warsaw: Instytut Badań Literackich, 1999), 5.

71. References to news segments from the Polish Film Chronicle (Polska Kronika Filmowa, PKF) follow the numeration in the card catalog of the Filmoteka Narodowa and the Repozytorium Cyfrowe Filmoteki Narodowej, as explained in the note preceding the list of news segments cited in this book on page 203. Thus, PKF 14/50:11 was the fourteenth newsreel in 1950 and the referenced news segment was the eleventh news story on that newsreel.

72. Tadeusz Makarczyński and Franciszek Fuchs, *Nowa sztuka* (Warsaw, 1950).

73. Ibid.

74. On the positive hero in socialist realism and his relationship to nineteenth-century narrative models, see Katerina Clark, *The Soviet Novel: History as Ritual* (Bloomington: Indiana University Press, 2000), 46–67. See also Wojciech Tomasik, "Proza narracyjna," in *Słownik realizmu socjalistycznego*, eds. Zdzisław Łapiński and Wojciech Tomasik (Kraków: Universitas, 2004); and Wojciech Tomasik, *Inżynieria dusz: Literatura realizmu socjalistycznego w planie "propagandy monumentalnej"* (Wrocław: Wydawnictwo Leopoldinum, 1999).

75. Hanna Gosk, "Literatura—rzecz poważna (O poezji wczesnych lat pięćdziesiątych poświęconej Warszawie)," *Poezja* 18, no. 1 (203) (1983): 90.

76. Ibid.

77. Marek Haltof, *Polish National Cinema* (New York: Berghahn Books, 2002), 56–64.

78. For a critical analysis of socialist realism in art and architecture, see Wojciech Włodarczyk, *Socrealizm: Sztuka polska w latach 1950–1954* (Kraków: Wydawnictwo Literackie, 1991). For a perspective on gender and socialist realism, see Ewa Toniak, *Olbrzymki: Kobiety i socrealizm* (Kraków: Korporacja ha!art, 2008).

79. Gosk makes this observation as regards poets of the early 1950s. See "Literatura—rzecz poważna," 89.

80. Ibid.

81. See Jane Leftwich Curry, ed., *The Black Book of Polish Censorship* (New York: Random House, 1984). For a description of the peculiarities of Polish censorship under communism, see Jan Kubik, *The Power of Symbols against the Symbols of Power: The Rise of Solidarity and the Fall of State Socialism in Poland* (University Park: Pennsylvania State University Press, 1994).

82. Bolesław Bierut, *O upowszechnienie kultury: Przemówienie Prezydenta Rzeczypospolitej Bolesława Bieruta na otwarciu radiostacji we Wrocławiu 16 listopada 1947* (Warsaw: Radiowy Instytut Wydawniczy, 1948). Cited according to Smulski, *Od Szczecina do . . .* , 13–14.

83. Cited according to Smulski, *Od Szczecina do . . .* , 15.

84. Makarczyński and Fuchs, *Nowa sztuka*.

85. "*Jurydyki*" were private settlements within a city or just outside the city walls that were not subject to city authorities and had their own laws. *Słownik języka polskiego*, ed. Witold Doroszewski et al. (Warsaw: Wiedza Powszechna, 1958–69), s.v. "jurydyka."

86. For an example of clashing conceptions of space, see my article "Intertextuality and Topography in Igor Ostachowicz's *Noc żywych Żydów*," in *Geograficzne przestrzenie utekstowione*, ed. Bożena Karwowska et al. (Białystok: Wydawnictwo Uniwersytetu w Białymstoku, 2017), 338–46. There I explain the different meanings assigned to Warsaw's Muranów by contemporary Poles and Jews. In particular, I underscore the difference between Muranów as part of contemporary Warsaw versus Muranów as the historical entity associated with the Warsaw ghetto. In addition to each spatiality created by the Polish or Jewish perspective, there is a third one created by the conflict between the first two.

Chapter 1

1. Bronisław Baczko, Jerzy Grabowski, and Edward Strzelecki, *Warszawa, stolica Polski*, ed. Kazimierz Saysse-Tobiczyk, 2nd ed. (Warsaw: Społeczny Fundusz

Odbudowy Stolicy, 1949). While this may have been the first such book published in Poland, other photobooks commemorating prewar Warsaw were published at this time in Switzerland (1945) and Stuttgart (1947). See Titus Burckhardt and Stefan Jasieński, *Warszawa Varsovie Warsaw Warschau 1945* (Basel, Switzerland: Urs-Graf at Basel and issued by the Polish soldiers of the 2nd Infantry Division interned in Switzerland, 1945). See also Krystyna Uszańska and Gabriela J. Lubomirska, *Warsaw: Album on the Polish Capital's Ancient Architecture, with an Introduction and Outline of the City's History up to the XIX Century* (Stuttgart: Kreuz-Verlag, 1947).

2. Baczko, Grabowski, and Strzelecki, *Warszawa, stolica Polski,* 7–8.

3. See Matthias Uecker, "The Face of the Weimar Republic: Photography, Physiognomy, and Propaganda in Weimar Germany," *Monatshefte* 99, no. 4 (2007): 469–84.

4. I use here the terms "Christian" and "Jewish" to acknowledge the diverging fate of these two groups in Nazi-occupied Poland.

5. *Encyklopedia Warszawy*, ed. Barbara Petrozolin-Skowrońska (Warsaw: PWN, 1994), s.v. "Ciborowski Adolf."

6. Adolf Ciborowski, *Warszawa: O zniszczeniu i odbudowie miasta* (Warsaw: Wydawnictwo "Polonia," 1964), 10.

7. Gerry Badger and Martin Parr, *The Photobook: A History*, vol. 1 (London: Phaidon, 2004), 6–7.

8. Ibid.

9. Patrizia Di Bello and Shamoon Zamir, "Introduction" in *The Photobook: From Talbot to Ruscha and Beyond,* eds. Patrizia Di Bello, Colette Wilson, and Shamoon Zamir (London: I. B.Tauris, 2012), 3–4.

10. For an exploration of the connection between memory, photography, and archeology, see Eric Downing, *After Images: Photography, Archeology, and Psychoanalysis and the Tradition of Bildung* (Detroit, Mich.: Wayne State University Press, 2006).

11. The Varsovian photobooks discussed in this chapter are excellent examples of books created by an editor or editorial team in contrast to auteur publications. For more on such corporate photobook creations, see Gerry Badger and Martin Parr, *The Photobook: A History*, vol. 2 (London: Phaidon, 2006), 204–33. In their analysis of photobooks, Di Bello and Zamir likewise call attention to the corporate nature of the photobook, noting that "Photobooks which combine images and texts tend also to be products of collaborative authorship." Di Bello, Wilson, and Zamir, *The Photobook: From Talbot to Ruscha and Beyond,* 5.

12. Single-author photobooks which highlighted Warsaw, first and foremost, included Olgierd Budrewicz and Edward Falkowski, *Warszawiacy,* ed. Ewa Karwowska (Warsaw: Wydawnictwo Interpress, 1970). See also Zbyszko Siemaszko and Dobrosław Kobielski, *Spojrzenia na Warszawę* (Warsaw: Krajowa Agencja Wydawnicza, 1987). Other types of Warsaw-related photobooks were published throughout the communist period. Some focused on specific neighborhoods or locations, others on specific historical events, such as the wartime defense of the capital. See, for example, Jerzy Piórkowski and Stefan Bałuk, *Miasto nieujarzmione* (Warsaw: Iskry, 1957). See also Emilia Borecka and Leonard Sempoliński, *Warszawa 1945* (Warsaw: PWN, 1975). Finally, the twenty-fifth anniversary of Warsaw's "liberation" by the Soviets saw numerous volumes dedicated to

Warsaw. This included a series of books sponsored by the illustrated weekly *The Capital* called "Poznaj Warszawę" ("Get to Know Warsaw") with separate volumes dedicated to Warsaw districts, such as Mokotów, Wola, and Żoliborz. These volumes were published roughly between 1969 and 1972.

13. According to the photography historian Wacław Żdżarski, the auteur photobook was almost nonexistent in Poland during the communist period. There seems to have been only one auteur publication, entitled *Jan Bułhak*, which was published in 1961 and featured a study of Bułhak's images a decade after his death. See Wacław Żdżarski, *Historia fotografii warszawskiej* (Warsaw: PWN, 1974), 311. Żdżarski is most likely referring to Lech Grabowski and Jan Bułhak, *Jan Bułhak* (Warsaw: Arkady, 1961).

14. See Lech Lechowicz, "Fotografia w narodowej potrzebie," in *Fotoeseje: Teksty o fotografii polskiej* (Warsaw: Fundacja Archeologia Fotografii, 2010), 7–18.

15. Ibid., 18, 21.

16. Ibid., 21.

17. Jan Bułhak, "Fotografia dla potrzeb krajoznawstwa i propagandy turystycznej," *Świat Fotografii* no. 1 (1946): 7. Cited according to Lechowicz, "Między politycznym bezpieczeństwem," in *Fotoeseje: Teksty o fotografii polskiej* (Warsaw: Fundacja Archeologia Fotografii, 2010), 75.

18. Ibid., 76.

19. Karolina Lewandowska, *Między dokumentalnością a eksperymentem: Krytyka fotograficzna w Polsce w latach 1946–1989* (Warsaw: Bęc Zmiana and Archeologia Fotografii, 2014), 65.

20. Ibid. See also Lechowicz, "Między politycznym bezpieczeństwem," 76–78.

21. Roland Barthes, "The Photographic Message," in *Image-Music-Text* (New York: Hill and Wang, 1977), 15–31.

22. Ibid., 15–16, 19.

23. Ibid., 20.

24. Zbigniew Grzybowski, Hubert Hilscher, and Leszek Wysznacki, *Warszawa 1945–1970*, trans. Regina Gorzkowska et al. (Warsaw: Wydawnictwo "Sport i Turystyka," 1970), 32–33.

25. See Agnieszka Ciecierska, "Radiowa Mapa Powstania Warszawskiego—walki o Prudential" (Radio Polska, 2014).

26. Wareckiego Square (plac Wareckiego) was called Napoleona Square (plac Napoleona) from 1921 to 1950 and was renamed in 1957 as Powstańców Warszawy Square (plac Powstańców Warszawy) to honor those who fought in the Warsaw Uprising. See Kwiryna Handke, *Słownik nazewnictwa Warszawy* (Warsaw: Slawistyczny Ośrodek Wydawniczy, 1998), 358, 64.

27. Uecker, "Face of the Weimar Republic," 470.

28. Barthes, "The Photographic Message," 31.

29. Badger and Parr, *Photobook*, vol. 1, 188.

30. In *The Photobook: A History*, Badger and Parr refer to what they call a photographic pamphlet published by the American War Information Unit in 1945, *KZ: Bildbericht aus fünf Konzentrationslagern* (*Photo Report from Five Concentration Camps*). They write: "The book shows, with a terse accompanying commentary, images from five of the concentration camps liberated by the allies in 1945—Buchenwald, Belsen, Gardelegen, Nordhausen and Ohrdruf. The

names of the camps—although now infamous—do not matter in a sense, for the pictures from each show a similar litany of horror." Ibid., 194.

31. Krzysztof Jabłoński, *Warszawa: Portret miasta*, ed. Stefan Muszyński (Warsaw: Arkady, 1979), 5.

32. Baczko, Grabowski, and Strzelecki, *Warszawa, stolica Polski*, 8.

33. Żdżarski, *Historia fotografii warszawskiej*, 223.

34. Grzegorz Piątek, "Koniec, który stał się początkiem / An End and a Beginning," in *Kronikarki / The Chroniclers (Zofia Chomętowska i Maria Chrząszczowa): Fotografie Warszawy 1945–1946 / Photographs of Warsaw 1945–1946*, ed. Karolina Lewandowska (Warsaw: Archeologia Fotografii, 2011), 305.

35. Żdżarski, *Historia fotografii warszawskiej*, 248.

36. The Polish Museum in Rapperswil, Switzerland, was founded in 1870 by Count Władysław Broël-Plater in the aftermath of the 1863 January Uprising.

37. Żdżarski, *Historia fotografii warszawskiej*, 248.

38. Ibid., 318. See also Anna Kotańska, "Dokumentacja fotograficzna wystaw: 'Warszawa wczoraj, dziś, jutro' (1938 r.) i 'Warszawa oskarża' (1945 r.) w zbiorach Muzeum Historycznego m. st. Warszawy," *Almanach Muzealny*, no. 2 (1999): 301–2.

39. Stanisław Lorentz was the director of the National Museum from 1936 to 1982. It is worth noting that May 3 is a national holiday in Poland celebrating the declaration of the Constitution of May 3, 1791.

40. For a detailed inventory of the exhibit, see Dariusz Kaczmarzyk, "Pamiętnik wystawy 'Warszawa oskarża' 3 maja 1945—28 stycznia 1946 w Muzeum Narodowym w Warszawie," *Rocznik Muzeum Narodowego w Warszawie* 20 (1976): 599–675.

41. Kotańska, "Dokumentacja fotograficzna," 300.

42. Kaczmarzyk, "Pamiętnik wystawy," 642.

43. This messianic reading of Poland's role in Europe was propagated in the early nineteenth century, particularly by the romantic poet-bard Adam Mickiewicz (1798–1855), in response to the partitioning of Poland. See Adam Mickiewicz, *Księgi narodu polskiego i pielgrzymstwa polskiego*, ed. Zbigniew Nowak, *Dzieła*, vol. 5, *Proza artystyczna i pisma krytyczne* (Warsaw: Czytelnik, 1996). I discuss Mickiewicz's messianism in relation to Tadeusz Konwicki's work in chapter 4.

44. Michael Meng, *Shattered Spaces: Encountering Jewish Ruins in Postwar Germany and Poland* (Cambridge, Mass.: Harvard University Press, 2011), 69–70, 74.

45. Kaczmarzyk, "Pamiętnik wystawy," 643.

46. Ibid., 599.

47. Cited according to Kotańska, "Dokumentacja fotograficzna," 311.

48. Kaczmarzyk, "Pamiętnik wystawy," 638.

49. Kotańska, "Dokumentacja fotograficzna," 291. *Warszawa wczoraj, dziś, jutro* presented such topics as Warsaw's history, the fight for national independence, arts and sciences, education and enlightenment, and health and social welfare. The exhibit included scale models of future projects, as well as Starzyński's plans for a metro system to be completed by the 1970s.

50. Kotańska, "Dokumentacja fotograficzna," 293.

51. Ibid., 302–4.

52. Ibid., 304.

53. Badger and Parr, *Photobook*, vol. 1, 187–88.

54. For an analysis of the relationship between Cocteau's text and Jahan's photographs, see Kathryn Brown, "Remembering the Occupation: La Mort et les statues by Pierre Jahan and Jean Cocteau," *Forum for Modern Language Studies* 49, no. 3 (2013): 286–99.

55. Badger and Parr, *Photobook*, vol. 1, 194–98.

56. On the importance of artifacts for spatial memory, see Jay Winter and Emmanuel Sivan, "Setting the Framework," in *War and Remembrance in the Twentieth Century*, eds. Jay Winter and Emmanuel Sivan (Cambridge: Cambridge University Press, 2000), 37–38.

57. Uszańska and Lubomirska, *Warsaw: Album on the Polish Capital's Ancient Architecture*, 6. Published in a bilingual edition, the introductory Polish and English texts differ slightly in tone; the English version places less emphasis on memory. The quoted material is my own translation from the Polish.

58. It is worth noting that this narrative cuts out references to a middle-class or aristocratic past of Warsaw, as well as a prewar multiethnic and multi-religious Warsaw. The uprisings and protests were presented in the context of peasant rebellions or workers' protests, ignoring the role of the nobility and aristocracy in these events. Note that in the original text, the events of 1794 are referred to as "the April days of 1794" rather than the "Kościuszko Uprising," which is the generally accepted nomenclature. Tadeusz Kościuszko (1746–1817) was a member of the *szlachta* or Polish nobility.

59. Baczko, Grabowski, and Strzelecki, *Warszawa, stolica Polski*, 15.

60. Ibid., 8.

61. The First Polish Army, also known as Berling's Army or the Kościuszko Infantry, was formed in 1943 and was subject to Soviet command. On the formation of the First Polish Army, see Norman Davies, *God's Playground: A History of Poland*, vol. 2, *1795 to the Present* (New York: Columbia University Press, 1982), 271–72.

62. Norman Davies, *Rising '44: The Battle for Warsaw* (New York: Viking, 2004), 391.

63. Baczko, Grabowski, and Strzelecki, *Warszawa, stolica Polski*, 15.

64. Ibid., 16.

65. Burckhardt and Jasieński, *Warszawa Varsovie Warsaw Warschau 1945*. This photobook was a multilingual publication in Polish, English, French, and German. Quotes in English are taken from the original.

66. Ibid., xv, xviii.

67. Ibid., xviii.

68. David Crowley, *Warsaw* (London: Reaktion, 2003), 28.

69. Baczko, Grabowski, and Strzelecki, *Warszawa, stolica Polski*, 15.

70. See "Słowo wstępne" by Janusz Zarzycki in *Warszawa: Krajobraz i architektura*, by Edmund Kupiecki and Ewa Biegańska (Warsaw: Arkady, 1963).

71. Ciborowski, *Warszawa: O zniszczeniu*, 8.

72. Baczko, Grabowski, and Strzelecki, *Warszawa, stolica Polski*, 15.

73. Ibid.

74. A poet and prose writer, Dobrowolski was first and foremost a propagandist. He was born in Warsaw and began his literary career in interwar Poland as a cofounder of the avant-garde literary circle "Kwadryga." During World War

II, he was a member of the Home Army and authored a number of songs on the Warsaw Uprising. After the war, Dobrowolski entered the ranks of the Polish People's Army, edited the monthly *Polska zbrojna (Armed Poland)*, became an active member of the communist party, wrote intensely during the short period of socialist realism, and worked for a time in the Ministry of Culture and Art. A fictional version of Dobrowolski is portrayed in Zbigniew Uniłowski's 1932 novel *Wspólny pokój (Shared Room)*.

75. Grzybowski, Hilscher, and Wysznacki, *Warszawa 1945–1970*, 4.

76. Ibid., 4–5.

77. Quoted from the English-language original, Stanisław Jankowski and Adolf Ciborowski, *Warsaw 1945 and Today* (Warsaw: Interpress, 1971), 6. For the Polish text, see Stanisław Jankowski and Adolf Ciborowski, *Warszawa 1945 i dziś* (Warsaw: Interpress, 1971).

78. Edmund Kupiecki and Ewa Biegańska, *Warszawa: Krajobraz i architektura* (Warsaw: Arkady, 1963), 9.

79. Budrewicz and Falkowski, *Warszawiacy*, 16.

80. Jankowski and Ciborowski, *Warsaw 1945 and Today*, 6.

81. Joanna B. Michlic and Antony Polonsky, "Introduction" in *The Neighbors Respond: The Controversy Over the Jedwabne Massacre in Poland*, eds. Joanna B. Michlic and Antony Polonsky (Princeton, N.J.: Princeton University Press, 2004), 6. Compare Michlic and Polonsky to Svetlana Boym, who writes that the tendency to count victims of the war within a national framework and without specifically acknowledging the Holocaust was common in the Soviet Union and its satellite countries. She writes: "the official GDR ideology, like the Soviet one, emphasized the anti-Fascist resistance and did not single out Jews as major victims of fascism." See Svetlana Boym, *The Future of Nostalgia* (New York: Basic Books, 2001), 201.

82. Baczko, Grabowski, and Strzelecki, *Warszawa, stolica Polski*, 72–73.

83. As Jacek Leociak demonstrates, the Warsaw Ghetto Uprising in April 1943 was not immediately referred to as an "uprising." See "'Zraniona pamięć': Rocznice powstania w getcie warszawskim w prasie polskiej (1944–1989)," in *Literatura polska wobec Zagłady*, eds. Alina Brodzka, Dorota Krawczyńska, and Jacek Leociak (Warsaw: Żydowski Instytut Historyczny, 2000), 29–49.

84. Bolesław Bierut, *Sześcioletni plan odbudowy Warszawy* (Warsaw: Książka i Wiedza, 1950), 201–12.

85. Compare with Meng, *Shattered Spaces*, 76.

86. Edmund Kupiecki, *Warszawa 1960* (Kraków: Arkady, 1960), 21.

87. Kupiecki and Biegańska, *Warszawa: Krajobraz i architektura*, image 105.

88. Pawiak Prison was the largest political prison in German-occupied Poland. The history of the prison, however, goes back to the nineteenth century. Originally built in the 1830s under the Russian partition of Poland, it served as a political prison after the January Uprising in 1863.

89. Kupiecki and Biegańska, *Warszawa: Krajobraz i architektura*, 104.

90. Jabłoński, *Warszawa: Portret miasta*, image 44. Note that the language adopted here is based on a Polish martyrological discourse.

91. Gerry Badger, "Sequencing the Photobook (part 2)," *Aperture* (2012): 3.

92. On the idea of temporal anachronies in narratology, see Gérard Genette, *Narrative Discourse: An Essay in Method* (Ithaca, N.Y.: Cornell University Press, 1980).

93. See Baczko, Grabowski, and Strzelecki, *Warszawa, stolica Polski*, 102–03, 32–39. See also Bierut, *Sześcioletni plan*, 228–30.

94. *Reconstruction of Towns in People's Poland: Warsaw—Poznań—Cracow—Gdańsk—Wrocław—Stalinogród*, special issue of the weekly *Stolica* (Warsaw, 1954).

95. Baczko, Grabowski, and Strzelecki, *Warszawa, stolica Polski*, 48.

96. On the exposure of Warsaw's older architectural elements due to wartime devastation, see Piątek, "Koniec," 284–85.

97. Baczko, Grabowski, and Strzelecki, *Warszawa, stolica Polski*, 40.

98. Ibid., 21.

99. Ibid., 63–64.

100. Originally erected in 1644, the Sigismund III Vasa Column is the oldest secular monument in Warsaw. It was toppled and severely damaged by the Germans during the 1944 Warsaw Uprising. In 1949, the statue of Sigismund was restored by conservationists and a new granite shaft was created to replace the nineteenth-century marble one that is now on display outside the Royal Castle.

101. Baczko, Grabowski, and Strzelecki, *Warszawa, stolica Polski*, 64.

102. Ibid., 80.

103. "Piękno Warszawy, której już nie ma, a którą wskrzesimy," *Stolica: Warszawski Tygodnik Ilustrowany*, November 3, 1946, 6.

Chapter 2

References to news segments from the Polish Film Chronicle (Polska Kronika Filmowa, PKF) follow the numeration in the card catalog of the Filmoteka Narodowa and the Repozytorium Cyfrowe Filmoteki Narodowej. The numbers before the colon refer to the edition and year the segment was released; those following the colon indicate the number of the news segment within that edition. Thus, for example, PKF 1/45:4 was the first newsreel in 1945 and the referenced news segment was the fourth news story on that newsreel. PKF news segments can be viewed at http://www.repozytorium.fn.org.pl.

1. Raymond Fielding, *The American Newsreel: A Complete History, 1911–1967* (Jefferson, N.C.: McFarland, 2006), 3.

2. While considered a weekly news report, the frequency of the PKF varied, particularly right after the war. See Wacław Świeżyński and Stanisław Ozimek, "Kroniki wojny i pokoju," in *Historia filmu polskiego: 1939–1956*, ed. Jerzy Toeplitz. (Warsaw: Wydawnictwo Artystyczne i Filmowe, 1974), 104–5.

3. Joshua Malitsky, *Post-Revolution Nonfiction Film: Building the Soviet and Cuban Nations* (Bloomington: Indiana University Press, 2013), 6–7.

4. On the manipulation of film elements in the newsreel, see Fielding, *The American Newsreel*. See also Malitsky, *Post-Revolution Nonfiction Film*; Ciara Chambers, *Ireland in the Newsreels* (Dublin: Irish Academic Press, 2012); and Sara Beth Levavy, "Immediate Mediation: A Narrative of the Newsreel and the Film," dissertation, Stanford University, 2013. As regards film as a tool of propaganda, see Nicholas Reeves, *The Power of Film Propaganda: Myth or Reality?* (London: Cassell, 1999).

5. Malitsky makes a similar point in reference to Soviet and Cuban nonfiction film. He writes: "these films and the networks through which they circulate do not just offer examples of new engagements with national space but *activate the process of imagining moving differently* through national space." Malitsky, *Post-Revolution Nonfiction Film*, 5.

6. Bolesław Michałek and Frank Turaj, *The Modern Cinema of Poland* (Bloomington: Indiana University Press, 1988), 2–3.

7. Jerzy Bossak, cited according to Frank Bren, *World Cinema 1: Poland* (London: Flicks Books, 1986), 4.

8. Ibid., 3–4.

9. Ibid., 3.

10. The precursor to the PKF, *Polska walcząca* (*Poland Embattled*), was a two-part newsreel dated January and November 1944 produced under the auspices of "Czołówka." The November newsreel became the basis for the first PKF edition. Świeżyński and Ozimek, "Kroniki," 101–2. In addition to the November newsreel, "Czołówka" (under the direction of Aleksander Ford) also produced the dramatic documentary *Majdanek—cmentarzysko Europy* (*Majdanek, the Burial Ground of Europe*), which was filmed on July 24–25, 1944, two days after the Majdanek concentration camp was liberated. This film was first screened along with the November newsreel at the Apollo movie theater in Lublin. These were not, however, the first newsreels produced in Poland. The interwar government's Polish Telegraphic Agency (PAT) began newsreel production in 1928. See Waldemar Grabowski, *Polska Agencja Telegraficzna 1918–1991* (Warsaw: Polska Agencja Prasowa, 2005).

11. Known initially by the name "Stowarzyszenie Propagandy Filmu Artystycznego Start," the group adopted the name "Stowarzyszenie Miłośników Filmu Artystycznego START" in 1931. See Marek Haltof, *Polish National Cinema* (New York: Berghahn Books, 2002), 37, 42. See also Sheila Skaff, *The Law of the Looking Glass: Cinema in Poland, 1896–1939* (Athens: Ohio University Press, 2008). I have adopted the translation of "START" from Janina Falkowska and Marek Haltof, *The New Polish Cinema* (Wiltshire, Eng.: Flicks Books, 2003), 99.

12. Jerzy Toeplitz, "Polska Kronika Filmowa—dorobek XX-lecia," *Zeszyty Prasoznawcze*, no. 3 (1964): 94–95.

13. Świeżyński and Ozimek, "Kroniki," 110.

14. For a more detailed description of the film industry in Poland after the war, see chapter 3.

15. *Słownik języka polskiego*, ed. Witold Doroszewski et al. (Warsaw: Wiedza Powszechna, 1958–69), s.v. "kronika."

16. The original title in Latin is *Gesta principum Polonorum*, meaning "the deeds of the Princes of the Poles."

17. Bolesław Prus, *Kroniki*, ed. Zygmunt Szweykowski, 16 vols. (Warsaw: PIW, 1966).

18. In contrast, the interwar newsreels produced by the Polish Telegraphic Agency (PAT) were referred to as "film weeklies" or "sound weeklies" (*Tygodnik Filmowy PAT* and later *Tygodnik Dźwiękowy PAT*), alluding to print newspapers or journals.

19. See Marek Cieśliński, *Piękniej niż w życiu: Polska Kronika Filmowa, 1944–1994* (Warsaw: Wydawnictwo "Trio," 2006).

20. On the role of film in Bolshevik propaganda, see Reeves, *Power of Film Propaganda*.

21. Cited according to Bren, *World Cinema 1*, 4.

22. Ibid., 3–4.

23. See Świeżyński and Ozimek, "Kroniki," 110. See also Cieśliński, *Piękniej niż w życiu*, 86–87. The distribution channels of the PKF were strictly controlled particularly after 1956, when the PKF introduced two editions of the newsreel: Edition A shown in the countryside, and Edition B reserved for large cities.

24. Ibid., 32.

25. Ibid. Vertov is best known as the father of cinéma vérité. For more on Vertov's style and influence in the Soviet context, see David C. Gillespie, *Early Soviet Cinema: Innovation, Ideology and Propaganda* (London: Wallflower, 2000). See also *Dziga Vertov: The Vertov Collection at the Austrian Film Museum*, eds. Barbara Kleiber-Wurm and Thomas Tode (Vienna: SYNEMA, 2006); Jeremy Hicks, *Dziga Vertov: Defining Documentary Film* (London: I. B. Tauris, 2007); and David Tomas, *Vertov, Snow, Farocki: Machine Vision and the Posthuman* (New York: Bloomsbury Academic, 2013).

26. Toeplitz, "Polska Kronika Filmowa," 95.

27. Cieśliński, *Piękniej niż w życiu*, 18.

28. Świeżyński and Ozimek, "Kroniki," 105. See also Cieśliński, *Piękniej niż w życiu*, 9.

29. Ibid., 28.

30. Ibid., 29–30.

31. Ibid., 32.

32. Cited according to Świeżyński and Ozimek, "Kroniki," 111–12. In turn, Świeżyński and Ozimek quote Bossak from Zbigniew Pitera, "Sprawozdanie z I Zjazdu Pracowników PKF," *Biuletyn Informacyjny Filmu Polskiego*, no. 14 (1946).

33. Quoted according to Cieśliński, *Piękniej niż w życiu*, 90. The original text can be found in the *Archiwum Akt Nowych* (zesp. KC PZPR, syng. 237/XIX–303).

34. Cieśliński, *Piękniej niż w życiu*, 15. See also Filip Łobodziński, "Życie po życiu," *Newsweek.pl*, May 24, 2009; and Krystyna Lubelska, "Kronika nie umyka," *Polityka.pl*, March 27, 2006. In Australia, Britain, Ireland, and the United States, the newsreel lost its popularity and disappeared from screens in the 1960s as television became the main source of audiovisual news. See Fielding, *The American Newsreel*. See also Chambers, *Ireland in the Newsreels*.

35. A newsreel was often made up of about a dozen short news segments. Exceptions were made for special events and holidays, when a newsreel could be devoted to one topic and last up to a half-hour. See, for example, PKF 20/52:1–21, "1 Maja 1952" (May 6, 1952).

36. A natural-sounding voice-over commentary is considered vital to the efficacy of newsreel propaganda. Brett Bowles discusses, for example, the failure of a 1940 French-language Nazi propaganda newsreel narrated by a non-native French speaker. See Brett Bowles, "German Newsreel Propaganda in France, 1940–1944," *Historical Journal of Film, Radio and Television* 24, no. 1 (2004): 51. In the Polish context, intonation tended to escape the control of censors, as did sarcasm, irony, or humor. Such was the case with those documentaries

considered part of the Czarna Seria (Black Series) made from around 1955 to 1958, which critiqued the shortcomings of the communist regime. The creators of the newsreels took liberties by recording ironic verbal commentaries that clashed with or countered the images on screen, or that alluded critically to current events. In such cases, the intonation of the speaker was often more important than the words themselves. Such commentary appeared in the PKF particularly during times of social upheaval, such as the June 1956 demonstrations in Poznań. See Łobodziński, "Życie po życiu." A similar tone appeared in reports on December 1970 and the start of the Solidarity movement in 1980.

37. Świeżyński and Ozimek, "Kroniki," 112.

38. See chapter 1 for a discussion of photobooks and the exhibit *Warszawa oskarża* (*Warsaw Accuses*). See also Michael Meng, *Shattered Spaces: Encountering Jewish Ruins in Postwar Germany and Poland* (Cambridge, Mass.: Harvard University Press, 2011), 69–70.

39. I define "normalization" as a transitional period moving from war trauma towards postwar peace and a period of post-trauma, and "normality" as a relative concept that is (re)defined by continually changing circumstances. See my article "Normalizacja a odbudowa Warszawy w obiektywie Polskiej Kroniki Filmowej (1945–1956)," in *(Nie)przezroczystość normalności w literaturze polskiej XX i XXI wieku*, eds. Hanna Gosk and Bożena Karwowska (Warsaw: Dom Wydawniczy Elipsa, 2014), 103.

40. As I mention earlier, the rhetoric of a "murdered" Warsaw was usually not part of the newsreel narrative about the capital, with "Warszawa wolna" being an exception. While the PKF did not dwell on the war in the context of Warsaw, of note are news segments on the prosecution of German war criminals that took place in the capital. See, for example, PKF 18/46:5, "Przybycie do Warszawy z Norymbergi zbrodniarzy hitlerowskich" (June 18, 1946), which shows the arrival in Warsaw of Rudolf Höss, commandant of Auschwitz from 1940 to 1944, who was extradited to Poland in May 1946. See also PKF 1/47:8, "Warszawa oskarża: Proces Fischera" (December 31, 1946), which reports on the trial of Ludwig Fischer, governor of the *Generalgouvernement*'s Warsaw District and the initiator of the Warsaw ghetto.

41. Though the average length of a shot in the film is six seconds, two of the longest shots (about ten seconds each) portray Bierut, then president of the National Home Council (KRN).

42. Marek Cieśliński, "Komentarz do PKF 4/45: Warszawa Wolna" (Warsaw: Repozytorium Cyfrowe Filmoteki Narodowej).

43. Throughout the rest of this book, the Palace of Culture and Science is also referred to as "the Palace of Culture" or "the Palace."

44. Świeżyński and Ozimek, "Kroniki," 103.

45. Cieśliński stresses this aspect of the PKF in his book *Piękniej niż w życiu*, whose title translates as "more beautiful than reality."

46. Despite the rejection of private enterprise under communism, private trade persisted in Poland. See, for example, PKF unused footage, no. 5015, "Bazary na Pańskiej i Ząbkowskiej" (September 5–11, 1950), which shows unused footage from an outdoor market in Warsaw in 1950. A critique of private enterprise and a "ground floor" Warsaw can also be found in photobooks. For example, in *MDM-Marszałkowska, 1730–1954* we read: "private initiative pushes its way

onto Marszałkowska . . . Single-floor ramshackle buildings with private shops pretend to be a city center . . . but ominous ruins still protrude from behind a shoddy veneer." See Stanisław Jankowski, *MDM-Marszałkowska, 1730–1954* (Warsaw: Czytelnik, 1955), 92–95.

47. See PKF 22/45:1, "Wręczenie listów uwierzytelniających Bierutowi przez ambasadora Francji" (August 18, 1945); PKF 22/45:2, "Wręczenie listów uwierzytelniających prezydentowi w Belwederze przez ambasadora USA" (August 18, 1945); PKF 28/45:1, "Wręczenie listów uwierzytelniających prezydentowi Bierutowi w Belwederze przez ambasadora Włoch" (October 4, 1945); PKF 28/45:2, "Wręczenie listów uwierzytelniających prezydentowi Bierutowi przez posła Wielkiego Księstwa Luxemburg" (October 4, 1945); and PKF 1/46:5, "Wręczenie listów uwierzytelniających w Belwederze przez posłów: Bułgarii, Danii, Holandii i Szwajcarii" (January 14, 1946).

48. See Meng, *Shattered Spaces*, 74.

49. PolskieRadio.pl, "Jan Zachwatowicz—udaremnił zamach Niemców na kulturę polską," Polskie Radio, http://www.polskieradio.pl/39/156/Artykul /909950,Jan-Zachwatowicz-udaremnil-zamach-Niemcow-na-kulture-polska. It is worth noting the difference between Zachwatowicz's approach and the approach adopted in the French village of Oradour-sur-Glane, which remains in a state of ruins as a site of memory and remembrance. I am indebted to Irene Masing-Delic for pointing this out.

50. Tadeusz Makarczyński, *Suita warszawska* (Narodowy Instytut Audiowizualny, 1946).

51. Wacław Świeżyński, "Film dokumentalny," in *Historia filmu polskiego: 1939–1956*, ed. Jerzy Toeplitz. (Warsaw: Wydawnictwo Artystyczne i Filmowe, 1974), 135.

52. Lutosławski was commissioned by Makarczyński to compose the music. For more on Lutosławski's composition, see Jan Topolski, "Suita warszawska (liner notes)," in *Lutosławski/świat (5 Disc CD Collection)*, ed. Adam Suprynowicz (Warsaw: Narodowy Instytut Audiowizualny, 2013).

53. Adolf Forbert's footage used in Makarczyński's film was originally intended for a different documentary short on postwar Warsaw by the composer and film director Andrzej Panufnik. Panufnik's film was set to Chopin's Ballade no. 4 in F-minor, Op. 52. According to Panufnik, his film was not released due to a "lack of ideological clarity and technical deficiencies." See Topolski, "Suita warszawska (liner notes)." See also "Ballada F-Moll," Filmpolski.pl: Internetowa baza filmu polskiego, http://www.filmpolski.pl/fp/index.php?film=427320.

54. On the various cultural functions of ruins, see "Archeology of Metropolis" in Svetlana Boym, *The Future of Nostalgia* (New York: Basic Books, 2001), 79.

55. Since the time of silent films, music has been used to evoke emotional responses in viewers and provide an interpretive framework to direct attention at relevant narrative and visual details. Music has been proven to have a significant impact on viewers' interpretation and memory of a filmic image. See Marilyn Boltz, "The Cognitive Processing of Film and Musical Soundtracks," *Memory & Cognition* 32, no. 7 (2004): 1194–205. See also Marilyn Boltz, "Musical Soundtracks as a Schematic Influence on the Cognitive Processing of Filmed Events," *Music Perception: An Interdisciplinary Journal* 18, no. 4 (2001): 427–54.

56. One of the most important streets before the war, Marszałkowska was almost completely destroyed during the Warsaw Ghetto Uprising in 1943 and the Warsaw Uprising in 1944. Bankowy Square was renamed Dzierżyńskiego Square in 1951 when the monument to Feliks Dzierżyński was erected.

57. See Jan Zachwatowicz, "Sprawozdanie kierownika Wydziału Architektoniczno-Zabytkowego Biura Odbudowy Stolicy na konferencję u Prezydenta Bolesława Bieruta 23 III 1945 r.," in *Warszawa: Stolica Polski Ludowej*, no. 2, ed. Jan Górski, vol. 11, *Studia warszawskie* (Warsaw: PWN, 1972), 271–74.

58. For details on this debate, see Jan Górski, "Dyskusje o odbudowie Warszawy w latach 1945–1946," in *Warszawa: Stolica Polski Ludowej*, no. 1, ed. Jan Górski, vol. 5, *Studia Warszawskie* (Warsaw: PWN, 1970), 75–140.

59. The Kiliński monument was removed (but not destroyed) by the Germans during the war. See *Encyklopedia Warszawy*, ed. Barbara Petrozolin-Skowrońska (Warsaw: PWN, 1994), s.v. "Pomnik Jana Kilińskiego."

60. Such mediation sometimes took a subtle but significant form of desacralizing religious spaces. See my article "Normalizacja a odbudowa Warszawy," 105–6.

61. Similar language was used in reference to the reconstruction of the Royal Castle in PKF 26/50:2, "Odbudowa Zamku Królewskiego" (June 21, 1950).

62. "*Zabytek*" cannot be translated into English directly. It is defined as "a work of art or literature (for example, a building, painting, statue, print, book) that has museum and historical value as a document of the past." *Słownik języka polskiego*, ed. Witold Doroszewski et al. (Warsaw: Wiedza Powszechna, 1958–69), s.v. "zabytek."

63. On the history of Mariensztat, see Andrzej Zahorski, *Warszawa za Sasów i Stanisława Augusta* (Warsaw: PIW, 1970), 60.

64. See PKF 36/46:4, "Odbudowa Warszawy" (October 23, 1946), particularly the section on the Łazienki Palace (00:02:02–12).

Chapter 3

1. On the effect of cultural texts on communal identity, in particular the relationship between the advent of the printing press and nationalism, see Benedict Anderson, *Imagined Communities: Reflections on the Origin and Spread of Nationalism* (New York: Verso, 1991).

2. For a database of Polish films organized by year of release, see *Filmpolski.pl: Internetowa baza filmu polskiego* (Warsaw: Państwowa Wyższa Szkoła Filmowa, Telewizyjna i Teatralna im. Leona Schillera w Łodzi, 1998–2013). Ewa Mazierska and Laura Rascaroli note that between 1945 and the 1960s, over forty films featured Warsaw. These films represented the communal effort to rebuild the capital after the war, the tragedy of wartime Warsaw, and Warsaw's distant past. See Ewa Mazierska and Laura Rascaroli, *From Moscow to Madrid: Postmodern Cities, European Cinema* (London: I. B. Tauris, 2003), 96–97.

3. Unlike in the newsreels, the workers in Ford's film are not "monumentalized" by the cinematography. Furthermore, the film shows the workers sweating and surrounded by mud and dirt. Construction equipment includes horses, not just the mechanized equipment featured in the newsreels. Finally, unlike in the newsreels, diegetic sound is used in the labor scenes of the film.

4. Of the twenty films set in Warsaw and produced between 1945 and 1956, one is a drama set before the war, seven are set during the war (six dramas and a musical), and eight are dramas set after the war.

5. Tadeusz Lubelski suggests that these movies were made according to the "strategy of the professional," which he defines as a way of making entertaining films according to a prewar model or in a "Hollywood style." See Tadeusz Lubelski, *Strategie autorskie w polskim filmie fabularnym lat 1945–1961* (Kraków: Uniwersytet Jagielloński, 1992), 56.

6. Richard Taylor, "A 'Cinema for the Millions': Soviet Socialist Realism and the Problem of Film Comedy," *Journal of Contemporary History* 18, no. 3 (1983): 454.

7. In addition to the cinematographers I have already mentioned, the camera operator and cinematographer Mieczysław Verocsy worked on three of the four comedies (as a cinematographer on *Treasure* and *Irena, Go Home!* and as a camera operator on *Adventure in Mariensztat*). Beginning his career just after the war, he was primarily involved in the creation of feature films, though he too dabbled in documentary. See Andrzej Bukowiecki, "Mieczysław Verocsy," Akademia Polskiego Filmu, http://www.akademiapolskiegofilmu.pl/pl/historia -polskiego-filmu/operatorzy/mieczyslaw-verocsy/353.

8. On cinema and popular culture in the Soviet Union, see Denise J. Youngblood, *Movies for the Masses: Popular Cinema and Soviet Society in the 1920s* (Cambridge: Cambridge University Press, 1992).

9. On the entertainment value of Polish films from the end of the war to 1960, see Bolesław Michałek's discussion of "film rozrywkowy" or narrative films for entertainment purposes in *Szkice o filmie polskim* (Warsaw: Wydawnictwa Artystyczne i Filmowe, 1960), 123.

10. Often attributed to Vladimir Lenin, the exact source of this quote is unclear. The Polish film critic Aleksander Ledóchowski attributes it to A. V. Lunacharsky, the first commissar of the Soviet Ministry of Education. See footnote 1 on page 119 in Piotr Zwierzchowski, *Pęknięty monolit: Konteksty polskiego kina socrealistycznego* (Bydgoszcz: Wydawnictwo Uniwersytetu Kazimierza Wielkiego, 2005). Regardless of the quote's source, it is clear that both Lenin and Lunacharsky considered cinema a vital tool for education and indoctrination. See Youngblood, *Movies for the Masses*, 35–38.

11. Marek Haltof, *Polish National Cinema* (New York: Berghahn Books, 2002), 49.

12. This was the case, for example, with the first postwar film, *Zakazane piosenki (Forbidden Songs)* (directed by Leonard Buczkowski, screenplay by Ludwik Starski), which was released in 1946, taken off screens almost immediately, reedited, and then rereleased in 1948. Similarly, Aleksander Ford's first film after the war, *Ulica Graniczna (Border Street)*, was not released until 1949, though the screenplay was written already in 1946 with production starting in 1947. And finally, Jerzy Zarzycki's *Miasto nieujarzmione (Unvanquished City)*, which began in 1945 as a screenplay written by Czesław Miłosz and Jerzy Andrzejewski, went through a number of screenplay and screen versions during a five-year period because it repeatedly failed to satisfy ideological demands. For more on *Forbidden Songs*, see Piotr Śmiałowski, "Pierwszy na zawsze," *Kino* 41, no. 475 (2007): 54–57. See also Alina Madej, *Kino, władza, publiczność: Kinematografia*

polska w latach 1944–1949 (Bielsko-Biała: Prasa Beskidzka, 2002), 116–33. For more on *Border Street,* see Marek Haltof, *Polish Film and the Holocaust: Politics and Memory* (New York: Berghahn Books, 2012), 53–73. See also Omer Bartov, *The "Jew" in Cinema: From The Golem to Don't Touch My Holocaust* (Bloomington: Indiana University Press, 2005), 179–86. For more on the history of *Unvanquished City,* see Czesław Miłosz, "Wyjaśnienia po latach," *Dialog: Miesięcznik Poświęcony Dramaturgii Współczesnej—Teatralnej, Filmowej, Radiowej, Telewizyjnej* 29, no. 9 [336] (1984): 116–17.

13. Bolesław Michałek and Frank Turaj, *The Modern Cinema of Poland* (Bloomington: Indiana University Press, 1988), 8–10. See also Haltof, *Polish National Cinema,* 56–71.

14. Alina Madej, "Zjazd filmowy w Wiśle, czyli dla każdego coś przykrego," *Kwartalnik Filmowy* no. 18 (1997): 207.

15. For more on censorship and the impact of the communist regime in Poland on the distribution of film, see Jane Leftwich Curry, ed., *The Black Book of Polish Censorship* (New York: Random House, 1984).

16. According to Marek Haltof, Ford—who headed Film Polski from 1945 to 1947—accumulated power and ran "the board in an almost dictatorial manner." Haltof, *Polish National Cinema,* 48.

17. Haltof, *Polish National Cinema,* 47–48.

18. Cited according to ibid., 47. See also Lubelski, *Strategie autorskie,* 39.

19. Zbigniew Pitera [Jan Łęczyca, pseud.], "O nowy realistyczny film polski," *Film,* no. 10 (1949). Cited according to Zwierzchowski, *Pęknięty monolit,* 123.

20. Haltof, *Polish National Cinema,* 47.

21. Madej, *Kino, władza, publiczność,* 120.

22. Zwierzchowski, *Pęknięty monolit,* 123.

23. Many filmmakers chose to emigrate rather than return to a Soviet-controlled Poland after the war. See Haltof, *Polish National Cinema,* 47; and Haltof, *Polish Film and the Holocaust,* 13.

24. Haltof, *Polish Film and the Holocaust,* 58.

25. Lubelski, *Strategie autorskie,* 59. See also Jerzy Armata, "Leonard Buczkowski," Akademia Polskiego Filmu, http://www.akademiapolskiegofilmu.pl/pl /historia-polskiego-filmu/rezyserzy/leonard-buczkowski/35.

26. On how Buczkowski, Starski, and Fethke navigated the problems of "commercial" film in the socialist realist context, see Zwierzchowski, *Pęknięty monolit,* 119–50.

27. Ibid., 124.

28. Madej, *Kino, władza, publiczność,* 120.

29. Danuta Szaflarska and Jerzy Duszyński were already well known to film audiences from their roles as a sister and brother, Halina and Roman Tokarski, in Buczkowski and Starski's *Forbidden Songs.*

30. The word "równy" in Polish has both concrete and abstract connotations. It can refer to something that is flat, level, or equal (as in amounts). It can also refer to the abstract value of equality between people. In *Treasure,* both meanings are relevant. "Równa Street" thus ironically refers to the landscape of the street, which is covered in rubble, and it also refers to the social equality portrayed in the film.

31. Monika Talarczyk-Gubała, *PRL się śmieje! Polska komedia filmowa lat 1945–1989* (Warsaw: Wydawnictwo "Trio," 2007), 35–36.

32. Grażyna Stachówna, "Socjalistyczne romanse, czyli gorzko-słodkie losy melodramatu w Peerelu," *Kino* 41, no. 476 (2007): 52. In Buczkowski's second Varsovian romantic comedy, *Adventure in Mariensztat*, he would forestall such criticism by describing the romance between the main characters as "the kind of private initiative that perfectly fits in with [the] economic plan."

33. Lubelski, *Strategie autorskie*, 62–63.

34. The simultaneous portrayal of chaos and order in *Treasure* comes almost a decade earlier than in the PKF and in the Black Series film *Warszawa 1956* (directed by Jerzy Bossak and Jarosław Brzozowski, 1956). See my discussion on this topic in chapter 4.

35. Compare this scene to such newsreels as PKF 25/46:6, "Młodzież jugosłowiańska przy uprzątaniu gruzów Warszawy" (August 6, 1946), and PKF 30/47:3, "Jugosłowianie przy pracy nad uprzątaniem gruzu w Warszawie" (July 23, 1947). In the movie, humor softens the propagandistic tone found in newsreels portraying similar volunteer efforts.

36. Witek's confusion parallels sentiments expressed in cultural artifacts such as the song "Na prawo most, na lewo most" ("A Bridge to the Left, A Bridge to the Right") and Adam Ważyk's "Poemat dla dorosłych" (1955; "A Poem for Adults"), which was one of the first texts to criticize the communist regime before the 1956 Thaw. The lyrics of "A Bridge to the Left, A Bridge to the Right" sing of Warsaw's changing landscape as something to be admired for its rapid day-to-day transformation. The refrain goes as follows: "A bridge to the left, a bridge to the right, / the Vistula flows below. / From second to second, from hour to hour, / the buildings continue to grow." In the first stanza of Ważyk's "A Poem for Adults," the poetic "I" mistakenly takes the wrong bus and is unable to figure out where he is because Warsaw has changed so much. For Ważyk, the changing landscape is something to be lamented. See my article "Normalizacja a odbudowa Warszawy w obiektywie Polskiej Kroniki Filmowej (1945–1956)," in *(Nie) przezroczystość normalności w literaturze polskiej XX i XXI wieku*, eds. Hanna Gosk and Bożena Karwowska (Warsaw: Dom Wydawniczy Elipsa, 2014), 101. See also David Crowley, *Warsaw* (London: Reaktion, 2003), 57–58.

37. Tadeusz Lubelski, "Nasza komedia narodowa," *Kwartalnik Filmowy* 67/68 (Autumn 2009): 295–96.

38. Tadeusz Lubelski makes a similar point. See ibid.

39. See Shumyatsky's 1935 *Cinematography for the Millions: An Attempt at Analysis*. Cited according to Taylor, "Cinema for the Millions," 453.

40. See Michałek and Turaj, *The Modern Cinema of Poland*, 13.

41. Both Korsakówna and Santor were members of the State Folk Group of Song and Dance "Mazowsze" that was formed by government decree in 1948. See "Mazowsze—historia," http://mazowsze.waw.pl/sub,pl,mazowsze—historia .html.

42. Zwierzchowski, *Pęknięty monolit*, 135–38.

43. This fairytale quality was a mark of Ludwik Starski's screenplays. See Tadeusz Szyma, "W starym kinie Ludwika Starskiego," *Kino* 40, no. 464 (2006): 72.

44. The Mariensztat Square scenes of the movie were actually filmed at the Film Polski studios in Łódź, where an outdoor set was created. See PKF 47/52:12, "Praca przy filmie 'Przygoda na Mariensztacie'" (November 12, 1952).

45. On the role of the establishing shot and its relationship to cinematic cartography, see Tom Conley, *Cartographic Cinema* (Minneapolis: University of Minnesota Press, 2007), 2.

46. Sue Beeton, *Film-Induced Tourism* (Clevedon, Eng.: Channel View Publications, 2005), 3–19. See also Dean MacCannell, *The Tourist: A New Theory of the Leisure Class* (Berkeley: University of California Press, 1999).

47. King Jan III Sobieski (1629-1696) was monarch of the Polish-Lithuanian Commonwealth from 1674 to 1696.

48. Bierut's Six-Year Plan for Warsaw's Reconstruction was presented on July 3, while the segment "We Are Visiting Warsaw" was released on November 24.

49. Unveiled in 1937, the Warsaw Mermaid was one of the few Varsovian monuments that remained intact after World War II and required very little repair.

50. Bożena Karwowska, "Metamorfozy pamięci—odbudowa Warszawy w narracji Poli Gojawiczyńskiej," in *Kobieta—Historia—Literatura* (Warsaw: Instytut Badań Literackich, 2016), 180.

51. In 1989, the statue of Feliks Dzierżyński was removed and the original name "Bankowy Square" was readopted. In 2001, the monument to Dzierżyński was replaced by one dedicated to the Polish romantic poet Juliusz Słowacki.

52. Conley, *Cartographic Cinema*, 1.

53. Monika Talarczyk-Gubała also calls attention to this framing of Warsaw in the film. See Talarczyk-Gubała, *PRL się śmieje!*, 38.

54. Tadeusz Lubelski notes that the comedic genre even went so far as to deride the socialist imagination of the ideal city as satisfying all the needs of the working class, as in the 1957 *Ewa chce spać* (*Ewa Wants to Sleep*) (directed by Tadeusz Chmielewski). See Lubelski, "Nasza komedia narodowa," 296.

Chapter 4

1. Jerzy S. Majewski and Tomasz Urzykowski, *Spacerownik: Pałac Kultury i Nauki; Socrealistyczna Warszawa* (Warsaw: Agora SA, 2015), 3.

2. While some sources indicate that the building was handed over to public use on July 22, I am following the date provided on the building's official website. See Pałac Kultury i Nauki w Warszawie, "Ciekawostki," http://www.pkin.pl/strefa-turysty-ciekawostki.

3. Ibid. The original height of the building was 756.8 feet; however, an antenna was added in 1994, raising it to its current height. In comparison, the Empire State Building boasts 102 floors, 2.7 million square feet of office space, and is 1,454 feet tall from the base to the top of the lightning rod/antenna. Its footprint, however, is significantly smaller than the Palace of Culture's, sitting on approximately two acres. See Empire State Realty Trust, "Empire State Building Fact Sheet," http://www.esbnyc.com/sites/default/files/esb_fact_sheet_4_9_14_4.pdf.

4. Pałac Kultury i Nauki w Warszawie, "Ciekawostki." In 1953, the tallest edifice in Europe was the Moscow State University building.

5. Pałac Kultury i Nauki w Warszawie, "W pałacu," http://www.pkin.pl/strefa-turysty-w-palacu.

6. Emilia Dłużewska, "Beata Chomątowska: Pałac Kultury to jest Polska [Rozmowa]," *Wyborcza.pl*, July 15, 2015.

7. For a discussion of these debates, see Konrad Rokicki, "Kłopotliwy dar: Pałac Kultury i Nauki," in *Zbudować Warszawę piękną: O nowy krajobraz*

stolicy (1944–1956), ed. Jerzy Kochanowski (Warsaw: Wydawnictwo "Trio," 2003), 198–207.

8. Dłużewska, "Beata Chomątowska."

9. Daniel Cooper Alarcón, "The Aztec Palimpsest: Toward a New Understanding of Aztlán, Cultural Identity and History," *Aztlán: A Journal of Chicano Studies* 19, no. 2 (1988): 35.

10. Tadeusz Sobolewski, "Balkon Konwickiego," *Gazeta Wyborcza*, August 17, 2009. See also Rokicki, "Kłopotliwy dar," 186.

11. David Crowley, *Warsaw* (London: Reaktion, 2003), 38. See also Rokicki, "Kłopotliwy dar," 127.

12. Jarosław Zieliński, *Pałac Kultury i Nauki* (Łódź: Księży Młyn Dom Wydawniczy, 2012), 47.

13. Rudnev and his cadre also visited Kazimierz nad Wisłą, Płock, Puławy, Czerwińsk, Nieborów, and Kielce. See Rokicki, "Kłopotliwy dar," 107, 91–92.

14. For a description of the Seven Sisters in the context of the history of the Palace of Culture, see Zieliński, *Pałac Kultury i Nauki*, 9–12.

15. Ibid., 7–8.

16. Ibid., 9.

17. Crowley, *Warsaw*, 38–47.

18. Rokicki, "Kłopotliwy dar," 110, 19, 48.

19. Wages were often cut to compensate for contingencies, such as construction errors, which had not been included in the budget. Furthermore, construction schedules were often interrupted because of shortages or delays in the delivery of materials. See ibid., 149–51, 58.

20. Crowley, *Warsaw*, 39.

21. Ibid., 40.

22. Teresa Torańska, *"Them": Stalin's Polish Puppets*, trans. Agnieszka Kolakowska (New York: Harper and Row, 1987), 307.

23. Syrkus was part of the architectural vanguard in interwar Poland and a coauthor of the modernist urban plan *Warszawa Funkcjonalna*.

24. Cited according to Rokicki, "Kłopotliwy dar," 114.

25. See ibid., 102–15.

26. Including Polish decorative elements in the design of the Palace of Culture was specifically done to satisfy detractors of the Palace, who claimed that such a building had no place in Warsaw. See Crowley, *Warsaw*, 40.

27. Rokicki, "Kłopotliwy dar," 107, 91–92.

28. Ibid., 113–14.

29. Ibid., 179.

30. Such an interpretation is supported by the unrealized project to build a Palace of the Soviets in Moscow on the site of the demolished Cathedral of Christ the Savior. Rokicki presents a similar interpretation of city centers as desacralized in ibid., 180–81. Another example of the desacralization of the city center is the Lenin Steel Works in the center of Nowa Huta, where the main avenue of the city leads directly to the factory gates. For more on Nowa Huta, see Katherine Lebow, *Unfinished Utopia: Nowa Huta, Stalinism, and Polish Society, 1949–56* (Ithaca, N.Y.: Cornell University Press, 2013). See also Kinga Pozniak, *Nowa Huta: Generations of Change in a Model Socialist Town* (Pittsburgh, Pa.: University of Pittsburgh Press, 2014).

31. Bolesław Bierut, *Sześcioletni plan odbudowy Warszawy* (Warsaw: Książka i Wiedza, 1950), 14th insert following p. 272.

32. The Six-Year Plan (1950–1955) was announced in 1948, while the Six-Year Plan for Warsaw's Reconstruction was announced in 1949.

33. Zieliński, *Pałac Kultury i Nauki*, 46.

34. Crowley, *Warsaw*, 43.

35. Rokicki, "Kłopotliwy dar," 187.

36. Leopold Tyrmand, *Zły* (Warsaw: Wydawnictwo MG, 2011), 125. Available in English as *The Man with the White Eyes*, trans. David Welsh (New York: Alfred A. Knopf, 1959).

37. English quote according to Leopold Tyrmand, *Diary 1954*, trans. Anita Krystyna Shelton and A. J. Wrobel (Evanston, Ill.: Northwestern University Press, 2014), 201–2.

38. Jerzy S. Majewski and Tomasz Urzykowski, "Pałac Kultury w popkulturze: Od socrealistycznych wierszy po atak Godzilli," *Wyborcza.pl*, July 18, 2015.

39. Ibid.

40. In the novel *Lalka* (1890; *The Doll*), Bolesław Prus ignored the architectural realities of imperial Russian administrative buildings and army barracks in Warsaw in order to create a literary space not occupied by foreign rule. See Józef Bachórz's introduction to Bolesław Prus, *Lalka* (Wrocław: Zakład Narodowy im. Ossolińskich, 1991), lxxxvii–xciii.

41. Wojciech Tymowski, "Pałac Kultury ma 60 lat. Tyle samo co Michał Ogórek [Rozmowa]," *Wyborcza.pl*, July 17, 2015.

42. Such events could not have happened without the explicit approval of the authorities and coincided with, as well as indicated, changes in party politics.

43. Rokicki, "Kłopotliwy dar," 171–72.

44. Przemysław Semczuk, "Kronikarz PRL," *Newsweek Polska*, January 2, 2011.

45. Warsaw's Fotoplastikon is a stereoscopic device for 3D viewing of old photographs from the early twentieth century and is akin to a *kaiserpanorama*.

46. The voice-over uses the word "pomnik," which can be translated as either "monument" or "memorial." The Polish word carries both connotations.

47. The Monument to Brotherhood in Arms was temporarily removed from its location in the Praga North neighborhood during the construction of the underground metro station at Wileński Square (plac Wileński) in 2011. In 2015, based on the monument's ideological meaning, city authorities voted to permanently remove it. See "Pomnik 'czterech śpiących' nie wróci na pl. Wileński," *Wiadomości.wp.pl*, February 26, 2015.

48. Rokicki, "Kłopotliwy dar," 191–92.

49. Crowley, *Warsaw*, 43.

50. Paul Coates, email correspondence with author, March 21, 2013.

51. The aesthetics of the Black Series continued in the PKF through the end of the communist period. See, for example, PKF 22/63:1, "Place Warszawy." In this segment, the slow urban development of Warsaw in the 1960s is critiqued through the ironic juxtaposition of image and voice-over.

52. Łukasz Kamiński, "Piosenki o Warszawie: 'Pałac' i 'Front wschodni' Dezertera," *Wyborcza.pl Warszawa*, September 23, 2005.

53. Stanisław Bereś [Stanisław Nowicki, pseud.], *Pół wieku czyśćca: Rozmowy z Tadeuszem Konwickim* (London: Aneks, 1986), 8.

54. Katarzyna Zechenter, *The Fiction of Tadeusz Konwicki: Coming to Terms with Post-war Polish History and Politics* (Lewiston, N.Y.: Edwin Mellen, 2007).

55. In my analysis of Konwicki, I follow Tadeusz Lubelski, who considers Konwicki's films and novels as parts of a greater textual whole despite the differences in form. He bases this conclusion on the stylistic and thematic coherence between Konwicki's literary and cinematic creations. See Tadeusz Lubelski, *Poetyka powieści i filmów Tadeusza Konwickiego: Na podstawie analiz utworów z lat 1947–1965* (Wrocław: Wydawnictwo Uniwersytetu Wrocławskiego, 1984), 14–15.

56. Konwicki's biography as presented here is a revised version of my encyclopedia entry "Tadeusz Konwicki," in *The Literary Encyclopedia*, December 20, 2016, http://www.litencyc.com/php/speople.php?rec=true&UID=12660.

57. In 1986, in an attempt to explain his early commitment to the communist party, Konwicki stated that "Marxism offered a certain rationalism" at a time when "what we had fought for [during the war] . . . had not been realized." Bereś, *Pół wieku czyśćca*, 63.

58. Tadeusz Konwicki, *Kompleks polski* (London: Index on Censorship, 1977). Available in English as *The Polish Complex*, trans. Richard Lourie (New York: Farrar, Straus and Giroux, 1982).

59. For a more detailed outline of Konwicki's evolution as a writer vis-à-vis the communist regime, see Edward Mozejko, "Beyond Ideology: The Prose of Tadeusz Konwicki," *The Review of Contemporary Fiction* 14, no. 3 (1994): 139–55.

60. Tadeusz Konwicki, *Zwierzoczłekoupiór* (Warsaw: Czytelnik, 1969). Available in English as *The Anthropos-Specter-Beast*, trans. George Korwin-Rodziszewski and Audrey Korwin-Rodziszewski (New York: S.G. Phillips, 1977).

61. Tadeusz Konwicki, *Nowy Świat i okolice; z rysunkami autora* (Warsaw: Czytelnik, 1986). Available in English as *New World Avenue and Vicinity*, trans. George Korwin-Rodziszewski and Audrey Korwin-Rodziszewski (New York: Farrar, Straus and Giroux, 1991).

62. Parenthetical citations for *Ascension* refer to the following edition: Tadeusz Konwicki, *Wniebowstąpienie* (Warsaw: Biblioteka Gazety Wyborczej, 2010). Under communism, harvest festivals were held as a celebration of the working class. Konwicki's text shows a clash between the socialist underpinnings of the Harvest Festival and the peasants in traditional folk dress roaming the streets of 1960s Warsaw.

63. Consider that Konwicki chose the word "ascension" (*wniebowstąpienie*) as the title, in contrast to the word "assumption" (*wniebowzięcie*), which would indicate divine intervention in the process of being assumed, body and soul, into heaven. For Czesław Miłosz's use of the phrase "New Faith," see Czesław Miłosz, *Zniewolony umysł* (Paris: Instytut Literacki, 1980).

64. Parenthetical citations for *A Minor Apocalypse* refer to the following edition: Tadeusz Konwicki, *Mała apokalipsa* (Warsaw: Wydawnictwo ALFA, 1989). For the English translation, see *A Minor Apocalypse*, trans. Richard Lourie (New York: Farrar, Straus and Giroux, 1983).

65. Judith Arlt and Wojciech Tomasik, *Mój Konwicki* (Kraków: Universitas, 2002), 21.

66. Parenthetical citations for *The Polish Complex* refer to the following edition: Tadeusz Konwicki, *Kompleks polski* (London: Index on Censorship, 1977).

67. Tadeusz Konwicki, *Lawa* (Warsaw: Telewizja Kino Polska, 1989), DVD.

68. Adam Mickiewicz, *Dziady*, ed. Zbigniew Nowak, *Dzieła*, vol. 3, *Dramaty* (Warsaw: Czytelnik, 1995), 161.

69. Mickiewicz also articulated his philosophy of messianism in *Księgi narodu polskiego i pielgrzymstwa polskiego* (1832; *Books of the Polish Nation and the Polish Pilgrimage*), where he cast Poland in the role of "Christ among Nations" ("Chrystus wśród narodów"), and as the savior of a Europe that had been brutally corrupted by the Austro-Hungarian, Prussian, and Russian empires. According to Mickiewicz, Poland's restoration as a nation was to bring European-wide redemption from this "Satanic Trinity" ("trójca szatańska"). See Adam Mickiewicz, *Księgi narodu polskiego i pielgrzymstwa polskiego*, ed. Zbigniew Nowak, *Dzieła*, vol. 5, *Proza artystyczna i pisma krytyczne* (Warsaw: Czytelnik, 1996), 5, 15.

70. Tadeusz Sobolewski, "Historia bez happy-endu," *Kino* 41, no. 477 (2007): 98.

71. Ibid.

72. Konwicki, *Lawa*, "Krzyk od Boga."

73. Holoubek recites the following first lines from the preface to *Forefathers' Eve*, Part 3: "For half a century, Poland represents, on the one hand, tireless and unrelenting brutality of tyrants, and on the other, boundless sacrifice and stubborn persistence of the people, such as has not been seen since the persecution of Christians. It seems as though kings have a Herod-like premonition of the manifestation of a new light on earth and of the nearness of their downfall, while the people believe more and more strongly in their rebirth and resurrection." In the remaining lines of the preface, Mickiewicz identifies the start of the "persecution of the Polish people" as 1822 (a year before his arrest), stating that "the history of Poland's martyrology spans many generations and countless victims . . . The epic verse, which we declare today, presents a few detailed sketches of this enormous picture, a few incidents from the time of persecution under the emperor Alexander . . . At that time a general persecution of the Polish people . . . began. Senator Novosiltsev . . . entered the scene." Mickiewicz, *Dziady*, 121.

74. On the persistence of Mickiewicz and his works in Polish culture, see Maria Janion, *Projekt krytyki fantazmatycznej: Szkice o egzystencjach ludzi i duchów* (Warsaw: Wydawnictwo PEN, 1991), 172.

75. Konwicki, *Lawa*, "Żałoba" and "Pamięć."

76. Ibid., "Modlitwa."

77. The closing of the play led to a series of student protests, which were brutally repressed, and students involved in the demonstrations were expelled from the University of Warsaw. By March of that year, the social turmoil spurred by the regime and conflicts within the communist party culminated in the expulsion of the majority of Poland's postwar Jewish community. These events led to an overhaul in the party hierarchy, as well as the political awakening of a new generation of young Poles, who directly felt the brutality of the communist authorities for the first time. See Dariusz Stola, "Fighting Against the Shadows: The Anti-Zionist Campaign of 1968," in *Antisemitism and Its Opponents in Modern Poland*, ed. Robert Blobaum (Ithaca, N.Y.: Cornell University Press, 2005), 284–300; Mikołaj Kunicki, "The Red and the Brown: Bolesław Piasecki, the Polish Communists, and the Anti-Zionist Campaign in Poland, 1967–1968," *East European*

Politics and Societies 19, no. 2 (2005): 185–225; and *1968, Forty Years After*, eds. Leszek W. Głuchowski and Antony Polonsky, vol. 21 of Polin: Studies in Polish Jewry (Oxford: Littman Library of Jewish Civilization, 2009).

78. Konwicki, *Lawa*, "Pamięć."

79. Mickiewicz, *Dziady*, 123.

80. Sobolewski, "Historia bez happy-endu."

81. Sobolewski, "Balkon Konwickiego."

82. Sobolewski, "Historia bez happy-endu."

83. See, for example, Michał Murawski, *Kompleks Pałacu: Życie społeczne stalinowskiego wieżowca w kapitalistycznej Warszawie*, trans. Ewa Klekot (Warsaw: Muzeum Warszawy, 2015).

84. For a comparison of how monuments to Stalin were treated in other regions of the Eastern bloc, see Hana Píchová, *The Case of the Missing Statue: A Historical and Literary Study of the Stalin Monument in Prague* (Řevnice: Arbor vitae, 2014).

LIST OF NEWS SEGMENTS FROM THE
POLISH FILM CHRONICLE

References to news segments from the Polish Film Chronicle (Polska Kronika Filmowa, PKF) follow the numeration in the card catalog of the Filmoteka Narodowa and the Repozytorium Cyfrowe Filmoteki Narodowej. The numbers before the colon refer to the edition and year the segment was released; those following the colon indicate the number of the news segment within that edition. Thus, PKF 1/45:4 was the first newsreel in 1945 and the referenced news segment was the fourth news story on that newsreel. PKF news segments can be viewed at http://www.repozytorium.fn.org.pl.

Borzechowa, Olga. "Goście z Chin." PKF 46/49:7, November 9, 1949, 00:00:33.
———. "Na Trasie W-Z." PKF 15/49:6, April 8, 1949, 00:02:27.
Borzechowa, Olga, and Wiktor Janik. "Odbudowa Warszawy. Budowa szybkościowca." PKF 38/49:2, September 1949, 00:02:29.
Borzechowa, Olga, and Karol Szczeciński. "Czyn lipcowy Warszawy." PKF 30/49:1, July 20, 1949, 00:04:15.
———. "Na Starym Mieście." PKF 49/49:6, December 1, 1949, 00:01:24.
———. "Zwiedzamy Warszawę." PKF 48/49:5, November 24, 1949, 00:00:59.
Borzechowa, Olga, and Mieczysław Wiesiołek. "Spacerkiem po WuZecie." PKF 33/49:6, August 10, 1949, 00:01:05.
Bossak, Jerzy, and Władysław Forbert. "Dziennikarze zagraniczni na Pradze." PKF 1/45:4, 1945, 00:01:35.
Bossak, Jerzy, Władysław Forbert, Stanisław Wohl, Adolf Forbert, Olgierd Samucewicz, and Eugeniusz Jefimow. "Warszawa wolna." PKF 4/45:1, January 2, 1945, 00:07:34.
Bossak, Jerzy, and Ludwik Perski. "Kongres satyryków." PKF 47/48:8, November 17, 1948, 00:01:04.
———. "Młodzież jugosłowiańska przy uprzątaniu gruzów Warszawy." PKF 25/46:6, August 6, 1946, 00:00:58.
———. "Trasa W-Z—makieta trasy i budowa." PKF 7/48:1–2, February 11, 1948, 00:02:18.
———. "Uprzątanie gruzów." PKF 19/46:3, June 27, 1946, 00:00:58.
———. "Warszawa oskarża. Proces Fischera." PKF 1/47:8, December 31, 1946, 00:01:20.
———. "Wręczenie listów uwierzytelniających prezydentowi Bierutowi przez posła Wielkiego Księstwa Luxemburg." PKF 28/45:2, October 4, 1945, 00:00:17.
Bossak, Jerzy, Ludwik Perski, Adolf Forbert, and Władysław Forbert. "Goście stolicy. Państwo Joliot w Warszawie." PKF 4/47:1, January 27, 1947, 00:01:24.

———. "Prezydent Bierut przy odgruzowywaniu rynku Starego Miasta." PKF 37/47:5, September 10, 1947, 00:01:02.

———. "W drodze do Moskwy. Bevin w drodze do Moskwy odwiedza Warszawę. Minister Bidault w Warszawie." PKF 11/47:1–2, March 13, 1947, 00:02:00.

Bossak, Jerzy, Ludwik Perski, and Władysław Forbert. "Wręczenie listów uwierzytelniających Bierutowi przez ambasadora Francji." PKF 22/45:1, August 18, 1945, 00:01:09.

Bossak, Jerzy, Ludwik Perski, Henryk Makarewicz, and Władysław Forbert. "Odbudowa Warszawy 'parterowej.'" PKF 17/46:6, June 11, 1946, 00:01:25.

Bossak, Jerzy, Ludwik Perski, and Sergiusz Sprudin. "Wręczenie listów uwierzytelniających w Belwederze przez posłów: Bułgarii, Danii, Holandii i Szwajcarii." PKF 1/46:5, January 14, 1946, 00:00:43.

Bossak, Jerzy, Ludwik Perski, and Karol Szczeciński. "Biuletyn Odbudowy Warszawy. Pomnik Kilińskiego wraca na dawne miejsce." PKF 30/46:5, September 10, 1946, 00:02:43.

———. "Delegacja angielskiej Partii Pracy zwiedza ruiny Warszawy." PKF 27/46:1, August 20, 1946, 00:00:45.

———. "Sekretarz Światowej Federacji Związków Zawodowych, Louis Saillant, zwiedza ruiny Warszawy." PKF 27/46:2, August 20, 1946, 00:00:39.

Bossak, Jerzy, Ludwik Perski, Karol Szczeciński, and Władysław Forbert. "Otwarcie mostu Poniatowskiego. Defilada ZWM i bratniej młodzieży z krajów socjalistycznych. Pierwszy tramwaj łączący Warszawę z Pragą przez most Poniatowskiego." PKF 24/46:1, July 31, 1946, 00:03:53.

Bossak, Jerzy, Ludwik Perski, Karol Szczeciński, and Antoni Wawrzyniak. "Odbudowa Warszawy." PKF 36/46:4, October 23, 1946, 00:02:39.

Forbert, Władysław. "Warszawa mistrza Canaletto." PKF 9/52:3, February 20, 1952, 00:02:35.

Fuchs, Franciszek, and Paweł Minkiewicz. "Studenci budują swój dom." PKF unused footage, no. 5024, August 28, 1950, 00:02:21.

Jefimow, Eugeniusz. "Pierwsze dni po wyzwoleniu Warszawy." PKF 7/45:1, February 1, 1945, 00:01:42.

Kaźmierczak, Wacław. "Defilada Tysiąclecia—Warszawa 22 lipca 1966 r." PKF 31A/66, 00:10:31.

Kędzierzawski, Janusz. "Trzydziestolatek." PKF 29/85:3, July 16, 1985, 00:01:02.

Lemańska, Helena. "1 Maja 1952." PKF 20/52:1–21, May 6, 1952.

———. "Na wczasach w Warszawie. Wczasy w Warszawie." PKF 8/53:4, February 18, 1953, 00:01:45.

———. "Wystawa plastyków. Pierwsza ogólnopolska wystawa plastyków w Muzeum Narodowym." PKF 14/50:11, March 29, 1950, 00:01:44.

———. "Ze świata. Moskiewski Pałac Nauki." PKF 42/52:12, October 8, 1952, 00:01:51.

Lemańska, Helena, and Władysław Forbert. "Nasz pradziadek. Fotoplastykon." PKF 51/53:11, September 11, 1953, 00:01:41.

Lemańska, Helena, and Franciszek Fuchs. "Dar przyjaźni. Podpisanie umowy o budowie Domu Kultury w Warszawie." PKF 17/52:1, April 15, 1952, 00:01:17.

Lemańska, Helena, Bogusław Lambach, Mieczysław Wiesiołek, and Wiktor Janik. "Warszawa. 1 Maja 1952." PKF 20/52:21, May 6, 1952, 00:06:25.

Lemańska, Helena, Franciszek Fuchs, and Karol Szczeciński. "Pałac Kultury i Nauki. Konferencja w Prezydium Rady Ministrów. Warty bierutowskie." PKF 19/52:1–4, April 29, 1952, 00:02:53.

Lemańska, Helena, Witold Jabłoński, and Władysław Forbert. "W ósmą rocznicę wyzwolenia stolicy. Pomnik Braterstwa. Budowa Pałacu Kultury i Nauki." PKF 4/53:3–8, January 14, 1953, 00:02:57.

Lemańska, Helena, Waldemar Kowalski, and Franciszek Fuchs. "Przyjaciele z Francji." PKF 41/50:6–7, October 4, 1950, 00:01:11.

Lemańska, Helena, Paweł Minkiewicz, Ryszard Kuźniarski, and Witold Jabłoński. "Stare mury Warszawy. Prace rekonstrukcyjne i konserwatorskie przy murach obronnych starej Warszawy." PKF 17/50:3, April 19, 1950, 00:01:09.

Lemańska, Helena, and Zdzisław Śluzar. "Wczasy w mieście. Młodzieżowy Dom Kultury." PKF 32/51:10, August 1, 1951, 00:01:11.

Lemańska, Helena, Janusz Sowiński, Władysław Forbert, Franciszek Fuchs, Sławomir Sławkowski, Mieczysław Wiesiołek, Zbigniew Raplewski, et al. "1 Maja 1953." PKF 19–20/53:1, May 7, 1953, 00:21:57.

Lemańska, Helena, and Karol Szczeciński. "Iglica w górę! Budowa Pałacu Kultury i Nauki. Montaż iglicy. Końcowe prace przy montażu konstrukcji wieży." PKF 47/53:4–6, November 4, 1953, 00:03:51.

———. "Marszałkowska latem 1950." PKF 29/50:4, June 11, 1950, 00:01:22.

———. "Miesiąc budowy socjalistycznej Warszawy. Odbudowa Warszawy." PKF 37/51:4, September 6, 1951, 00:01:39.

———. "Młoda Starówka. Odbudowa Starówki." PKF 49/52:2–4, November 26, 1952, 00:01:49.

———. "Na szczycie Pałacu. Obudowa iglicy. Rząd na terenie PKiN. Pałac Kultury—iglica. Pałac Kultury—efekty nocne." PKF 49/53:1–4, November 19, 1953, 00:02:42.

———. "Odbudowa Starego Miasta." PKF 12/52:4, March 12, 1952, 00:01:53.

———. "Odbudowa Zamku Królewskiego." PKF 26/50:2, June 21, 1950, 00:01:14.

Lemańska, Helena, Karol Szczeciński, and Leonard Zajączkowski. "Za złotówki na SFOS. Społeczny fundusz odbudowy Warszawy. Z tematu kroniki 38 'Odbudowa Warszawy.'" PKF 40/51:4–5, September 26, 1951, 00:01:42.

Lemańska, Helena, and Mieczysław Wiesiołek. "Praca przy filmie 'Przygoda na Mariensztacie.'" PKF 47/52:12, November 12, 1952, 00:01:16.

Lemańska, Helena, Mieczysław Wiesiołek, Karol Szczeciński, Władysław Forbert, and Olgierd Samucewicz. "Rośnie Pałac Przyjaźni. Otoczenie Pałacu Kultury i Nauki." PKF 47/52:2–9, November 12, 1952, 00:03:17.

Lemańska, Helena, Leonard Zajączkowski, and Karol Szczeciński. "Budujemy nową Warszawę. MDM odgruzowanie. Budowa trasy NS. Sportowcy francuscy odgruzowują Warszawę." PKF 39/50:3–7, September 30, 1950, 00:03:37.

"Pałac Nauki." PKF 13/51:11, March 21, 1951, 00:01:00.

Perski, Ludwik, and Jerzy Bossak. "Jugosłowianie przy pracy nad uprzątaniem gruzu w Warszawie." PKF 30/47:3, July 23, 1947, 00:00:49.

———. "Osiedle na Mariensztacie." PKF 32/48:3, August 4, 1948, 00:00:48.

———. "Wręczenie listów uwierzytelniających prezydentowi Bierutowi w Belwederze przez ambasadora Włoch." PKF 28/45:1, October 4, 1945, 00:0037.

Perski, Ludwik, Jerzy Bossak, Adolf Forbert, and Karol Szczeciński. "Warszawa przyszłości. Odbudowa Warszawy. Plany BOS." PKF 30/47:1–2, July 23, 1947, 00:01:30.

Perski, Ludwik, Jerzy Bossak, and Władysław Forbert. "Dziennikarze zagraniczni w Warszawie. Zwiedzanie miasta." PKF 19/45:4, July 21, 1945, 00:00:48.

———. "Wręczenie listów uwierzytelniających prezydentowi w Belwederze przez ambasadora USA." PKF 22/45:2, August 18, 1945, 00:00:36.

Perski, Ludwik, Jerzy Bossak, Władysław Forbert, and Karol Szczeciński. "Studenci porządkują ulice Warszawy." PKF 16/46:7, May 31, 1946, 00:00:43.

Perski, Ludwik, Jerzy Bossak, and Henryk Makarewicz. "Konferencja w Biurze Odbudowy Stolicy w Warszawie." PKF 8–9/46:7, March 16, 1946, 00:00:34.

———. "Wizyta Hoovera w Polsce." PKF 11/46:1, April 6, 1946, 00:01:11.

Perski, Ludwik, Jerzy Bossak, and Karol Szczeciński. "Przybycie do Warszawy z Norymbergi zbrodniarzy hitlerowskich." PKF 18/46:5, June 18, 1946, 00:01:39.

———. "Z frontu odbudowy—Warszawa. Budowa Domu Słowa Polskiego." PKF 14/48:1, April 1948, 00:01:24.

Perski, Ludwik, Jerzy Bossak, Karol Szczeciński, and Władysław Forbert. "Prezydent Bierut i premier wśród robotników zatrudnionych przy odbudowie mostu Poniatowskiego." PKF 18/46:4, June 18, 1946, 00:01:46.

Raplewski, Zbigniew, and Jerzy Snoch. "Dźwig elektryczny na M.D.M." PKF unused footage, no. 5309, December 15, 1950, 00:00:59.

Szczeciński, Karol. "Na budowie Pałacu Przyjaźni." PKF 33/52:1, August 6, 1952, 00:01:56.

———. "Na rusztowaniach Warszawy. Budowa MDM. Materiał do filmu Warszawa, ul. Krucza i Marszałkowska." PKF 16/51:4–5, April 11, 1951, 00:01:09.

———. "Na Starówce. Odbudowa Starego Miasta." PKF 7/51:3, February 7, 1951, 00:01:18.

———. "Spacerkiem po MDM." PKF 34/52:2–3, August 13, 1951, 00:01:31.

———. "W rocznicę wyzwolenia Warszawy. Warszawa w szóstą rocznicę wyzwolenia. Widok zburzonej Warszawy." PKF 4/51:1–2, January 17, 1951, 00:02:05.

———. "Warszawskie wrześnie." PKF 40/52:6–7, September 24, 1952, 00:02:33.

Szczeciński, Karol, and Jerzy Dmowski. "Bazary na Pańskiej i Ząbkowskiej." PKF unused footage, no. 5015, September 5–11, 1950, 00:09:03.

Szczeciński, Karol, Henryk Kucharzuk, and Jerzy Dmowski. "MDM (odgruzowanie)." PKF unused footage, no. 4971, August 1950, 00:03:16.

Wiesiołek, Mieczysław, and Waldemar Kowalski. "Tramwaj na Marszałkowskiej." PKF unused footage, no. 3224, November 23, 1948, 00:02:25.

Wionczek, Roman. "Place Warszawy." PKF 22/63:1, 00:01:28.

Alarcón, Daniel Cooper. "The Aztec Palimpsest: Toward a New Understanding of Aztlán, Cultural Identity and History." *Aztlán: A Journal of Chicano Studies* 19, no. 2 (1988): 33–68.

Anderson, Benedict. *Imagined Communities: Reflections on the Origin and Spread of Nationalism.* New York: Verso, 1991.

Andreson, Harry, Rich Thomas, Emily Newhall, Theodore Stanger, Ron Moreau, and Elizabeth Bailey. "Poland Under the Heel." *Newsweek*, December 28, 1981.

Arias, Santa, and Barney Warf, eds. *The Spatial Turn: Interdisciplinary Perspectives.* London: Routledge, 2009.

Arlt, Judith, and Wojciech Tomasik. *Mój Konwicki.* Kraków: Universitas, 2002.

Armata, Jerzy. "Leonard Buczkowski." Akademia Polskiego Filmu, http://www.akademiapolskiegofilmu.pl/pl/historia-polskiego-filmu/rezyserzy/leonard-buczkowski/35.

Auerbach, Karen. *The House at Ujazdowskie 16: Jewish Families in Warsaw after the Holocaust.* Bloomington: Indiana University Press, 2013.

Bachelard, Gaston. *The Poetics of Space.* New York: Orion, 1964.

Baczko, Bronisław, Jerzy Grabowski, and Edward Strzelecki. *Warszawa, stolica Polski.* Edited by Kazimierz Saysse-Tobiczyk. 2nd ed. Warsaw: Społeczny Fundusz Odbudowy Stolicy, 1949.

Bachórz, Józef. Introduction to *Lalka*, by Bolesław Prus, V–CLII. Wrocław: Zakład Narodowy im. Ossolińskich, 1991.

Badger, Gerry. "Sequencing the Photobook (part 2)." *Aperture* (December 2012): 3.

Badger, Gerry, and Martin Parr. *The Photobook: A History.* Vol. 1. London: Phaidon, 2004.

———. *The Photobook: A History.* Vol. 2. London: Phaidon, 2006.

Barthes, Roland. "The Photographic Message." Translated by Stephan Heath. In *Image-Music-Text*, 15–31. New York: Hill and Wang, 1977.

Bartov, Omer. *The "Jew" in Cinema: From The Golem to Don't Touch My Holocaust.* Bloomington: Indiana University Press, 2005.

Beeton, Sue. *Film-Induced Tourism.* Clevedon, Eng.: Channel View Publications, 2005.

Bellotto, Bernardo, and Mieczysław Wallis. *Canaletto, malarz Warszawy.* 5th ed. Warsaw: Auriga, 1961.

Benjamin, Walter. "The Work of Art in the Age of Mechanical Reproduction." Translated by Harry Zohn. In *Illuminations*, edited by Hannah Arendt, 217–51. New York: Schocken, 2007.

Bereś, Stanisław [Stanisław Nowicki, pseud.]. *Pół wieku czyśćca: Rozmowy z Tadeuszem Konwickim*. London: Aneks, 1986.

Białoszewski, Miron. *A Memoir of the Warsaw Uprising*. Translated by Madeline G. Levine. New York: New York Review of Books Classics, 2015.

———. *Pamiętnik z powstania warszawskiego*. Warsaw: PIW, 1970.

Biblioteka Uniwersytecka w Warszawie. "O Bibliotece / Historia / 1915–1999: Biblioteka Uniwersytecka w Warszawie." www.buw.uw.edu.pl.

Bierut, Bolesław. *O upowszechnienie kultury: Przemówienie Prezydenta Rzeczypospolitej Bolesława Bieruta na otwarciu radiostacji we Wrocławiu 16 listopada 1947*. Warsaw: Radiowy Instytut Wydawniczy, 1948.

———. *Sześcioletni plan odbudowy Warszawy*. Warsaw: Książka i Wiedza, 1950.

Bierut, Bolesław, and Hilary Minc. *Plan sześcioletni*. Warsaw: Książka i Wiedza, 1950.

Bolton, Jonathan. "Writing in a Polluted Semiosphere: Everyday Life in Lotman, Foucault, and de Certeau." In *Lotman and Cultural Studies: Encounters and Extensions*, edited by Andreas Schönle, 320–44. Madison: University of Wisconsin Press, 2006.

Boltz, Marilyn G. "The Cognitive Processing of Film and Musical Soundtracks." *Memory & Cognition* 32, no. 7 (2004): 1194–205.

———. "Musical Soundtracks as a Schematic Influence on the Cognitive Processing of Filmed Events." *Music Perception: An Interdisciplinary Journal* 18, no. 4 (2001): 427–54.

Borecka, Emilia, and Leonard Sempoliński. *Warszawa 1945*. Warsaw: PWN, 1975.

Bowles, Brett. "German Newsreel Propaganda in France, 1940–1944." *Historical Journal of Film, Radio and Television* 24, no. 1 (2004): 45–67.

Boym, Svetlana. *The Future of Nostalgia*. New York: Basic Books, 2001.

Bren, Frank. *World Cinema 1: Poland*. Flicks Books, 1986.

Brown, Kathryn. "Remembering the Occupation: La Mort et les statues by Pierre Jahan and Jean Cocteau." *Forum for Modern Language Studies* 49, no. 3 (2013): 286–99.

Budrewicz, Olgierd, and Edward Falkowski. *Warszawiacy*. Edited by Ewa Karwowska. Warsaw: Wydawnictwo Interpress, 1970.

Bukowiecki, Andrzej. "Mieczysław Verocsy." Akademia Polskiego Filmu, http://www.akademiapolskiegofilmu.pl/pl/historia-polskiego-filmu/operatorzy/mieczyslaw-verocsy/353.

Bułhak, Jan. "Fotografia dla potrzeb krajoznawstwa i propagandy turystycznej." *Świat Fotografii*, no. 1 (1946).

Burckhardt, Titus, and Stefan Jasieński. *Warszawa Varsovie Warsaw Warschau 1945*. Basel, Switz.: Urs-Graf at Basel and issued by the Polish soldiers of the 2nd Infantry Division interned in Switzerland, 1945.

Chambers, Ciara. *Ireland in the Newsreels*. Dublin: Irish Academic Press, 2012.

Ciborowski, Adolf. *Warszawa: O zniszczeniu i odbudowie miasta*. Warsaw: Wydawnictwo "Polonia," 1964.

Ciecierska, Agnieszka. "Radiowa Mapa Powstania Warszawskiego—walki o Prudential." 04:32: Radio Polska, 2014.

Cieśliński, Marek. "Komentarz do PKF 4/45: Warszawa wolna." Warsaw: Repozytorium Cyfrowe Filmoteki Narodowej.

————. *Piękniej niż w życiu: Polska Kronika Filmowa, 1944–1994*. Warsaw: Wydawnictwo "Trio," 2006.

Clark, Katerina. *The Soviet Novel: History as Ritual*. Bloomington: Indiana University Press, 2000.

Conley, Tom. *Cartographic Cinema*. Minneapolis: University of Minnesota Press, 2007.

Corrsin, Stephen D. *Warsaw before the First World War: Poles and Jews in the Third City of the Russian Empire, 1880–1914*. New York: Columbia University Press, 1989.

Crowley, David. "Paris or Moscow? Warsaw Architects and the Image of the Modern City in the 1950s." In *Imagining the West in Eastern Europe and the Soviet Union*, edited by György Péteri, 105–30. Pittsburgh, Pa.: University of Pittsburgh Press, 2010.

————. *Warsaw*. London: Reaktion, 2003.

Curry, Jane Leftwich, ed. *The Black Book of Polish Censorship*. New York: Random House, 1984.

Davies, Norman. *God's Playground: A History of Poland*. Vol. 2, *1795 to the Present*. New York: Columbia University Press, 1982.

————. *Rising '44: The Battle for Warsaw*. New York: Viking, 2004.

de Certeau, Michel. *The Practice of Everyday Life*. Translated by Steven Rendall. Berkeley: University of California Press, 1984.

Di Bello, Patrizia, Colette Wilson, and Shamoon Zamir, eds. *The Photobook: From Talbot to Ruscha and Beyond*. London: I. B. Tauris, 2012.

Dillon, Sarah. *The Palimpsest: Literature, Criticism, Theory*. London: Continuum, 2007.

Dłużewska, Emilia. "Beata Chomątowska: Pałac Kultury to jest Polska [Rozmowa]." *Wyborcza.pl*, July 15, 2015.

Downing, Eric. *After Images: Photography, Archeology, and Psychoanalysis and the Tradition of Bildung*. Detroit, Mich.: Wayne State University Press, 2006.

Dziga Vertov: The Vertov Collection at the Austrian Film Museum. Edited by Barbara Kleiber-Wurm and Thomas Tode. Vienna: SYNEMA, 2006.

Empire State Realty Trust. "Empire State Building Fact Sheet." http://www.esbnyc.com/sites/default/files/esb_fact_sheet_4_9_14_4.pdf.

Encyklopedia Warszawy, edited by Barbara Petrozolin-Skowrońska. Warsaw: PWN, 1994.

Falkowska, Janina, and Marek Haltof. *The New Polish Cinema*. Wiltshire, Eng.: Flicks Books, 2003.

Fielding, Raymond. *The American Newsreel: A Complete History, 1911–1967*. Jefferson, N.C.: McFarland, 2006.

"Filmpolski.pl: Internetowa baza filmu polskiego." Warsaw: Państwowa Wyższa Szkoła Filmowa, Telewizyjna i Teatralna im. Leona Schillera w Łodzi, 1998–2013.

Fisher, Jaimey, and Barbara Mennel, eds. *Spatial Turns: Space, Place, and Mobility in German Literary and Visual Culture*. Amsterdam: Rodopi, 2010.

Fuchs, Anne. *After the Dresden Bombing: Pathways of Memory, 1945 to the Present*. Houndmills, Eng.: Palgrave Macmillan, 2012.

Gajewski, Dariusz. *Warszawa*. 105 min. Poland: Gutek Film, 2003.

Genette, Gérard. *Narrative Discourse: An Essay in Method.* Ithaca, N.Y.: Cornell University Press, 1980.

Gerstenberger, Katharina. *Writing the New Berlin: The German Capital in Post-Wall Literature.* Rochester, N.Y., and Woodbridge, Eng.: Camden House and Boydell and Brewer, 2008.

Gillespie, David C. *Early Soviet Cinema: Innovation, Ideology and Propaganda.* London: Wallflower, 2000.

Głuchowski, Leszek W., and Antony Polonsky, eds. *1968, Forty Years After.* Vol. 21 of Polin: Studies in Polish Jewry. Oxford: Littman Library of Jewish Civilization, 2009.

Gomułka, Władysław. *Pamiętniki.* Vol. 2. Edited by Andrzej Werblan. Warsaw: Polska Oficyna Wydawnicza "BGW," 1994.

Górski, Jan. "Dyskusje o odbudowie Warszawy w latach 1945–1946." In *Warszawa: Stolica Polski Ludowej,* no. 1, edited by Jan Górski, 75–140. Vol. 5, *Studia Warszawskie.* Warsaw: PWN, 1970.

Gosk, Hanna. "Literatura—rzecz poważna (O poezji wczesnych lat pięćdziesiątych poświęconej Warszawie)." *Poezja* 18, no. 1 (203) (January 1983): 89–99.

Grabowski, Lech, and Jan Bułhak. *Jan Bułhak.* Warsaw: Arkady, 1961.

Grabowski, Waldemar. *Polska Agencja Telegraficzna 1918–1991.* Warsaw: Polska Agencja Prasowa, 2005.

Grzybowski, Zbigniew, Hubert Hilscher, and Leszek Wysznacki. *Warszawa 1945–1970.* Translated by Regina Gorzkowska, Ludwik Kaduczek, Maria Wołaczka, Małgorzata Bester and Nina Perczyńska. Warsaw: Wydawnictwo "Sport i Turystyka," 1970.

Haltof, Marek. *Polish Film and the Holocaust: Politics and Memory.* New York: Berghahn Books, 2012.

———. *Polish National Cinema.* New York: Berghahn Books, 2002.

Handke, Kwiryna. *Słownik nazewnictwa Warszawy.* Warsaw: Slawistyczny Ośrodek Wydawniczy, 1998.

Hess-Lüttich, Ernest W. B. "*Spatial Turn*: On the Concept of Space in Cultural Geography and Literary Theory." *meta-carto-semiotics: Journal for Theoretical Cartography* 5 (2012): 1–11.

Hicks, Jeremy. *Dziga Vertov: Defining Documentary Film.* London: I. B. Tauris, 2007.

Historia filmu polskiego: 1939–1956. Edited by Jerzy Toeplitz. Warsaw: Wydawnictwa Artystyczne i Filmowe, 1974.

Jabłoński, Krzysztof. *Warszawa: Portret miasta.* Edited by Stefan Muszyński. Warsaw: Arkady, 1979.

Jakubowski, Józef. *Dekret o odbudowie Warszawy.* Lublin: Wydawnictwo Lubelskie, 1980.

Janion, Maria. *Projekt krytyki fantazmatycznej: Szkice o egzystencjach ludzi i duchów.* Warsaw: Wydawnictwo PEN, 1991.

Jankowski, Stanisław. *MDM-Marszałkowska, 1730–1954.* Warsaw: Czytelnik, 1955.

———. "Warsaw: Destruction, Secret Town Planning, 1939–44, and Postwar Reconstruction." In *Rebuilding Europe's Bombed Cities,* edited by Jeffry M. Diefendorf, 77–93. New York: St. Martin's, 1990.

Jankowski, Stanisław and Adolf Ciborowski. *Warsaw 1945 and Today.* Warsaw: Interpress, 1971.

———. *Warszawa 1945 i dziś*. Warsaw: Interpress, 1971.

Jarosiński, Zbigniew. *Nadwiślański socrealizm*. Warsaw: Instytut Badań Literackich, 1999.

Kaczmarzyk, Dariusz. "Pamiętnik wystawy 'Warszawa oskarża' 3 maja 1945—28 stycznia 1946 w Muzeum Narodowym w Warszawie." *Rocznik Muzeum Narodowego w Warszawie* 20 (1976): 599–675.

Kamiński, Łukasz. "Piosenki o Warszawie: 'Pałac' i 'Front wschodni' Dezertera." *Wyborcza.pl Warszawa*, September 23, 2005.

Kapuściński, Ryszard. *Imperium*. New York: Alfred A. Knopf, 1994.

Karwowska, Bożena. "Metamorfozy pamięci—odbudowa Warszawy w narracji Poli Gojawiczyńskiej." In *Kobieta—Historia—Literatura*, 178–90. Warsaw: Instytut Badań Literackich, 2016.

Kohlrausch, Martin. "*Warszawa Funkcjonalna*: Radical Urbanism and the International Discourse on Planning in the Interwar Period." In *Races to Modernity: Metropolitan Aspirations in Eastern Europe, 1890–1940*, edited by Jan C. Behrends and Martin Kohlrausch, 205–31. Budapest: Central European University Press, 2014.

Konwicki, Tadeusz. *The Anthropos-Specter-Beast*. Translated by George Korwin-Rodziszewski and Audrey Korwin-Rodziszewski. New York: S. G. Phillips, 1977.

———. *Kompleks polski*. London: Index on Censorship, 1977.

———. *Lawa*. Warsaw: Telewizja Kino Polska, 1989. DVD.

———. *Mała apokalipsa*. Warsaw: Wydawnictwo ALFA, 1989.

———. *A Minor Apocalypse*. Translated by Richard Lourie. New York: Farrar, Straus and Giroux, 1983.

———. *New World Avenue and Vicinity*. Translated by George Korwin-Rodziszewski and Audrey Korwin-Rodziszewski. New York: Farrar, Straus and Giroux, 1991.

———. *Nowy Świat i okolice; z rysunkami autora*. Warsaw: Czytelnik, 1986.

———. *The Polish Complex*. Translated by Richard Lourie. New York: Farrar, Straus and Giroux, 1982.

———. *Wniebowstąpienie*. Warsaw: Biblioteka Gazety Wyborczej, 2010.

———. *Zwierzoczłekoupiór*. Warsaw: Czytelnik, 1969.

Kotańska, Anna. "Dokumentacja fotograficzna wystaw: 'Warszawa wczoraj, dziś, jutro' (1938 r.) i 'Warszawa oskarża' (1945 r.) w zbiorach Muzeum Historycznego m. st. Warszawy." *Almanach Muzealny*, no. 2 (1999): 291–313.

Kubik, Jan. *The Power of Symbols against the Symbols of Power: The Rise of Solidarity and the Fall of State Socialism in Poland*. University Park: Pennsylvania State University Press, 1994.

Kunicki, Mikołaj. "The Red and the Brown: Bolesław Piasecki, the Polish Communists, and the Anti-Zionist Campaign in Poland, 1967–1968." *East European Politics and Societies* 19, no. 2 (2005).

Kupiecki, Edmund. *Warszawa 1960*. Kraków: Arkady, 1960.

Kupiecki, Edmund, and Ewa Biegańska. *Warszawa: Krajobraz i architektura*. Warsaw: Arkady, 1963.

Lebow, Katherine. *Unfinished Utopia: Nowa Huta, Stalinism, and Polish Society, 1949–56*. Ithaca, N.Y.: Cornell University Press, 2013.

Lechowicz, Lech. "Fotografia w narodowej potrzebie." In *Fotoeseje: Teksty o fotografii polskiej*, 7–24. Warsaw: Fundacja Archeologia Fotografii, 2010.

————. "Między politycznym bezpieczeństwem a polityczną poprawnością: Rozważania nad sztuką medialną w Polsce dekad powojennych." In *Fotoeseje: Teksty o fotografii polskiej*, 7–24. Warsaw: Fundacja Archeologia Fotografii, 2010.

Leociak, Jacek. "'Zraniona pamięć': Rocznice powstania w getcie warszawskim w prasie polskiej (1944–1989)." In *Literatura polska wobec Zagłady*, edited by Alina Brodzka, Dorota Krawczyńska, and Jacek Leociak, 29–49. Warsaw: Żydowski Instytut Historyczny, 2000.

Leslie, Esther. "Siegfried Kracauer and Walter Benjamin: Memory from Weimar to Hitler." In *Histories, Theories, Debates*, edited by Susannah Radstone and Bill Schwarz, 123–35. New York: Fordham University Press, 2010.

Levavy, Sara Beth. "Immediate Mediation: A Narrative of the Newsreel and the Film." Dissertation, Stanford University, 2013.

Lewandowska, Karolina. *Między dokumentalnością a eksperymentem: Krytyka fotograficzna w Polsce w latach 1946–1989*. Warsaw: Bęc Zmiana and Archeologia Fotografii, 2014.

Łobodziński, Filip. "Życie po życiu." *Newsweek.pl*, May 24, 2009.

Lotman, Jurij M., and Boris A. Uspenskij. Authors' Introduction to *The Semiotics of Russian Culture*, edited by Ann Shukman and Boris Andreevich Uspenskij, ix–xiv. Ann Arbor: Department of Slavic Languages and Literatures, University of Michigan, 1984.

Lubelska, Krystyna. "Kronika nie umyka." *Polityka.pl*, March 27, 2006.

Lubelski, Tadeusz. "Nasza komedia narodowa." *Kwartalnik Filmowy* 67/68 (Autumn 2009): 286–303.

————. *Poetyka powieści i filmów Tadeusza Konwickiego: Na podstawie analiz utworów z lat 1947–1965*. Wrocław: Wydawnictwo Uniwersytetu Wrocławskiego, 1984.

————. *Strategie autorskie w polskim filmie fabularnym lat 1945–1961*. Kraków: Uniwersytet Jagielloński, 1992.

MacCannell, Dean. *The Tourist: A New Theory of the Leisure Class*. Berkeley: University of California Press, 1999.

Madej, Alina. *Kino, władza, publiczność: Kinematografia polska w latach 1944–1949*. Bielsko-Biała: Prasa Beskidzka, 2002.

————. "Zjazd filmowy w Wiśle, czyli dla każdego coś przykrego." *Kwartalnik Filmowy*, no. 18 (1997): 207–14.

Majewski, Jerzy S., and Tomasz Urzykowski. "Pałac Kultury w popkulturze: Od socrealistycznych wierszy po atak Godzilli." *Wyborcza.pl*, July 18, 2015.

————. *Spacerownik: Pałac Kultury i Nauki; Socrealistyczna Warszawa*. Warsaw: Agora SA, 2015.

Majewski, Piotr. "Jak zbudować 'Zamek socjalistyczny'?: Polityczne konteksty odbudowy Zamku Królewskiego w Warszawie w latach 1944–1956." In *Zbudować Warszawę piękną: O nowy krajobraz stolicy (1944–1956)*, edited by Jerzy Kochanowski, 25–95. Warsaw: Wydawnictwo "Trio," 2003.

Makarczyński, Tadeusz. *Suita warszawska*. 00:18:28: Narodowy Instytut Audiowizualny, 1946.

Makarczyński, Tadeusz, and Franciszek Fuchs. *Nowa sztuka*. Warsaw, 1950.

Malitsky, Joshua. *Post-Revolution Nonfiction Film: Building the Soviet and Cuban Nations*. Bloomington: Indiana University Press, 2013.

Mandelker, Amy. "Logosphere and Semiosphere: Bakhtin, Russian Organicism, and the Semiotics of Culture." In *Bakhtin in Contexts: Across the Disciplines*, edited by Amy Mandelker, 177–90. Evanston, Ill.: Northwestern University Press, 1995.

Markiewicz, Tomasz. "Prywatna odbudowa Warszawy." In *Zbudować Warszawę piękną: O nowy krajobraz stolicy (1944–1956)*, edited by Jerzy Kochanowski, 214–58. Warsaw: Wydawnictwo "Trio," 2003.

Mazierska, Ewa, and Laura Rascaroli. *From Moscow to Madrid: Postmodern Cities, European Cinema*. London: I. B. Tauris, 2003.

"Mazowsze—historia." http://mazowsze.waw.pl/sub,pl,mazowsze—historia.html.

Melo e Castro, Paul. *Shades of Grey: 1960s Lisbon in Novel, Film and Photobook*. London: Maney Publishing for the MHRA, 2011.

Meng, Michael. *Shattered Spaces: Encountering Jewish Ruins in Postwar Germany and Poland*. Cambridge, Mass.: Harvard University Press, 2011.

Merleau-Ponty, Maurice. *Phenomenology of Perception*. Translated by Donald A. Landes. London: Routledge, 2012.

Michałek, Bolesław. *Szkice o filmie polskim*. Warsaw: Wydawnictwa Artystyczne i Filmowe, 1960.

Michałek, Bolesław, and Frank Turaj. *The Modern Cinema of Poland*. Bloomington: Indiana University Press, 1988.

Michlic, Joanna B., and Antony Polonsky. "Introduction" in *The Neighbors Respond: The Controversy Over the Jedwabne Massacre in Poland*, edited by Joanna B. Michlic and Antony Polonsky, 1–43. Princeton, N.J.: Princeton University Press, 2004.

Mickiewicz, Adam. *Dziady*. In *Dzieła*, vol. 3, *Dramaty*. Edited by Zbigniew Nowak. Warsaw: Czytelnik, 1995.

———. *Księgi narodu polskiego i pielgrzymstwa polskiego*. In *Dzieła*, vol. 5, *Proza artystyczna i pisma krytyczne*. Edited by Zbigniew Nowak. Warsaw: Czytelnik, 1996.

Miller, J. Hillis. *Topographies*. Stanford, Calif.: Stanford University Press, 1995.

Miłosz, Czesław. "Wyjaśnienia po latach." *Dialog: Miesięcznik Poświęcony Dramaturgii Współczesnej—Teatralnej, Filmowej, Radiowej, Telewizyjnej* 29, no. 9 [336] (1984): 116–17.

———. *Zniewolony umysł*. Paris: Instytut Literacki, 1980.

Moretti, Franco. *Atlas of the European Novel, 1800–1900*. London: Verso, 1998.

———. *Graphs, Maps, Trees: Abstract Models for a Literary History*. London: Verso, 2005.

Mozejko, Edward. "Beyond Ideology: The Prose of Tadeusz Konwicki." *The Review of Contemporary Fiction* 14, no. 3 (1994): 139–55.

Murawski, Michał. *Kompleks Pałacu: Życie społeczne stalinowskiego wieżowca w kapitalistycznej Warszawie*. Translated by Ewa Klekot. Warsaw: Muzeum Warszawy, 2015.

Nöth, Winfried. "The Topography of Yuri Lotman's Semiosphere." *International Journal of Cultural Studies* 18, no. 1 (2015): 11–26.

Ostachowicz, Igor. *Noc żywych Żydów*. Warsaw: Wydawnictwo W.A.B., 2012.

Pałac Kultury i Nauki w Warszawie. "Ciekawostki." http://www.pkin.pl/strefa-turysty-ciekawostki.

Pałac Kultury i Nauki w Warszawie. "W pałacu." http://www.pkin.pl/strefa-turysty
-w-palacu.

Piątek, Grzegorz. "Koniec, który stał się początkiem / An End and a Beginning." Translated by Marcin Wawrzyńczak and Katarzyna Bartoszyńska. In
*Kronikarki / The Chroniclers (Zofia Chomętowska i Maria Chrząszczowa):
Fotografie Warszawy 1945–1946 / Photographs of Warsaw 1945–1946*, edited
by Karolina Lewandowska, 274–91. Warsaw: Archeologia Fotografii, 2011.

Píchová, Hana. *The Case of the Missing Statue: A Historical and Literary Study
of the Stalin Monument in Prague.* Řevnice: Arbor vitae, 2014.

"Piękno Warszawy, której już nie ma, a którą wskrzesimy." *Stolica: Warszawski
Tygodnik Ilustrowany*, November 3, 1946, 6–8.

Piórkowski, Jerzy, and Stefan Bałuk. *Miasto nieujarzmione.* Warsaw: Iskry, 1957.

Pitera, Zbigniew [Jan Łęczyca, pseud.]. "O nowy realistyczny film polski." *Film*,
no. 10 (1949): 3.

Pitera, Zbigniew. "Sprawozdanie z I Zjazdu Pracowników PKF." *Biuletyn Informacyjny Filmu Polskiego*, no. 14 (1946).

PolskieRadio.pl. "Jan Zachwatowicz—udaremnił zamach Niemców na kulturę
polską."PolskieRadio.http://www.polskieradio.pl/39/156/Artykul/909950,Jan
-Zachwatowicz-udaremnil-zamach-Niemcow-na-kulture-polska.

"Pomnik 'czterech śpiących' nie wróci na pl. Wileński." *Wiadomości.wp.pl.* February 26, 2015.

Pozniak, Kinga. *Nowa Huta: Generations of Change in a Model Socialist Town.*
Pittsburgh, Pa.: University of Pittsburgh Press, 2014.

Prus, Bolesław. *The Doll.* Translated by David Welsh and revised by Dariusz
Tołczyk and Anna Zaranko. Budapest: Central European University Press,
1996.

———. *Kroniki.* Edited by Zygmunt Szweykowski. 16 vols. Warsaw: PIW, 1966.

———. *Lalka.* Wrocław: Zakład Narodowy im. Ossolińskich, 1991.

*Reconstruction of Towns in People's Poland: Warsaw—Poznań—Cracow—
Gdańsk—Wrocław—Stalinogród.* Special issue of the weekly *Stolica.* Warsaw,
1954.

Reeves, Nicholas. *The Power of Film Propaganda: Myth or Reality?* London:
Cassell, 1999.

Rokicki, Konrad. "Kłopotliwy dar: Pałac Kultury i Nauki." In *Zbudować
Warszawę piękną: O nowy krajobraz stolicy (1944–1956)*, edited by Jerzy
Kochanowski, 97–209. Warsaw: Wydawnictwo "Trio," 2003.

Ross, Silvia M. *Tuscan Spaces: Literary Constructions of Place.* Toronto: University of Toronto Press, 2010.

Rudnicki, Adolf. "The Crystal Stream." In *Art from the Ashes: A Holocaust
Anthology*, edited by Lawrence L. Langer. New York: Oxford University Press,
1995.

———. "Czysty nurt." In *Sto jeden.* Kraków: Wydawnictwo Literackie, 1984.

Schlögel, Karl. *W przestrzeni czas czytamy: O historii cywilizacji i geopolityce.*
Translated by Łukasz Musiał and Izabela Drozdowska. Poznań: Wydawnictwo
Poznańskie, 2009.

Sejm of the Republic of Poland. Ustawa z dnia 3 lipca 1947 r. o odbudowie m. st.
Warszawy (Dz.U. 1947 nr 52 poz. 268).

Semczuk, Przemysław. "Kronikarz PRL." *Newsweek Polska*, January 2, 2011.

Siemaszko, Zbyszko, and Dobrosław Kobielski. *Spojrzenia na Warszawę*. Warsaw: Krajowa Agencja Wydawnicza, 1987.

Singer, Isaac Bashevis. *The Family Moskat*. New York: Farrar, Straus and Giroux, 1950.

Skaff, Sheila. *The Law of the Looking Glass: Cinema in Poland, 1896–1939*. Athens: Ohio University Press, 2008.

Skrzeszewska, Bronisława. "O pomocy Związku Radzieckiego dla Warszawy w pierwszym okresie po jej wyzwoleniu." In *Warszawa: Stolica Polski Ludowej*, no. 1, edited by Jan Górski, 209–22. Vol. 5, *Studia Warszawskie*. Warsaw: PWN, 1970.

Słonimski, Antoni. *Wspomnienia warszawskie*. Warsaw: Czytelnik, 1957.

Śmiałowski, Piotr. "Pierwszy na zawsze." *Kino* 41, no. 475 (January 2007): 54–57.

Smulski, Jerzy. *Od Szczecina do . . . Października: Studia o literaturze polskiej lat pięćdziesiątych*. Toruń: Wydawnictwo Uniwersytetu Mikołaja Kopernika, 2002.

Sobolewski, Tadeusz. "Balkon Konwickiego." *Gazeta Wyborcza*, August 17, 2009.

———. "Historia bez happy-endu." *Kino* 41, no. 477 (March 2007): 98.

Stachówna, Grażyna. "Socjalistyczne romanse, czyli gorzko-słodkie losy melodramatu w Peerelu." *Kino* 41, no. 476 (2007): 52.

Steedman, Marek. "State Power, Hegemony, and Memory: Lotman and Gramsci." In *Lotman and Cultural Studies: Encounters and Extensions*, edited by Andreas Schönle, 136–58. Madison: University of Wisconsin Press, 2006.

Stola, Dariusz. "Fighting against the Shadows: The Anti-Zionist Campaign of 1968." In *Antisemitism and Its Opponents in Modern Poland*, edited by Robert Blobaum, 284–300. Ithaca, N.Y.: Cornell University Press, 2005.

Świeżyński, Wacław. "Film dokumentalny." In *Historia filmu polskiego: 1939–1956*, edited by Jerzy Toeplitz, 110–43. Warsaw: Wydawnictwa Artystyczne i Filmowe, 1974.

Świeżyński, Wacław, and Stanisław Ozimek. "Kroniki wojny i pokoju." In *Historia filmu polskiego: 1939–1956*, edited by Jerzy Toeplitz, 101–10. Warsaw: Wydawnictwa Artystyczne i Filmowe, 1974.

Szyma, Tadeusz. "W starym kinie Ludwika Starskiego." *Kino* 40, no. 464 (2006): 72.

Talarczyk-Gubała, Monika. *PRL się śmieje! Polska komedia filmowa lat 1945–1989*. Warsaw: Wydawnictwo "Trio," 2007.

Taylor, Richard. "A 'Cinema for the Millions': Soviet Socialist Realism and the Problem of Film Comedy." *Journal of Contemporary History* 18, no. 3 (1983): 439–61.

Toeplitz, Jerzy. "Polska Kronika Filmowa—dorobek XX-lecia." *Zeszyty Prasoznawcze*, no. 3 (1964).

Tołwiński, Stanisław. "Czy były wątpliwości co do budowy nowej Warszawy na dawnym miejscu?" In *Warszawa: Stolica Polski Ludowej*, no. 2, edited by Jan Górski, 45–53. Vol. 11, *Studia Warszawskie*. Warsaw: PWN, 1972.

Tomas, David. *Vertov, Snow, Farocki: Machine Vision and the Posthuman*. New York: Bloomsbury Academic, 2013.

Tomasik, Wojciech. *Inżynieria dusz: Literatura realizmu socjalistycznego w planie "propagandy monumentalnej."* Wrocław: Wydawnictwo Leopoldinum, 1999.

————. "Proza narracyjna." In *Słownik realizmu socjalistycznego*, edited by Zdzisław Łapiński and Wojciech Tomasik. Kraków: Universitas, 2004.

————. "Warsaw in 1945–55: The Emergence of a New Chronotope." In *The Phoney Peace: Power and Culture in Central Europe, 1945–49*, edited by Robert B. Pynsent, 328–36. London: School of Slavonic and East European Studies, University of London, 2000.

Toniak, Ewa. *Olbrzymki: Kobiety i socrealizm*. Kraków: Korporacja ha!art, 2008.

Topolski, Jan. "Suita warszawska (liner notes)." In *Lutosławski/świat (5 Disc CD Collection)*, edited by Adam Suprynowicz. Warsaw: Narodowy Instytut Audiowizualny, 2013.

Torańska, Teresa. *"Them": Stalin's Polish Puppets*. Translated by Agnieszka Kolakowska. New York: Harper and Row, 1987.

Tymowski, Wojciech. "Pałac Kultury ma 60 lat. Tyle samo co Michał Ogórek [Rozmowa]." *Wyborcza.pl*, July 17, 2015.

Tyrmand, Leopold. *Diary 1954*. Translated by Anita Krystyna Shelton and A. J. Wrobel. Evanston, Ill.: Northwestern University Press, 2014.

————. *The Man with the White Eyes*. Translated by David Welsh. New York: Alfred A. Knopf, 1959.

————. *Zły*. Warsaw: Wydawnictwo MG, 2011.

Uecker, Matthias. "The Face of the Weimar Republic: Photography, Physiognomy, and Propaganda in Weimar Germany." *Monatshefte* 99, no. 4 (2007): 469–84.

Uniłowski, Zbigniew. *Wspólny pokój i inne utwory*. Wrocław: Zakład Narodowy im. Ossolińskich, 1976.

Uszańska, Krystyna, and Gabriela J. Lubomirska. *Warsaw: Album on the Polish Capital's Ancient Architecture, with an Introduction and Outline of the City's History up to the XIX Century*. Stuttgart: Kreuz-Verlag, 1947.

Vale, Lawrence J. *Architecture, Power, and National Identity*. New Haven, Conn.: Yale University Press, 1992.

Wampuszyc, Ewa. "Intertextuality and Topography in Igor Ostachowicz's *Noc żywych Żydów*." In *Geograficzne przestrzenie utekstowione*, edited by Bożena Karwowska, Elżbieta Konończuk, Elżbieta Sidoruk, and Ewa Wampuszyc. Białystok: Wydawnictwo Uniwersytetu w Białymstoku, 2017.

————. "Normalizacja a odbudowa Warszawy w obiektywie Polskiej Kroniki Filmowej (1945–1956)." In *(Nie)przezroczystość normalności w literaturze polskiej XX i XXI wieku*, edited by Hanna Gosk and Bożena Karwowska, 98–109. Warsaw: Dom Wydawniczy Elipsa, 2014.

————. "Socialism, Synecdoche, and Tadeusz Konwicki's Palace of Culture." *East European Politics and Societies* 27, no. 2 (2013): 224–40.

————. "Tadeusz Konwicki." In *The Literary Encyclopedia*, entry edited by Roman Koropeckyj. December 20, 2016. http://www.litencyc.com/php/speople .php?rec=true&UID=12660.

"Warszawski wrzesień." *Stolica: Warszawski Tygodnik Ilustrowany*. September 18, 1949.

Ważyk, Adam. "Poemat dla dorosłych." *Nowa Kultura*, no. 34 (August 21, 1955).

Werlen, Benno. *Sozialgeographie: Eine Einführung*. Bern: Haupt, 2000.

Widdis, Emma. *Visions of a New Land: Soviet Film from the Revolution to the Second World War*. New Haven, Conn.: Yale University Press, 2003.

Williams, Raymond. *The Country and the City*. New York: Oxford University Press, 1973.

Winter, Jay, and Emmanuel Sivan, "Setting the Framework." In *War and Remembrance in the Twentieth Century*, edited by Jay Winter and Emmanuel Sivan, 6–39. Cambridge: Cambridge University Press, 2000.

Włodarczyk, Wojciech. *Socrealizm: Sztuka polska w latach 1950–1954*. Kraków: Wydawnictwo Literackie, 1991.

Wynot, Edward D. *Warsaw between the World Wars: Profile of the Capital City in a Developing Land, 1918–1939*. New York: Columbia University Press, 1983.

Youngblood, Denise J. *Movies for the Masses: Popular Cinema and Soviet Society in the 1920s*. Cambridge: Cambridge University Press, 1992.

Zachwatowicz, Jan. "Sprawozdanie kierownika Wydziału Architektoniczno-Zabytkowego Biura Odbudowy Stolicy na konferencję u Prezydenta Bolesława Bieruta 23 III 1945 r." In *Warszawa: Stolica Polski Ludowej*, no. 2, edited by Jan Górski, 271–74. Vol. 11, Studia warszawskie. Warsaw: PWN, 1972.

Zahorski, Andrzej. *Warszawa za Sasów i Stanisława Augusta*. Warsaw: PIW, 1970.

Zaleski, Marek, ed. *Warszawa Miłosza*. Warsaw: Stowarzyszenie "Pro Cultura Litteraria," Wydawnictwo PAN, 2013.

Żdżarski, Wacław. *Historia fotografii warszawskiej*. Warsaw: PWN, 1974.

Zechenter, Katarzyna. *The Fiction of Tadeusz Konwicki: Coming to Terms with Post-war Polish History and Politics*. Lewiston, N.Y.: Edwin Mellen, 2007.

Zieliński, Jarosław. *Pałac Kultury i Nauki*. Łódź: Księży Młyn Dom Wydawniczy, 2012.

Zwierzchowski, Piotr. *Pęknięty monolit: Konteksty polskiego kina socrealistycznego*. Bydgoszcz: Wydawnictwo Uniwersytetu Kazimierza Wielkiego, 2005.

INDEX

Page numbers in **boldface** refer to illustrations.